About the Author

MICHAEL HARRISON abandoned his plans for a career as an architect in favour of becoming a journalist and fiction writer. His first book, a novel, appeared in 1934 and since then he has written twenty more novels. He has more recently turned his talents to non-fiction, and his writings on Sherlock Holmes and the history of London have brought him wide readership and acclaim on both sides of the Atlantic.

In recent years, Michael Harrison has concentrated on 'puzzle-solving' books, tackling intricate problems and providing some highly interesting answers. FIRE FROM HEAVEN is an outstanding example of his efforts in this field.

FIRE FROM HEAVEN

by

Michael Harrison

SKOOB BOOKS PUBLISHING

LONDON

Published by
SKOOB BOOKS PUBLISHING LTD
Skoob Esoterica Series
19 Bury Place
Bloomsbury
London WC1A 2JH

ISBN   1 871438 65 9   Paper

Typeset by Moss Database in ITC Garamond
Printed in Singapore by Thomson Printing Company

In all affection, to my friend of
many years, Geraldine Collins Beskin,
once of The Atlantis Bookshop, through
whose kindly offices this book is to
enjoy its fourth edition.

And in most affectionate memory of her
Mother, Kathleen Collins, under whose
gentle but efficient rule, The Atlantis
Bookshop flourished, to the rich enjoyment
of us all.

CONTENTS

ACKNOWLEDGMENTS

All research is a matter of more or less considerable labour, but the research preliminary to the writing of this book involved both considerable and even more considerable difficulty. As is made clear in the book, there exists a deep and widespread prejudice, not so much against Spontaneous Combustion, as against the *possibility* that it might be a fact. The resolute obstinacy with which the 'learned' reject the factuality of this phenomenon is really startling to the striving-to-be-objective historian. The majority of medical men, coroners or not; police and other relevant authorities; all behave, when confronted with the phenomenon of spontaneous combustion, as did the eighteenth-century French philosopher, when told that his theories did not seem to accord with the observed facts. 'Then', said he, arrogantly, '*so much the worse for the facts!*'

This widespread prejudice against the admission of even the phenomenon's possibility has greatly reduced the number of 'gratefully acknowledged' names which are normally to be found at the beginning of my non-fiction books; here are a mere two dozen, compared with the several dozen in any book on no 'awkward' subject – and even within this small number there are one or two of the still unconvinced. One of these, a friend of mine, is a physician of distinction and established practice. In sending me the last of the several articles and press cuttings that he had so kindly and diligently collected for me, he wrote, 'I still can't accept that there's any such thing as spontaneous combustion.' (Perhaps, after he has read this book, his non-belief will not be so assured?)

Here then, set out in alphabetical order, are the names of those persons or institutions which – convinced, half-convinced or wholly unconvinced – have, by providing needed information or permission to quote copyright material, helped in the production of this book – the first complete study of the phenomenon of spontaneous combustion. Miss Jacqueline Aubertin, for generously undertaken research, especially at the Bodleian and other libraries; Professor M. J. Boyd, of Queen's University, Belfast, Ireland for an important reference to ancient 'superstition' and ritual; Mrs Kathleen Collins and Miss Geraldine Collins, of the *Atlantis Bookshop*, Museum Street, London, for directing me to source material, for loan of rare books, and – above all – for consistently encouraging support in my quest for information; Mr Kalman Cziszar, Reference Librarian, Pontiac Public Library, for a courteous prompt reply to my letter of enquiry; Mr Michael, Assistant Vice-Chancellor for Academic Affairs, University of Tennessee, for putting me on the path to the identification of 'Mr H.', the Fire-struck Professor of Mathematics; Professor O. W. Dilke, Department of Latin, Leeds University, England, for a scholar's scholarly and friendly exposition of some classical facts; Mr Anthony Fusco, Attorney-at-Law, Morgantown, West Virginia, for help in tracking down source material; Mr Vincent Gaddis, both for encouragement and for his generous permission to use and quote from his fascinating book, *Mysterious Fires and Lights*; Mr Eric Gaskell, for calling my attention to the Grafin von Görlitz and to the picture from *Diogenes*; Mr J. H. H. Gaute, of the Medico-Legal Society, for a useful hint on source material; Dr D. J. Gee, MB, BS, etc, Lecturer in Forensic Medicine, Leeds University, for the facts in his excellent article in *Medicine, Science and the Law*, Vol 5, 1965, pp 37-8; Mr R. J. Gregory, QPM, Chief Constable of the West Yorkshire Metropolitan Police for kind permission to use the photograph (Plate 2) originally illustrating Dr D. J. Gee's

ii

article; Dr Dudley A. Hart, MD, of Harley Street, London, for backing at an important moment; Mr R. T. Hewitt, OBE, MA, Executive Director, the Royal Society of Medicine, for admitting me to that distinguished body and for making me free of its incomparable library and archives; Mr Brian Inglis, the well-known publicist, author, telecaster, and editor, for having so kindly procured details of cases of SHC not previously known to me, thus making it possible for me to include them in the second edition of this book; Dr Banesh Hoffman, the eminent U.S. physicist and mathematician, for having read and annotated the original edition of this book, and for having offered me valuable and gratefully accepted comments; Mr John A. Keel, the well-known U.S. historian and philosopher of the 'off-beat' fact, for valuable introductions to both books and persons, and for permission to quote from his excellent *Anomaly; A journal of Forteana*; Dr K. D. Keele, MD, FRCP, for an enjoyable and instructive lecture at Trinity College, Oxford, and some productive ideas from his *Leonardo da Vinci – Movement of the Heart and Blood*; Mr David McKay, David McKay Company, New York, for *trying* courteously to find me an out-of-print book; Mr James Magruder II, Managing Editor, The Oakland Press, Pontiac, Michigan, for an offer of help; Mr Aubrey Noakes, the historian, for his friendly interest and his search for valuable references in a number of libraries; Dr Donald A. Redmond, Librarian, Queen's College, Kingston, Ontario, for kindly researching relevant literature; Professor Keith Simpson, the distinguished British pathologist, for some important references and an esteemed introduction to the Department of Forensic Medicine, Guy's Hospital; Dr Gavin Thurston, MRCP, Barrister-at-Law, Her Majesty's Coroner for Inner West London, for encouraging correspondence (though Dr Thurston is *not* among the convinced!), and for permission to use the valuable article in *The Medico-Legal Journal*, 1961, 29, Pt 4, pp 100ff; Mr J. D. Walker, MBE, Her

Majesty's Coroner for the Metropolitan District of Leeds, for information on an essential photograph; Miss Ann Y. Wilkinson, for the use of quotations from her article, 'Bleak House: From Faraday to Judgement Day'; Dr J. E. Windrow, of the George Peabody College for Teachers (assisted by Mrs Eads, of the Tennessee State Library, and Miss Judith Sommervold, of Peabody College), Nashville, Tennessee, for finding me the facts about Mr. James Hamilton, of the University of Nashville, and for sending me illustrative and historical material with kind permission to use both in my book; Dr Edward Van Liere, Dean Emeritus of the Medical Center, University of West Virginia, for replying to some important questions; Julian Wolff, MD, of New York, who – though not an accepter of spontaneous combustion as a fact – generously sought out and supplied me with much relevant source material, notably the article on Dr Krogman's experiences and reported opinions, quoted in the notes at the end of this book.

To various public and private institutions, some new to me, some known for many years, I also tender my thanks; the staffs of the British Museum Library, the Buckingham Palace Road Library, were as helpful as they have always been. The service of the Photographic Section of the Royal Society of Medicine deserves a special mention, while in opening up their library to me, the Dickens Fellowship brought some important early references to spontaneous combustion to my notice. I record my thanks to the librarians of the *Daily Telegraph* and of the London office of *The Liverpool Post and Echo* for finding me the particulars of Miss Phyllis Newcombe's and Mrs Mary Carpenter's tragic deaths respectively, and I acknowledge, with thanks, the permission of the publisher and editor of *The Philadelphia Enquirer* for permission to quote from the article, 'The Case of the Cinder Woman', from the issue of 15 June 1974.

I have reserved until the last, for special mention, the very talented authors, Sheila Ostrander and Lynn Schroeder, of *PSI – Psychic Discoveries Behind the Iron Curtain*, by far the best popular account of Russian work in the field of parapsychology. As I have gratefully acknowledged in the text, it has given me much information on the Kirlians' experiments. At the same time, and still in connection with Russian scientific activities, I should like to thank the Novosti (APN) Press Agency, Moscow, and its helpful London representatives, for finding and giving me permission to use the photographs of the 'Kirlian Effect'.

FOREWORD

No previous subject on which I have chosen to write has excited such interest as has Spontaneous Combustion. The number of readers' letters has far exceeded any produced by an earlier book, and the fact that I have received them from all over the world (one has just arrived from Kuching, Malaysia) testifies to the literally universal interest that not so much SHC as its 'study in depth' arouses over the widest spectrum of society, in women as well as in men, in the young no less than in the middle-aged and old.

What is more, these many letters are, most of them, constructively informative; they not only express the writers' interest in my book and its subject, they give me the writers' opinions, and very many provide relevant and pertinent information. Some adversely criticize, of course – that is to be expected by any author – but the adverse criticisms are few, and I have taken great pleasure in the fact that generally my own opinions have been favourably received. The pleasure is the greater, since I am aware that SHC is among the most explosively controversial subjects on which I could have chosen to write.

Research – especially when the fact sought has yet to be found – is a continuing matter; and ever since I published my book in England, I have been adding to the corpus of knowledge on the subject of SHC, through the information received from readers as well as through my own investigations. On the publication of the paperback edition in England, I was able to add considerably to the book, and the same opportunity was given to me, I am happy to say, in the publication of the American edition, where I was able to print, for the first time, the details of my own 'breakthrough' in the matter of the Water-Fire connection.

I wish that I had space here to acknowledge by name all those – especially readers – who have provided me with information. Alas!, I have not that space, but I would not care to close this foreword without thanking Mr Bayard Grimshaw, of Rochdale, England, for his kindness in supplying me with the details of the 'slow-vaulting' of 1776, and Mr Ray Bexley, of Fulham, London, for having called my attention to the truly remarkable passage from the Chinese classic of Wu Ch'eng-en (c. 1505-80), *Monkey*. To all those who have helped me, my warmest thanks.

'What you have learnt,' said the Patriarch, 'will preserve your youthful appearance and increase the length of your life; but after five hundred years Heaven will send down lightning which will finish you off, unless you have the sagacity to avoid it. After another five hundred years Heaven will send down a fire that will devour you. This fire is of a peculiar kind. It is neither common fire nor celestial fire, *but springs up from within and consumes the vitals, reducing the whole frame to ashes . . .*'

Monkey by Wu Ch'eng-en, a famous sixteenth century Chinese classic translated by Arthur Waley.
[Author's emphasis]

1

A WORD WITHOUT WARNING

When they found Mrs Thomas Cochrane, a widow, what was left of her was still seated in the armchair 'stuffed with pillows and cushions', in which she had dropped off to sleep. Mrs Cochrane had been 'burned beyond recognition', but neither pillows nor cushions had been even scorched.

Mr and Mrs. Kiley an elderly couple of fixed habits, died together – both burned to death – but in chintz-covered easy chairs of which the chintz had not been singed. Billy Thomas Peterson, of Pontiac, Michigan, was found dying in his car after a passing motorist had seen smoke coming from Peterson's garage. Billy was also burnt: 'His left arm was so badly burned that the skin rolled off. His genitals had been charred to a crisp. His nose, mouth and ears were burned'. And a plastic religious statue on the dashboard had melted in the intense heat.

But nothing else was even singed – *not even Peterson's underwear.*

Mrs Madge Knight died in a hospital at Chichester, Sussex, on 6 December 1943, of toxaemia following severe burns to her back. Lying in bed at home, *something* had burned her, so that she screamed out with the pain, and a doctor, called in, had to anaesthetize her before he could dress the burns. But her nightgown was not burned or even scorched.

All five – five out of perhaps as many thousands of such cases – were victims of what our remotest ancestors called 'The Fire from Heaven', and is now called 'Spontaneous Human Combustion'. It is of this mysterious and frightening phenomenon – as mysterious and frightening today as it was when Elijah called down 'The Fire from Heaven' to confound the priests of Baal – that this book will treat.

When I call Spontaneous Human Combustion – SHC for short - a mysterious phenomenon, I do not refer solely to the basic fact that it is burning, fatal or non-fatal, to which no cause may be assigned; I refer also to the fact that, so far as 'informed medical opinion' is generally concerned, it is, not so much taboo, as what we may exactly call a 'non-subject'. The bibliography at the back of this book lists only a fraction of the literature, technical and lay, on the subject; yet a leading U.S. pathologist, writing on the subject of one of the most baffling cases of SHC – that of Mrs Mary Reeser, of St Petersburg, Florida – does not hesitate to affirm that he is 'aware of only one other recorded instance of such an occurrence, and that was in a work of fiction: Charles Dickens's *Bleak House*'. When a medical scientist of this eminence refuses to credit, not merely the fact of SHC (he does not), but the full record of the phenomenon over the past three centuries, we may hardly wonder that our coroners and police chiefs are reluctant to admit to its being even a possibility.

Yet that the Fire does exist – does strike down in what seems to us (but cannot be) a totally haphazard way – is a fact now beyond rejection by ordinary commonsense observation. And, far from there having been only one other recorded instance – in a work of fiction – our newspapers, year after year, are full of such cases.

In bringing this book up to date for the paperback edition I had no difficulty in finding cases of SHC which date to this present year; and should any further revision of this book be called for, I am sure that we shall have no more difficulty in updating that. For, like a lot of other things, Spontaneous Human Combustion is always with us, and must be, since so much intentional suppression of the facts has always been practised by authority, a great deal more common than even those who unreservedly accept the fact of the phenomenon realize.

How do we define Spontaneous Human Combustion? Simply damage to the human body – partial or total – by a fire whose origins we cannot state with certainty. It is probable that the adjective 'spontaneous' is, like many another popular term, a bit wide of the mark; and that SHC is no more 'spontaneous' than the fires which break out in a bundle of oily rags in a ship's paintlocker, in a haystack, in a coal-dump, whose cause we may explain (or think that we may). One of these days – and perhaps in a not so distant future – we may explain why human beings do catch fire; but at present we do not know why they do – and, for want of a better term, we might as well stick for the moment to the time-hallowed expression, Spontaneous Human Combustion. There is nothing wrong in Dr Gavin Thurston's writing to me to say that 'I can state without qualification that no such phenomenon as Spontaneous Combustion exists, or has ever occurred . . . the combustion is not spontaneous, it has always been started by external fire'. Just so. But it is in the determined effort to seek *and find* his hypothetical 'external fire' that the majority of the world's coroners and other medico-legal experts have not only obscured both the facts and the issue, but have seriously impeded the prospects of our finding the *true* cause of SHC (which, I may add, is closely allied to the unexplained combustion of some non-human and even non-living things). The real trouble in all this effort to determine the cause of 'unexplained' fire deaths or fire injuries (there seem to be more deaths than mere injuries, by the way) is the obstinate decision of the enquirers that a cause will and *must* be found at all costs. The pages of this book will amply and distressingly demonstrate the general attitude of authority towards SHC; and will demonstrate, too, that authority will always find the evidence (in this as in other matters) that it *wishes* to find.

Not all authority is so resolutely opposed to assuming that SHC *must* have what is called a 'logical explanation' – and even among coroners there is a healthy, broadminded attitude towards the 'unexplainedness' of the unexplained.

Thus the Dublin City coroner, Dr P. J. Bofin, though, as he said, he had never before encountered a case like that of Mrs Margaret Hogan, an 89-year-old widow,[1] 'immediately recognized the signs of Spontaneous Human Combustion,' giving his opinion in words which deserve to be recorded here:

> There is no doubt that the woman died from burning. The circumstances of the burning are unusual, and would conform to what is called Spontaneous Combustion. Spontaneous Combustion does not mean that the fires are in fact spontaneous in origin. It's simply a term carried on in forensic literature to describe a set of circumstances in which a Person is burned to death without an obvious source of fire . . .

The inquest on Mrs Hogan, whom 'an intensive, devastating fire' reduced to 'a mere pile of ashes', was held on 3 April 1970, and was fully reported in the Irish press, the most detailed account being given, over a month later, in *The Irish Times* of 12 May 1970.

As a death by SCH, that of Mrs Hogan was typical, even to the fact that the small fire by which she had been sitting had gone out, nothing remaining in the grate but 'just a shovelful of blackened cinders', and that, though all sorts of suggestions were put forward as to how the fire could have managed to ignite the old lady, none could be found to be in any way satisfactory. And – again relating this fire

---

[1] See page 112

death to the now 'classic' pattern of SHC – though Mrs Hogan's body had been completely burned save for her feet, only a small square of linoleum beneath her charred (but not seriously burned) armchair was charred.

Mention of the informative newspaper report brings me to another important point: that the record of, and evidence for, SHC, is to be found more in the pages of tabloids than in the pages of the medical and medico-legal journals, which deal with SHC only rarely and in usually a decidedly selective manner, whereas the newspapers report the facts without comment, and far more frequently. My book makes it clear how much I, and other researchers into the pheno- menon of SHC and allied pyrotechnics, owe to the con- tinuous reporting of the world's press.

It is the fashion to-day to describe all manifestations of energy, from a thunderstorm to human thought, as 'elec- trical in nature' and my research into SHC and allied manifestations if 'unexplained' (though not, one hopes, inexplicable) over-heating have inclined me more and more to the belief that *all* forms of heat connected with human beings are part of one wide thermal spectrum of which SHC is but a part – and perhaps not the most important part, at that. For the Fire from Heaven seems, often enough, to have taken up its habitation here on earth; striking, not rarely and haphazardly, but frequently and with strong evidence of control.

When we come to the chapter which deals with that poltergeist activity connected with fire, we shall see that the Fire lives, as it were, in the walls of 'fire-haunted' houses, to be summoned forth by those who 'know the right words', as demons, for our ancestors, were to be summoned by 'the right words'. And the Fire seems, too, to live in – to be permanently inherent in – certain persons of unusual physico-mental pattern, from the hyperthermic 'Father Pio' (Father Forgione, of Foggia), who can survive a body temperature of nearly 120°F (49°C), to the Russian tele-kinetic medium, Nina Kulagina, who, apparently, has the power to burst spontaneously into flames.

In an interview with the London *Sunday People* (14 March 1976), the distinguished Soviet parapsychologist, Professor Genady Sergeyev, had this to say of Madame Kulagina:

> She can draw energy somehow from all around her . . . On several occasions the force rushing into her body left burn-marks up to 4 inches long on her arms and hands . . . I was with her once when her clothing caught fire from this energy flow – it literally flamed up. I helped to put out the flames, and saved some of the burned clothing as an exhibit.

The case of Lily White, whose clothing was often des-troyed by fire – though without harming the wearer *(Chapter 14)* – and that of Mrs Charles H. *(Chapter 11)* are but two out of dozens whose 'absorption of energy at abnormal levels' causes them to return that energy, often in highly inconvenient ways. One is struck by the suspicion that the 'returned energy' apparent as the giving of electrical shocks or the emission of sparks and that apparent as flame with the power to consume materials are forms of energy different only in degree, and not at all in essence – a point which will be discussed in this book.

Just as the energy which manifests itself in the various types of 'thermal irregularity', from ordinary 'causeless' fever to the almost total combustion of the human body, is but one kind of energy, so may anyone, of whatever sex, age, class, race, creed or bodily state, fall a victim to the Fire. When I wrote the first edition of this book, I was under the impression that very young children were exempt from this strangest of all human dooms; but I have since found that I was wrong. I have discovered at least one case of a death by what was obviously SHC, in which the victim was a boy of only eleven months; and I have no doubt now that further research will reveal other cases involving very young children. The case of the 11-month-old boy was reported in the London *Daily Telegraph* for 4 January 1939, and it was of interest to me to see that the story described the incineration of the boy by 'Spontaneous Combustion'. The boy, Peter Seaton, had been put to bed, and was supposedly fast asleep when a visitor to the house, Harold Edwin Huxstep, a friend of the family, heard screams of terror, and rushed upstairs to the room in which Peter had his bed.

But there could be no rescue of Peter by Mr Huxstep.

'It seemed', he said, 'as if I had opened the door of a furnace. There was a mass of flames, which shot out, burning my face and flinging me back across the hall. It was humanly impossible to get Peter out'.

And what had caused this conflagration, so powerfully all-consuming that it had not only destroyed completely the body of the child, but had raged with such intensity that, in Mr Huxstep's vivid phrase, it seemed to him as though he had opened the door of a furnace? Superintendent E. H. Davies, of the London Fire Brigade, who carried out a minute search of the room, could give no answer save that there had been nothing in the room which could have initiated even a small fire, let alone a blaze of the shocking intensity which had destroyed little Peter, but had left most of the furniture untouched. This is a case of particular importance in that the age of the victim outlawed the usual 'suggestions' made whenever children are concerned: that they were 'playing with matches'; that they had 'brought a bottle of gasoline into the room', 'had been messing around with the electric switches', and so on. There was no question that 11-month-old Peter Seaton had been put to bed already half asleep, and that certainly he had had no *explicable* hand in causing the holocaust which had destroyed him.

As I said, 'broadminded' coroners and others investigating fire deaths in which no *apparent* cause is discoverable, are willing to ascribe the fire (and resultant death) to 'Spontaneous Human Combustion', for, as Dr Bofin, the Dublin City Coroner, expressed it: SHC is 'simply a term . . . to describe a set of circumstances in which a person is burned to death without an obvious source of fire'.

This is true enough – so far as it goes; but it does not go far enough, and it contains a dangerous ambiguity. For death or injury by SHC is not merely caused by a fire which has 'no obvious source'; it is caused by a fire which, like the recently discovered 'poly-water', has, as we may say, 'its own rules'. And it was this special – and specialized – behaviour on the part of 'SHC fire' which so impressed the Ancient World that it was then attributed a divine origin, and named, as we have seen, 'The Fire from Heaven'. For it is not primarily the absence of an 'obvious source of fire' which entitles us to classify a fire death or fire injury as one belonging to an SHC category; our so classifying the fire depends primarily on the curiously abnormal aspects of the fire's behaviour. Briefly, ordinary 'normal' fire consumes anything and everything inflammable or combustible; even the smallest flame will go on to burn up anything which is capable of being burned; the ordinary fire will die out only when it has exhausted the materials on which to feed.

Not so the fire of SHC: it has a *selective* property that our much more observant ancestors saw only as a selective function; and it is for the evidences of this selectivity, and not for the negative evidence of a missing 'obvious source of fire' that our coroners, police officials and firemen should be looking to know how to classify a fire as belonging to the SHC type. For what ordinary fire may effect almost total combustion of the human body inside its unburnt clothing, may burn both body and clothes, but spare (save for the slightest scorching) the armchair in which the victim was

11

sitting when the highly selective Fire struck – why and how we do not yet know. It isn't as though the Fire burned without heat – Mr Huxstep opened the door of little Peter's room, and it was as though 'I had opened the door of a furnace . . . a mass of flames, which shot out, burning my face and flinging me back across the hall'. But even the most inflammable things may be untouched by this genuinely great heat – I call it 'genuinely great', since it has more than a merely subjective intensity. When they found Grace Pett, of Ipswich, 'like a half-burned wooden log; a heap of cinders covered with a white ash', a paper screen standing within a few inches of the fierce fire which had consumed Mrs Pett was unscorched; the equally fierce fire which had burned up George Turner in the cab of his truck had not even caught some oil spilled on the seat beside him – and certainly in the case of *all* the numerous fire deaths in cars mentioned in this book, the highly inflammable gasoline never caught fire. What the Fire does and how it behaves in its highly idiosyncratic way, it is the purpose of this book to describe.

As I said, the men of the Ancient World interpreted the highly selective behaviour of the Fire – burning the specific object of its attack, and leaving all 'irrelevant' adjacent material untouched, as the undeniable evidence of purpose. When the drunken old soldier clambered up to the hayloft in Colchester, on Sunday, 19 February 1888, he fell asleep 'in the immediate proximity of dry woodwork and hay, loose and in bundles'. The fire completely consumed the old soldier; the highly inflammable hay was not even scorched. In a letter to me, Mr Edward Campbell, the literary editor of the London *Evening News,* suggests that all victims of the Fire may be the subjects of a conscious or unconscious intention to harm, on the part of those who have the power of projecting (and, he should have added, *directing)* lethal heat. Certainly the author of that part of the Book of Kings which deals with the prophet, Elijah the Tishbite, would agree with Mr Campbell about the controllability of the Fire.

Shocked by the fact that King Ahab had forsaken the true God of Israel for the false Canaanite gods, Elijah the prophet decided to expose both the false gods and the four hundred and fifty Baalimite priests whom Ahab had imported to serve them. Elijah asked Ahab for permission to arrange a test of the rival gods' powers; a sacrifice would be laid out on a Baalimite altar, and a similar sacrifice on an altar of Elijah's making. Then, said the prophet, each side would pray that the sacrifice be burned by the power of its respective god or gods (the prophet, of course, prayed to only One).

All day the Baalimites prayed, and nothing happened, even though, in their frenzy, they gashed themselves with knives, so that the blood poured out.

As last, when the evening had come, Elijah ordered that four barrels of water should be emptied over his stone-and-wood altar, and that this should be done four times – sixteen barrels - full in all. And he also ordered that water should be poured into the trench that he had dug around the altar.

Then Elijah prayed.

Then the fire of the Lord fell, and consumed the burnt sacrifice, and the wood, and the stones, and the dust, and licked up the water that was in the trench.

– that totality of combustion, in fact, which is always, it seems, within the capacity of the Fire from Heaven.

The author of Psalm 97 is even more explicit in stating where the Fire is, Who controls it – and for what purpose.

1. The Lord reigneth; let the earth rejoice; let the multitude of isles be glad *thereof*.

13

2. Clouds and darkness are round about him; righteousness and judgment *are* the habitation of his throne.
3. A fire goeth before him, and burneth up his enemies round about.

The very practical opinion – based on commonsense observation and clear-thinking – is, however poetically and even 'mystically' expressed, that the Fire that we encounter in SHC and allied phenomena is fire which is directed from a clearly definable point of origin, and against a specifically designated victim. To what extent modern thinking agrees with the opinion of the prophets of the Ancient World – the thinkers, the seers, the philosophers, the priests of all the Ancient World (not merely that part of it whose opinions are recorded in the Old Testament) – this book will, I trust, make clear.

An attempt will be made to find, if not the precise nature of the Fire, then at least some hypotheses which may indicate in which direction we may look for the truth.

What will, I know, be apparent, is the growing conviction among all who have studied the phenomena of SHC, that Fire is not an isolated phenomenon, but is linked, in ways that we do not as yet understand, with many other aspects of what may be classified under the general heading of the Phenomena of the Strange, or the Phenomena of the Unexplained. That, for one thing, SHC phenomena and poltergeist phenomena may be linked at certain times is now beyond question – and it is in the study of fire in poltergeist 'hauntings' that, I think, we shall come first to establishing the connection between the manifestations of the Fire and the originating Will to Harm. Certainly the fires broke out in the school to which reluctant 12-year-old Willie Brough was sent because unhappy Willie hated the school; and that there was a connection between Jennie Bramwell's unhappiness and the *several hundred* fires at her foster-parents' house is, I think, beyond argument. There are many other such cases, in which the very real 'fiery poltergeist' has been summoned by an unhappy child's subconscious will to change things to his or her own liking – in Willie Brough's case the school trustees obligingly sent him packing there and then!

Perhaps the most impressive demonstration of the manner in which the Fire may be linked with poltergeist activity – it is one of the more recent, too – is the account of what happened to the van Reenan family of Plettenberg Bay, South Africa, as told in the *National Enquirer* for 4 November 1975. The whole affair of the van Reenans 'fiery persecutions' will be told later in this book, but the case is mentioned here as one more example of the close link between poltergeist activity and the Fire from Heaven.

What the reader should bear in mind is that the Fire and all those other manifestations of the strange which may or may not be associated with it are phenomena of the *unexplained* – and *not* of the inexplicable. If we have no way yet of explaining the highly individual behaviour of the Fire from Heaven – behaviour which sets it apart from all other forms of fire – be sure that we shall have that needed explanation sooner or later. There is no mystery in human experience which does – or even may – remain a mystery for ever.

2

'SHE DIED BY THE VISITATION OF GOD'

On Whit Monday, 1725, Le Lion d'Or, the best inn of the ancient city of Rheims, was full; and the landlord, Jean Millet, had retired early, knowing that he had to be up at dawn on the following day, for the heavy work of the Whit Tuesday Fair. Most of the servants were in bed. Two or three stayed up to attend to late drinkers in the bistro and Madame Millet remained downstairs to see to the eventual locking-up.

At about 2:30 on the Tuesday morning, Millet woke with a start: the smell of burning had awakened him. Tugging on his old dressing-gown, and not waiting to light his flat candlestick, he opened the door of his bedroom and ran down the corridor to the head of the stairs, banging on each door as he passed, shouting, 'Fire! Fire! Get up and get downstairs to safety!'. Within seconds, servants and guests were hurrying down in the wake of the landlord. In the great entrance hall, with logs still red in its man-high fireplace, was the fire – but it was not any part of the hotel which was burning; it was the landlord's wife, Nicole Millet. Burning – and dead.

The Lieutenant of Police, accompanied by two gendarmes from the barracks, was making his rounds when the commotion from Le Lion d'Or brought him quickly to the open door of the inn. He entered, saw the smoking corpse of Madame Millet in the *unburnt* armchair before the fire, and with that rapidity in fixing guilt for which the French police

16

have always been noted, at once charged the innkeeper with having murdered his wife.

It was as well that, among the guests awakened that night by Millet's shouts of 'Fire!' and kept awake by the foul smell of the burning body, was a young surgeon named Claude-Nicholas le Cât, not yet fully qualified, but already highly respected by his superiors at the Hôtel Dieu in Rheims.

Le Cât had not rushed pell-mell down the stairs with the other terrified guests, but had followed more slowly. Now he came into the large hall just in time to hear the Lieutenant of Police order the landlord's arrest.

'One moment, if you please, Monsieur le Lieutenant', said the young surgeon, pushing his way through the crowd – most of them with their handkerchiefs to their noses – assembled around the smoking and almost totally destroyed corpse. 'Why are you arresting this man?'

'Because it is evident that he has just murdered his wife!'

'Is it so evident? Why *he*? Why not some other person?'

'Who else would wish to do her harm?'

'Why should the landlord here wish to do her harm?'

'Because', said one of the gendarmes, 'she gave him hell; drank like a fish, and spent all the profits on her boozing. *That's* why!'

Le Cât now addressed himself directly to Millet. 'Is this true, Monsieur le Patron?'

'Is what true, sir? That I murdered my poor wife? No, that indeed is not true. I went to bed early – to my own room; since tomorrow – to-day, rather – is the great fair. My wife slept in her own room which she shares – shared – with a servant. She must have come down again . . . for a final drink. I swear that I did not kill her!'

A slatternly woman of thirty or so now pushed her way through the throng of people. Addressing no one in particular, she shouted:

'Yes, that's true. Madame and I went upstairs. I got into my bed and Madame got into hers. And then . . . I'd just got into my first sleep, when a noise awoke me: it was Madame getting out of her bed. I heard her open and close the door, and her footsteps going down the corridor. Then I fell asleep again and woke to hear Monsieur shouting that the place was afire'.

Le Cât nodded, and again addressed himself to Millet.

'I am inclined to believe that you did not kill your wife', he said. 'But now: as for these other things which have been said – are *they* true? Did your wife drink heavily? I see . . . All the time . . . ? And was it her habit to take a bottle and drink it up as she sat before the fire?'

'I think I may say', said Millet with evident reluctance, 'that I do not recall her ever having gone to bed sober these past twenty years. But I did not kill her, Monsieur; I *swear* that I did not kill her!'

Le Cât turned to the Lieutenant of Police. 'Indeed he did not, and you may safely release him from custody. If you doubt my authority to be so precise in this matter, pray ask yourself by what *human* agency such *total* combustion might be effected? Look, I ask you! – only the skull and the very extremities remain; almost the entire body is consumed – and that completely.

'But, Monsieur, look further. Observe how, despite the almost total destruction of the body, this chair in which the dead woman was sitting is hardly burned. True, the leather is somewhat scorched, the varnish of the woodwork some-what bubbled . . . But how could a fire procured by ordinary criminal intent have managed to burn the body in its entirety, while still leaving unharmed the chair in which this poor woman was sitting?'

'And who are you, Sir, that you speak with such author-ity?'

'I am Claude-Nicholas le Cât, born in Blérancourt, and present Assistant-Surgeon at the Hôtel Dieu in this city.'

The Lieutenant of Police made a deep bow, doffing his three-cornered hat in a sarcastic manner.

'You are not a Doctor of Medicine? Not yet, eh? Well, Monsieur Assistant-Surgeon, when you are a fully qualified Doctor of Medicine, perhaps we shall be more inclined to listen to what you have to say.

'For the present, I say that there appears to be strong *primâ facie* evidence that Monsieur le Patron did kill his wife − probably by pouring her bottle over her, and setting the spirit alight. You ask why the chair wasn't burned? Because, as soon as she felt herself on fire, she jumped up − and fell back into the chair again only when the body had been entirely consumed, and the flames had been quenched for want of fuel. If you have any real evidence to give, you shall have your opportunity at either the inquest or the trial − or both. And now, Monsieur Millet, I shall ask you to accompany me to the Prefecture'.

The freeing of Millet was no simple matter: both the Coroner and the President of the Assize Court were reluctant to accept the evidence of facts which even to-day are treated as non-facts by some of the world's leading medical men, who flatly deny the phenomenon of spontaneous human combustion.

Indeed, Millet had been condemned to death before le Cât's eloquent presentation of an impressive mass of historical precedents for Madame Millet's death reversed the court's opinion, and permitted the landlord of Le Lion d'Or to return to his inn.

'We find', said the president, 'after having heard the well-presented arguments of Monsieur le Cât, that the prisoner did not kill his wife'.

'But if he did not', the Lieutenant muttered obstinately, 'how then did she die?'

'She died', said le Cât, solemnly, 'by *the visitation of God*'.

At the inquest held by the Coroner for the city of Rheims on the body of Nicole Millet, the evidence given by le Cât caused a sensation, not only in Rheims, but throughout France and Europe. For it was le Cât's evidence which inspired another Frenchman, Jonas Dupont, to collect all available evidence concerning the type of death which had killed Nicole Millet. Nearly forty years after le Cât had almost outwitted the credulity of the Rheims coroner's court, Dupont published the first full account of the phenomenon of the spontaneous combustion of the human body: *De Incendiis Corporis Humani Spontaneis,* the first edition of which is dated 1763 at Leyden.

Reading over the evidence of le Cât in the Millet case, one is struck by the fact that he is guided throughout by an opinion which was never challenged until the present century, and which still influences the findings of present-day coroners and forensic scientists: that the so-called spontaneous combustion of the human body finds *a* principal, if not *the* principal, 'triggering' in the fact that the subject is a heavy drinker of *ardent spirits* (not of wine or beer).

Already, by le Cât's day, there was ample evidence that it was not only the heavy drinkers, such as Madame Millet, who were so strangely attacked by this 'Fire from Heaven'.

A noted case of the spontaneous combustion of a non-drinker was that of the Contessa Cornelia di Bandi – a case which must have come to le Cât's ears, because of the curious and terrifying features of her death. The alarm was given by some neighbours because from the windows of the Countess's room there trickled out a yellowish, utterly loathsome half-liquid smoke, whose very smell terrified her little lapdog.

THOMÆ *19?*
BARTHOLINI

A C T A

MEDICA & PHILOSO-
PHICA HAFNIENSIA

Ann. 1671. & 1672.

Cum æneis figuris.

Justus Höeg?
Haga comitum?
15 May 1674?

HAFNIÆ,

Sumptibus PETRI HAUBOLD Acad. Bibl.
Typis GEORGII GÖDIANI, Typogr. Reg.
cIↄ IↃC LXXIII.

11

Though Thomas Bartholin's famous *Acta*, published at Copenhagen in 1673, treats of spontaneous combustion only incidentally, he is the first medical scientist to treat the phenomenon seriously and objectively. *Copyright: The British Library.*

SPECIMEN PATHOLOGICO-MEDICUM
INAUGURALE

DE

INCENDIIS CORPORIS HUMANI SPONTANEIS,

Q U O D,

FAVENTE SUMMO NUMINE,

Ex Auctoritate MAGNIFICI RECTORIS

D. DAVIDIS van ROYEN,
MEDICINAE DOCTORIS. BOTANICES IN ACAD.
LUGD. BAT. PROFESSORIS ORDINARII:

NEC NON

Ampliſſimi SENATUS ACADEMICI *Conſenſu,*
& *Nobiliſſimae* FACULTATIS MEDICAE *Decreto,*

PRO GRADU DOCTORATUS,

Summisque in MEDICINA Honoribus & Privilegiis
ritè ac legitimè conſequendis,

Eruditorum Examini ſubmittit

I O N A S   D U P O N T,
AMST. BAT.

Ad diem 16. *Decembris* M. D. CC. LXIII. *H. L. Q. S.*

Intima pars homini vero flagravit ad oſſa:
Flagravit ſtomacho flamma, ut fornacibus intus.
LUCRET.

LUGDUNI BATAVORUM,
Apud THEODORUM HAAK, Bibliop.

The classic of spontaneous combustion: Jonas Dupont's pioneer work on 'the spontaneous combustion of the human body', published at Leyden, December 1763. With this outstandingly important medical work the scientific study of spontaneous combustion may be said to have begun. *Copyright: The British Library.*

Sir David Brewster, in his *Letters on Natural Magic*, calls this 'one of the most remarkable cases of spontaneous combustion'. He thus describes the death of 'the Countess Cornelia Zangari and Bandi[2] of Cesena':

This lady, who was in the sixty-second year of her age, retired to bed in her usual health. Here she spent above three hours in familiar conversation with her maid and in saying her prayers: and having at last fallen asleep, the door of her chamber was shut. As her maid was not summoned at the usual hour, she went into the bed-room to wake her mistress; but receiving no answer she opened the window [i.e. drew back the curtains], and saw her corpse on the floor in the most dreadful condition. At the distance of four feet from the bed there was a heap of ashes. Her legs, with the stockings on, remained untouched, and the head, half-burned, lay between them. Nearly all the rest of the body was reduced to ashes. The air in the room was charged with floating soot. A small oil lamp on the floor was covered with ashes but had no oil in it; and in two candlesticks, which stood upright upon a table, the cotton wick of both the candles was left, and the tallow of both had disappeared. The bed was not injured, and the blankets and sheets were raised on one side as if a person had risen from it. From an examination of all the circumstances of this case, it has been generally supposed that an internal combustion had taken place; that the lady had risen from her bed to cool herself, and that, on her way to open the window, the combustion had overpowered her, and consumed her body by a process in which no flame was produced which could set fire to the furniture or the floor. The Marquis Scipio Maffei was informed by an Italian nobleman who passed through Cesena a few days after the event, that he heard it stated in that town, that the Countess Zangari was in the habit,

---

[2]   So correctly – and uniquely – described by the meticulous Scottish scientist.   But the forms 'Countess Cornelia di Bandi' or 'Countess di Bandi' have become acceptable through usage, and have been adopted by me in this book. MH

when she felt herself indisposed, of washing all her body with
camphorated spirit of wine.

Here, though the victim did not drink alcohol, was the
reasonably presumed presence of alcohol – camphorated
spirit of wine – among the physical circumstances in which
the Countess died. But it is true that in the majority of
these spontaneous combustions there was a well-established
history of drinking.

Grace Pett, a fisherman's wife of the parish of St Clements, Ipswich, England – as dedicated to drunkenness as the
Countess had been devoted to sobriety – went up in smoke
on the evening of 9 April 1744. Only a few years later her
case was followed by that of widow Mary Clewes, 'of
indifferent character, and much addicted to drinking'. Mrs
Clewes, unlike many another widow, paid her dead husband
the compliment of sincere grief and consoled herself in her
solitary condition with two pints of rum a day.

Perhaps the assumed connection between over-indulgence
in alcohol and spontaneous combustion seemed more
apparent in the eighteenth-century, for the reason that few
of the lower classes did *not* drink. The Contessa Cornelia di
Bandi was an exception to the general rule of spontaneous
combustions, not so much because she did not drink, as
because she came from the aristocracy. In all the history of
spontaneous combustion, few in modern times have been
above the social level of the lower-middle class. Speaking
generally – I shall mention the exceptions later – the
aristocracy and upper and upper-middle classes do not seem
to have been threatened with this oddest of all human
dooms.

The eighteenth-century took pride in calling itself the
Age of Reason. A more appropriate title would have been
the Age of Reasoning. It was an age as interested in mysterious phenomena as even the most ignorantly superstitious

period of the Middle Ages could have been, but the eighteenth century differed from all preceding periods in that it *always* sought a 'rational' explanation.

It is this earnest enquiry after non-mystical, eminently factual (and so completely credible) explanations which made the eighteenth the mother-century of the modern world. It is from this enquiry-obsessed century that all modern technology begins. From this century come present-day chemistry, physics, metallurgy, electrical theory and practice – and it is significant to note that one of the fathers of modern chemistry, the German chemist Andreas Sigismund Marggraf, pioneered modern chemical analysis when, in 1758, he began to study the behaviour of *flame* through a spectroscope. He noted that it was possible to distinguish between the salts of sodium and those of potassium by observing the different colours that they imparted to a flame: yellow and lavender respectively.

About the same time that Marggraf was peering through his spectroscope, opening up the chemical secrets of Nature with a flame, the ten-year-old Antoine-Laurent de Lavoisier found himself wondering why things burned. A little later he would be embarking on such profound research in which the last great survival of alchemical thinking – 'Phlogiston, the Principle of Combustion' by Marggraf – was to be swept away. With French imagination but still typically eighteenth-century reason, Lavoisier, in determining the chemical composition of air, showed once and for all the rôle of oxygen in combustion. Before the French terrorists sent him to the guillotine, Lavoisier had given chemistry its modern nomenclature; had stated the law of the conservation of mass; had made the first steps in the measurement of heat; and had given the world the metric system. But it was his work on heat and combustibility in particular which brought him honour.

Indeed, until we realize that the eighteenth century was fascinated – and fascinated 'rationally' – by heat and its various manifestations, we shall not be able to understand the fascination that 'thermal aberrations' such as spontaneous combustion had for the men of that time.

In an article in the *Medico-Legal Journal* (29: 1961), Dr Gavin Thurston discusses a modern case of 'preternatural combustibility' and looks at past opinions on this subject. 'The present case', he writes, 'shows most of the features listed by the older authorities, *except that the deceased woman was not a heavy drinker* [my italics – M.H.]. Why drink has so often been mentioned in the past is not clear, unless it is that the habitual drinker is more likely to fall into a grate than the average person'.

I shall return to Dr Thurston and his views later; but here it is essential to correct the dangerous implications of a remark that wider reading on his part would have made impossible: 'A point that has never been made before is that all these cases *[i.e. of 'preternatural combustibility']* have happened indoors, usually near to the hearth'.

The only permissible comment on this statement is that it is untrue. Many cases have occurred out-of-doors. A New England doctor, B. H. Hartwell, driving through a wood in 1891, was able to extinguish the flames spouting from a young woman's back, and, from my own reading, I would say that the majority of cases which occur indoors are not in close proximity to the grate.

The 'reason' why an addiction to drink was always put forward as a predetermining condition for the occurrence of spontaneous combustion was that, in an age when drinking was the rule rather than the exception, any statistical analysis of any type of accident would have shown drinkers in the majority.

Where the victim had been provably abstemious, this apparent exception was never permitted to challenge the

24

'inviolate' rule that, somehow, alcohol and spontaneous combustion were joined in a cause-and-effect linkage.

Indeed, even in the case of the abstemious Contessa di Bandi, drink – or, rather, alcohol – was not absent. At the enquiry into her loathsome death, it was stated, as I have mentioned, that she had been in the habit of rubbing her body with camphorated spirits. The eighteenth century, in its determination to 'explain rationally' the burning of a human body, always looked for a first cause; in these cases, some flame or other source of heat. The *London Medical and Surgical Journal* for 25 November 1837, in an article which surveys recent cases of 'alleged spontaneous combustion'. remarks that 'Dr Paris[3] thinks that . . . combustion never originates spontaneously', and this even though Paris goes on to recall that, in the case of Grace Pett of Ipswich, England, quoted above, 'There was no fire in the grate; a candle had burnt into the socket near the body' *(i.e. the candle had nothing to do with the death of Grace Pett, who had been found in the morning 'like a half-burned wooden log; a heap of cinders covered with a white ash').*

As we examine the surprisingly varied aspects of this strange visitation we shall see that contemporary medical science is as faithfully wedded to a preconceived opinion as were the men of the past.

Modern forensic scientists examine the corpses of the victims of 'preternatural combustibility' in the certainty that there is no such phenomenon as spontaneous combustion, and that 'therefore' some igniting agency *must* have been present even if no traces of its existence may be found.

With no apparent consciousness of self-contradiction, the expert medical supporters of the no-fire-no-combustion theory will admit – quite without reluctance, it seems – that

---

[3] *See Bibliography.*

there *may* be cases where the generating heat is not only not discernible, but may even not have been present.

Once again let me quote Dr Gavin Thurston:

> This is an account of a case illustrating the phenomenon of preternatural combustibility. Instances are extremely rare and have been described from time to time over the centuries, but, as will be shown, authenticity has often been doubted and the condition lies near the borderland of fact and myth. Nevertheless, there are undisputed instances, and this seems to be one, where the body has burned in its own substance, without external fuel, and in which there has been a remarkable absence of damage to surrounding inflammable objects.

Now the given reason why most modern experts in this field reject the phrase 'spontaneous combustion', in favour of the phrase 'preternatural combustibility', is that in these cases there has been no *spontaneous* generation of body-consuming heat, but the body has been ignited by some 'external fuel'. Yet, in the passage quoted above, Dr Thurston not only gives one case in which the absence of 'external fuel' was proved, but also mentions that, in the historical record, there have been other 'undisputed instances' of the same fuelless generation of intense heat.

Although modern medical scientists try, as eagerly as did their predecessors of the seventeenth, eighteenth and nineteenth-centuries, to rationalize the phenomenon of spontaneous (or 'preternatural') combustion, the modern attitude is different – fundamentally different, indeed – from that of past times.

In the past, they sought to rationalize the phenomenon because it was a matter of absorbing interest to professional and layman alike; to-day the experts seek to rationalize the phenomenon in order to dismiss it from discussion. I have seen the entry 'Spontaneous Combustion' again and again under the heading 'Suspected Cause of Fire', in the report sheets of the London Fire Brigade, yet an enquiry made to the press officer may well lead the enquirer to believe that there is not only such thing as spontaneous combustion, but that no such entry could ever have appeared on the sheets.

And, despite the fact that coroners are sitting year by year on such cases, any literary reference to the phenomenon in the specialist journals *always* treats it as though it belonged only in the folklore of times past.

Thus: 'Little is heard nowadays on this macabre subject, which in the first half of the nineteenth century attracted much notice' (article in the *British Medical Journal* in the 'Nova et Vetera' column, 21 May 1938); 'Sir, your note in the *Journal* of May 21 (p. 1106) on spontaneous human combustion is very interesting. It is surprising how common was the belief in its occurrence some hundred years ago' (letter in the *British Medical Journal*, from L. A. Parry, FRCS, 4 June 1938); 'Sir, the subject of spontaneous combustion apparently attracted the attention, not only of the medical profession, but of the laity, one hundred years ago' (Letter in the *British Medical Journal*, from Gavin Thurston, MRCP, 18 June 1938).

Very many more letters, covering a period of several years, could be cited to support the fact that modern medical science, faced with the impossibility of presenting a true explanation of this phenomenon, prefers not to discuss it. (One might almost add: even to think about it!)

A fellow-member of the Crime Writers' Association, Professor Keith Simpson, writes to me that:

I have not seen a case, in forty years' practice, where I have been satisfied that the body burning is literally spontaneous, and the case referred to in detail by Prof. Gee of Leeds (who is a particularly careful observer and supports his views in his account [in *Medicine, Science and Law*, 1965, 5, 37] of another case by some experiments with fat and other tissues) supports my own view that: '. . . though fat when deteriorating and oily

27

can burn, some other condition has to be present to start fire. About 250°C is necessary and the body itself will not do this. (Of course, as soon as ignition is effected, the fat will burn at a far lower temperature).'

So, as in Gee's case (and I suspect also in Thurston's) a smouldering fire, embers, some other source of heat, or the ignition of gas near the body (as by a pilot light) is enough. The decomposing oily body fat will then burn. Methane, also produced in the decomposing body, needs heat or a spark – even a static electric discharge will do it – to take fire.

There can be no doubt of Professor Simpson's authority to speak on medical matters – especially those connected with forensic medicine. But, again, we find the expert arguing his case on (not so much the evidence, as) *selected evidence. Professor Simpson ignores both the historical record regarding the difficulty of burning bodies when others are burning them,* and the fact that many cases of combustion, spontaneous or 'preternatural', have affected living persons.

Widely read as he is in this particular subject, Professor Simpson makes no reference to the fact, referred to in Dr Thurston's article already quoted: 'Nevertheless, there are undisputed instances . . . where the body was burned in its own substance, without external fuel . . .'

The fascination that spontaneous combustion exercised over 'the laity' at the beginning of the nineteenth-century is responsible for the fact that the two 'classic' descriptions of death by spontaneous combustion are not to be found in the medical references (the principal of which will be listed later) but in the works of two novelists: Captain Frederick Marryat, RN (1792-1848) and Charles Dickens (1812-70).

3

INVESTIGATING
THE PHENOMENON

It is one thing to tell an awkward fact to go away; it is another when that fact refuses, and one is left with the choice of trying to ignore the fact or of explaining it. Spontaneous combustion, by its willful persistence in occurring, refused to go away; and it had therefore to be explained.

Vested interests, in the study of spontaneous combustion as elsewhere, warred obstinately against the truly objective elucidation of the mystery inherent in the phenomenon. The 'problem of alcohol' was a preoccupation with the do-gooders of the newly dawned nineteenth-century, and these were quick to seize on the 'lessons' to be derived from deaths by spontaneous combustion – though, perhaps, 'awful warnings' would be the preferable phrase.

One of the first verifiable cases of out-of-doors spontaneous combustion was that of John Anderson of Nairn, Scotland, a recognized heavy drinker, who was found 'smouldering' and dying by the roadside outside his native town. The fullest 'moral' advantage was taken of John's 'awful' death by the *Glasgow Temperance Journal*, which was the only one to report this case in full.

There had, of course, been many earlier cases, from that of the old woman who had been mysteriously consumed in Copenhagen in 1692, through all the eighteenth-century cases to deaths of this type in Massachusetts in 1802, in Ireland in 1810, and in other parts of the United States and in Canada in 1837.

However, scepticism has its advantages; and the earnest attempts, not so much to disprove the phenomenon of spontaneous combustion, as to find a rational explanation for it, caught the attention of patient investigators. The classic authorities to establish their reputation in these studies – more, indeed, by the thoroughness of their research rather than by their pioneering in it – were J. A. Paris and J. S. M. Fonblanque, whose joint *Medical Jurisprudence* was published in London in 1833, and T. R. and J. B. Beck, the 6th edition of whose *Elements of Medical Jurisprudence* appeared in 1838. Paris and Fonblanque are superior to the Becks in that the former were honestly objective enough to adduce positive evidence for the 'defence' – that is, for those who *did* believe in the possibility of spontaneous combustion; the Becks are superior in filling out the historical record. Together, these two partnerships have provided a corpus of fact and speculation, in respect of spontaneous combustion, on which every succeeding researcher has necessarily built.

In several instances, the Becks repeat the conclusions of Paris and Fonblanque; no harm in that, save that the later researchers seem often to ignore the implications, not only of the facts that their own research has uncovered, but also of those that they have 'borrowed' from the earlier work.

All the same, few dedicated researchers toil on without any original discovery as reward for their dedication: it was the Beck book which recorded[4] the significant fact that, throughout the almost total combustion of Grace Pett (see p.12) the clothes of a child and a paper screen, both close to the burning body, escaped even the slightest scorching. And in Paris and Fonblanque's book are found the sig-

---

[4]   Outside of a newspaper report, the first mention of this case is to be found in Sir David Brewster's *Letters on Natural Magic (1823)*.

nificant facts that water, far from extinguishing the 'spontaneous' fire, rather feeds it; and that the incidence of spontaneous combustion is universal.

Paris and Fonblanque were not the first to remark on the fact that to consume a human body at the stake to the extent to which the average victim of spontaneous combustion is consumed called for 'large quantities of fuel', and they quote the relevant complaints of public executioners of the costliness of burning felons.

Where one of their 'considered findings' runs counter to established fact is in their stating — and this has been stated since, and (against all the evidence) is still being stated — that 'new, highly inflammable products become formed in the body by decomposition, which explains the rapid combustion of these cases'. This is too much even for Dr Thurston, the opponent of the 'spontaneous' theory. In an article in *The Medico-Legal Journal* he comments: '[Beck and Beck] do not, however, indicate the nature of the decomposition, nor explain the apparent good health of the victims shortly before combustion occurs'.

Nor, for that matter, do the modern researchers — now seemingly pinning their solution on the presence of 'methane in the dead body' — explain the preternatural combustion of *living* bodies, phenomena for which ample evidence exists.

Thurston notes, in respect of the classic authorities that he himself quotes, the significant fact that 'none of the authorities which will presently be quoted have personally examined cases of this kind . . .'.

Just so; and it is with this feeling that they are, at best, dealing with second-hand (usually 'lay') reports, and, at worst, the recollections of gross self-deception, that the researchers into the phenomenon move so cautiously; always more ready to reject than to accept. There is nothing which can equal the convincing power of subject experience.

The unconvinced, for whom no subjective experience is available, is a man impossible to convince by hearsay alone. He refuses to believe. Just such an arrogant disbeliever was J. L. Casper, in whose *Handbook of the Practice of Forensic Medicine* (London, 1861) the 'myth' of spontaneous combustion received its most severe trouncing to date. Considering that this work was offered as a guide to examining police surgeons, coroners and others concerned with the reasons for sudden – and particularly unusual – deaths, Casper's plenary denunciation of the 'myth' and its supporters can hardly have had the effect intended. If these almost totally consumed bodies, in *their almost totally unconsumed clothes*, had not died by 'spontaneous combustion', by *what* had they died? Casper does not say – for him the denunciation of the 'myth' is sufficient: 'It is sad to think, that in an earnest scientific work, in this year of grace 1861, we must still treat of the fable of spontaneous combustion, the very proof of whose existence rests on the testimony of perfectly untrustworthy non-professionals'.

The denunciation continues for four large pages, and is noteworthy, if not admirable, for the patent expression of a xenophobia remarkable even in a German caught up in the heady excitement of Bismarckian chauvinism. From an attack on the 'fable' of spontaneous combustion, he passes to an attack on all those 'backward' countries from which the reports of the phenomenon have come, and ends up with this dig at 'the selected enemy', France:

> . . . moreover, it must be remembered, *as an incontrovertible fact* [my italics – MH], that the mass of the French people are more credulous than the Germans, and this helps to explain why France has been the birthplace of 'spontaneous combustion,' of which it is to be hoped that we shall hear no more in relation to the science of medical jurisprudence.

32

Dr Thurston succinctly remarks: 'As Casper does not recognize such a condition, no attempt at explanation is necessary or offered' – small help, indeed, to a police surgeon or coroner invited to explain to a lay jury how a healthy human being turned into a 'fetid, greasy mass'.

In at least one important respect, serious medical observers of the phenomenon – both before and after the publication of *Handbook of the Practice of Forensic Medicine* – differ from Casper in that, though they may fail to offer an acceptable explanation of spontaneous (or preternatural) combustion, they do admit to the unreserved recognition of the phenomenon itself.

In Mr John Michell's *City of Revelation* I find this arresting passage:

> In the course of the following chapters we shall examine a certain way of thought . . . The attraction of this Philosophy is that it professes to interpret a wide and varied range of phenomena by means of a few simple laws, which are those of natural growth and movement. Its masters are both mystics and logicians, *insisting that nothing be accepted as true that can not be proved so in two ways: by reason and poetic intuition.*

Dickens is unusual – not unique, fortunately – among the great, and particularly so among the great-*and*-popular, novelists in that he could bring to bear both reason and poetic intuition on the examination of phenomena which interested him. The Gothic bias of his feverishly observant mind drew him magnetically to the unexplained and the inexplicable; and of all these mysteries of our everyday, none had for him so powerful an attraction as the phenomenon of spontaneous combustion. It is for this reason that, though written (as Casper would sneeringly say) by an untrustworthy non-professional, Dickens' description of a death by this malignant visitation of uncontrollable heat ranks with Marryat's as one of the two classic descriptions of all time.

Dickens, of course, is as obsessed here, as in any other consideration of cosmic irregularity, with the moral implications of Krook's death. If Dickens highlights the horror of Krook's dying, it is only because Dickens the moralist wishes to show that, here at any rate, the horror of the punishment matches even in its terrifying impact on all the senses (but particularly those of smell and sight) the horror of that greatest sin of all: wrong done by complacent indifference. Observe how Dickens, by drawing the domestic cat into the *dramatis personae,* indicates that, not only the abominably dehumanized victim, not only the two horrified discoverers of the charred and molten body, Guppy and Weevle, but all creation, symbolized by the cat, is somehow involved in this dramatic, horrifying presentation of crime and punishment.

'What's the matter with the cat?' says Mr Guppy. 'Look at her!'
'Mad, I think. And no wonder, in this evil place'.

A very great sin has been, not so much expiated, as punished, in the dark, evil house; in the dark, evil alley; but the 'good' men are not themselves innocent − in this symbolic drama, and drama of symbolism, Dickens pretty fairly distributes guilt.

The two men advance fearfully into the boozy old miser's room:

Mr Guppy takes the light. They go down, more dead than alive, and holding one another, push open the door of the back shop. The cat has retreated close to it, and stands snarling − not at them, at something on the ground, before the fire. There is a very little fire left in the grate, but there is a smoldering suffocating vapour in the room, and a dark greasy coating on the walls and ceiling. The chairs and table, and the bottle so

34

rarely absent from the table, all stand as usual. On one chairback, hang the old man's hairy cap and coat.

So that the old man must be *somewhere* in the room . . . He is.

They advance slowly . . . The cat remains where they found her, still snarling at the something on the ground, before the fire and between the two chairs. What is it? Hold up the light.

Here is a small burnt patch of flooring; here is the tinder from a little bundle of burnt paper, but not so light as usual, seeming to be steeped in something; and here is – is it the cinder of a small charred and broken log of wood sprinkled with white ashes, or is it coal? Oh Horror, he is here! and this from which we run away, striking out the light and overturning one another into the street, is all that represents him.

Even in the facetious handling of the coroner's inquest, the always reliable Dickens adheres strictly to the classic pattern of fact:

At last come the coroner and his enquiry, like as before, except that the coroner cherishes this case as being out of the common way, and tells the gentlemen of the jury, in his private capacity, that 'that would seem to be an unlucky house next door, gentlemen, a destined house; but so we sometimes find it, and these are mysteries we can't account for!'

4

THE NATURE OF
PRETERNATURAL FIRE

'Science', said the late Charles Fort, 'is very much like the American Civil War. No matter which side had won, it would still be an American victory.'

Science has taken up what appear to be two sides in this matter of spontaneous combustion: one side affirming that the phenomenon does not exist (that is, all fires which seem to be of the 'spontaneous' type are just . . . well, fires), the other side affirming that, though there are deaths (the mere injuries — non-fatal — are always ignored) which seem to have an appearance of the mysterious about them, this is simply because the correct explanation has not, as yet, been conveniently forthcoming. This side of science affirms that spontaneous combustion is not, as so many people claim, 'inexplicable' but merely unexplained — and here science may well be right. It is, however, not going to bring us any nearer to the desired explanation if science insists on a too selective choice of its evidence.

Only one researcher, so far, has had anything original, anything constructive, to say about spontaneous combustion: this was Charles Fort, the iconoclast who used broken idols to provide the foundations for the sanest philosophy with which the mind of man has ever been driven mad.

Spontaneous combustion fascinated Fort as much as it fascinated Dickens, and it is sad to reflect that Dickens never had a chance of reading Fort. If Dickens, one may say, was *romantically* Gothic, Fort *was constructively* Gothic. He demolished almost every 'accepted fact', 'undeniable truth', incontrovertible evidence'. Scientists hated him, and still hate him. Scientists made him laugh.

He looked closer at spontaneous combustion, and, indeed, every other anomalous phenomenon, than any man had looked since the armchair philosophers of the seventeenth-century. But he looked with a far keener eye, and in consequence he saw more. And he saw more because he was able, through the normal twentieth-century press clipping services, to gather far more material for examination than was ever available to a Michel de Montaigne, Thomas Browne, John Aubrey, John Evelyn or a Robert Burton.

Fort was an obsessive investigator of the Odd; and by collecting facts that science had not only not explained, but had never attempted to explain, and in presenting these anomalies, he was quick to point out the bizarre and disturbing implicatons of his findings.

After having described some *very* odd cases involving spontaneous combustion – not all of them fatal – Fort then comments:

> I think that our data relate, not to 'spontaneous combustion of human bodies', but to things or beings, that, with a flaming process, consume men and women, but like werewolves or alleged werewolves, mostly pick out women.

But before we go on to consider those cases collected by Fort – cases different from all previously cited cases in that they are Fort-picked to support his individual theories – let us consider the fact that, by the mid-nineteenth-century, all the evidence had been collected by which the unusual nature of 'preternatural fire' might have been plainly set forth – but was not.

It was not so much that facts were misrepresented by the relevant science, as that facts were suppressed, or that false 'facts' were irresponsibly or carelessly introduced into the record, as, for example, Dr Thurston's statement, *complelely unsupported by evidence completely available to him,* that 'all the cases have happened indoors, usually near to the hearth.'

Now, by the first years of the nineteenth century, 'six essential preliminary conditions' had supposedly been discovered by the investigators – 'six essential preliminary conditions' without which the phenomenon of spontaneous combustion could not or, at least, was most unlikely to occur. These 'essential conditions' had not changed either the nature or their number by 1938, nor, indeed, have they changed since. The six are:

1. The victim is a chronic alcoholic.
2. The victim is an elderly female.
3. A lamp or other source of ignition, 'which might have occasioned the fire', is always present. Sometimes the heat source is a grate.
4. The victim is corpulent (so as to make easier the post-mortem generation of 'inflammable gases').
5. The victim is a solitary – or, at least, dies alone.
6. The victim is 'usually' a pipe-smoker.

To these 'essential preliminaries', I must now add the features which distinguished a 'spontaneous' or 'preternatural' fire from any other fire of normal type.

1. Little damage is done to combustible substances – clothes, furniture, etc. – even in the closest contact with the body.
2. There is a residue of greasy ashes.
3. There is almost total consumption of the body.
4. The extremities usually escape serious burning; certainly hands and feet – and often the head – are never totally consumed.

Now, briefly to recapitulate my objections to the above 'findings', in addition to the *facts* given above, I may add:

1. Though females form the majority of the victims – to-day, as in the past – they neither did nor do make up the *totality* of the victims. Both women *and* men are 'taken', and of the women, some are 'elderly', some middle-aged down to young; and – as we shall see – some of the more striking cases have involved adolescent girls. The only very rare sex-age-group represented in the record is that of the *boy,* pre- or post-pubescent.

   The only case of a pre-pubescent Fire-victim known to me is that of the 11-month-old boy, Peter Seaton, of Peckham Rye, London, the strange circumstances of whose death I touched on in the opening chapter of this book. So far, little Peter remains the unique member of that age-group to which he belongs.

2. I have mentioned the claim that all the victims are 'elderly females', in order to dispose of the 'sex-classifications' first. I will now turn to the statement that 'the victim is a chronic alcoholic'. Now, this is pure folklore, sustained by the novelists (as we might expect) – Balzac, Dickens and Zola – but admitted to be an 'inconstant' even by the coroners. Thus Dr Thurston, reporting a modern case: 'A slim widow, aged 69, lived alone in a small terraced house. She was in poor health, tottery on her legs, and was under treatment for high blood pressure and mild Parkinson's disease. *Her habits were abstemious* [my italics – MH], and she took half a grain of a barbiturate each bedtime.'

   This woman's case will be examined in detail later – she died 'with an unusual amount of smoke and sparks coming from her chimney' – but here notice that she *was not corpulent, in poor health* (the 'health' of the victims was also, if not an essential, then at least a 'normal' condition), and that 'her habits were abstemious.'

   At this point, established medical opinion begins to question itself. Desperately trying to salvage some prestige from the older 'authorities', Dr Thurston comments: 'The present case shows *most of the features listed by the older authorities* [my italics – MH], except that the deceased woman was not a heavy drinker . . .'

This is quite disingenuous, even for one of committed medical opinion.

When Dr Thurston says that 'the present case shows most of the features listed by the older authorities', he must surely be bearing in mind that he himself has given the six 'essential conditions' postulated by these 'older authorities', but only *three* – that is, *only fifty per cent* – of the 'essential conditions' were present in this case.

Now, if three out of six 'essential conditions' may be, in actuality, dispensed with, how 'essential' are these 'essentials'?

There was, though it was not mentioned in Dr Thurston's report, another 'essential condition' – the victim seems to have been dead before the fire flamed which burnt her up to a cinder. But the number of reported cases in which the victim has been alive forms a large proportion of the total.

3. 'A source of heat' – pipe, lamp, grate, etc. – is *always* mentioned in all inquests, even though it is often clear that, for all the presence of a 'source of heat' in the room in which the victim dies, it could not have been the pipe, lamp, grate, etc. which caused the ignition of the body. Why this 'heat source' is *always* mentioned will be examined later. But here it may be pointed out that, in the first place, several modern deaths by spontaneous combustion have occurred where there was no source of heat, and that, in the second place, the 'essential' presence of a source of heat has never been established in the case of some *living* victims.

4. 'The post-mortem generation of inflammable gases' is possible really only by the adipose condition of the 'always corpulent' victim – he or she supplied fuel for the 'candle effect' to be mentioned later. An examination of the cases shows that the

40

victims may be both fat and slim – *see* the case mentioned above. *All* reported living cases appear to have been, if not slim, then at least not fat. Neither the servant-girl from Binbrook Farm nor the young woman found flaming in a wood at Ayer, Massachusetts, was fat. One might comment 'perhaps that's why they didn't die!' – except that 'the slim widow of 69' *did* die, and so did many a non-corpulent other.

5. 'The victim is a solitary' – the victim 'lives alone'. Well, this is *often* true – but again there are striking exceptions to this rule, as the case of the Kileys, reported in the *Hampshire* (England) *Advertiser* of 4 March 1905, makes clear.

This strange affair happened at Butlock's Heath, a village near Southampton, where an elderly couple, Mr and Mrs John Kiley, lived alone in what may be described as 'modest retired comfort'.

On the *morning* of 26 February neighbours heard what they afterwards described to the coroner as 'a scratching sound', which, whatever its indescribability at the inquest, seemed to the neighbours to be sufficiently unusual and sufficiently alarming to justify their 'breaking and entering' the Kiley house. They found the house's interior in flames.

Old Mr Kiley was lying burned to death on the floor of the living room; his wife, also burned to death, was in an easy chair in the same room. Both bodies were, it was afterwards reported, 'badly charred, but recognizable.'

When the police were called, and carried through a minute examination of the premises, they noted with satisfaction that a table had been overturned and that there was an oil-lamp, its glass shade and chimney smashed, lying on the floor.

The obvious explanation – ?

Yes, except for one disturbing fact: in no circumstance could the falling of the lamp have started the fire which burnt Mr and Mrs Kiley. No wonder that the jury brought in the verdict 'accidental death – but by what means we are unable to say.'

Not pressed by the coroner to delve too deeply or to think too much, the jury took home with them the recollection of some curious and quite inexplicable facts. Both bodies, at the moment of death, had been fully dressed – as was evident from 'fragments of clothes' not quite consumed by the intense heat. Now this piece of evidence has far-reaching implications not at all insisted upon by the coroner.

That the Kileys, *elderly people of fixed habits,* had died still fully dressed, indicates the *probability* (it is, of course, no more) that they had died before going up to their bedroom, a fact – or probability – which might have indicated the time or death, except for one unaccountable discrepancy: if the Kileys had been struck down before their usual time of going to bed (say at some time between 10 and 11 p.m.), why was the house not in flames until some seven to eight hours later?

And why, if the Kileys, being still down in their living-room and so, presumably, still 'up', had been awake, did they not call for help? The neighbours, inquisitive as all country people habitually are, had heard – and investigated – the strange 'scratching noise', but had heard no cry for help. The Kileys then, had been burnt to death – charred almost to unrecognizability – in a *strictly localized* fire which had not become a *general* fire until hours later.

But who overturned the table? Mr Kiley, with the first sharp bite of the Fire from Heaven on him, making a desperate effort to open the door of room and house, and summon help?

The easy chair was of the type known then as a 'saddle-bag', upholstered in cut-plush and with a loose cover of chintz.

For all Mrs Kiley's charred condition, the loose cover was not even singed.

Supposing that many – most – of the victims of spontaneous combustion are dead when the Fire hits them, it is nevertheless a fact that the Fire strikes both the living and the dead. The case of Father Bertholi has become a 'classic'; an awkward 'classic', really, seeing that it offends against the 'rules', in this context.

Father Bertholi, not an alcoholic, not corpulent, not by any means 'an elderly female', and certainly not a man of evil life, suddenly cried out in agony – when those who heard his screams rushed to his aid, they found him enveloped in blue flames, that, with some difficulty, they beat out with their hands and coats. The eminent Italian surgeon, Battaglia, being called, examined Father Bertholi, and found that part of one of the priest's arms had been totally consumed. Battaglia dressed the burns, which were (apart from those on the arm) extensive, and put Father Bertholi to bed.

The mortification which quickly succeeded Dr Battaglia's ministrations may or may not have had to do with the Fire; it was a century preceding that in which Lister and Semmelweiss clearly demonstrated the connection between 'dirt' and disease, and Dr Battaglia, and not the Fire, may have caused the mortification of the priest's wounds.

This horrible mortification was succeeded by an intense thirst, and soon Father Bertholi fell into a coma, from which he never awakened. Judging by the description of his condition, as given in the *London Medical and Surgical Journal* of 25 November 1837, the coma provided a merciful release from his sufferings: 'While the coma was present, the body was so putrid that it exhaled an insupportable odour. Worms crawled from the body while yet alive, and the nails of the left hand separated . . .'

It should be noted, in passing, that this responsible medical journal is one of the few *early* authorities which does not insist on the 'essential' condition of corpulency:

'. . . In many of the cases recorded, the sufferers were addicted to intoxication; but not in all. They were either fat *or very lean*[5] . . . or very much debilitated; though some exceptions to this state of things have occurred.'

This comment is interesting; it shows that at least one early nineteenth-century medical editor accepted both 'under-weight' or 'emaciated' and 'debilitated' (that is, the reverse of 'healthy') as, if not exactly normally predisposing conditions in spontaneous combustion, then conditions which were found. This is in direct contrast with Dr Thurston's commenting on the 'generally healthy' condition of the victims.

The semantic connection between 'alcohol' and the Fire was far more apparent to our ancestors when the phrase 'ardent spirits' was still comprehensible to a Latin-taught society as 'burning spirits' (Latin, *ardens,* 'burning').

But even before the introduction of distilled liquors into Europe, through the School of Salerno in the twelfth-century, there were reports of persons who seemed to have a startling affinity with fire or light or both.

The legend of the men who can set fire to materials with their 'dragon-breath' is one of great antiquity and widely scattered: Charles Fort suggests that there were once such men, inheriting what was once a necessary quality in the days when fire was needed but not obtainable by mechanical means.

Theodoric the Great (AD 455-526), King of the Ostrogoths and of Italy, had a body so curiously fashioned that, when rubbed, it would give off flames; and some centuries

---

[5]   My italics: MH. Cf case of the 'slim widow of 69' on page 39.

later, still in Italy, the renowned Bookseller of Pisa astonished his fellow-citizens by the luminescence radiating from his otherwise ordinary body.

All 'flame' is not fatal – sometimes not even hot – and the incidence of the 'flame', from the harmless luminescence of the Pisan bookseller, through the (alarming but) equally harmless blue flames of the Ostrogothic king, to the painful and terrifying 'wing-flames' of the Binbrook servant-girl, represents but an infinite number of degrees *of the same phenomenon;* a phenomenon that it is the purpose of this book to examine and, if possible, to explain.

There is obviously an intimate connection between the more harmless (as well as the more dangerous) of these 'flame-phenomena' and the *cosmozants* of static electricity, which play about the masts of ships at sea. Normally harmless, this 'static' *was* still responsible for the loss of the *Hindenburg.*

It is thought that one of the gas-bags filled with hydrogen had begun to leak even before the giant German dirigible had arrived at her Lakehurst, N.J. mooring-mast. On the thousands of square feet of the airship's 'skin' an immense charge of static electricity had built up during, and because of, her swift passage through the air. The discharge of this static ignited the escaping hydrogen, with results that we know. A recent film suggested that the explosion was caused by sabotage; but the official enquiry would seem to confirm that static electricity *was* the prime cause of the disaster.

Following Spanish practice, we call this discharge 'St Elmo's Fire'. The Romans called a single flame of St Elmo's Fire 'Helen'; a double flame, 'Castor and Pollux.' (*See Note* p. 339).

I have examined elsewhere the socio-religious results of the Black Death.[6] What is relevant here is that the fact of death – indiscriminately striking, universally encountered, death – became associated in the European public mind with the 'spirits' distilled from wine and cereals, introduced through Italy two centuries earlier.

Contemporary medical science did nothing to discourage the belief that the ingestion – the *intemperate* ingestion – of highly volatile and inflammable liquids rendered the taker thereof volatile . . . and inflammable.

Unchecked – indeed, encouraged – by the medical profession, the common people believed that the heavy drinking of spirits made the sweat stink of brimstone; made underwear dangerously explosive;[7] that the combing of a drunkard's hair caused blue flames to spring up as from the fur of 'electrified' cats.

Doctors gravely warned their inebriate patients to keep well away from open flames – even those of candles. (And, since people *have* gone up in smoke, who shall say that those who took the doctors' advice were not saved from the burning . . . ?)

It is no denigration of the great eighteenth-century chemists' discoveries in the field of combustibility that one may ask if their 'sweeping-away into the limbo of exploded beliefs' really proved the non-existence of phlogiston, the alchemists' 'principle of combustibility?' All that Cavendish, Priestley and Lavoisier really did was to analyze the gases whose behaviour had already been extraordinarily well

---

[6] In *The Roots of Witchcraft* (Skoob Books Publishing Ltd, London, forthcoming).

[7] What lay behind this 'popular fallacy'? – the crackling and 'St. Elmo's Fire' of the static charge in silk or even linen underwear?

stated – particularly by Boyle – in the previous century. In extracting the highly inflammable hydrogen from water, did Cavendish really disprove the existence of a 'principle of combustibility'? Did Priestley, when he isolated oxygen from the air? If present-day chemists and physicists can 'explain' why metallic sodium ignites on contact with water, phosphorus on contact with air, does that deny to these two substances that quality of inflammability which, said the alchemists and their successors, was inherent, not so much in, say, metallic sodium and phosphorus by themselves, as in the *situation* of metallic sodium in immediate proximity with water, of phosphorus in immediate proximity with air?

What the modern scientists do is not so much to state new facts as to measure, with a precision inaccessible to our alchemical-age ancestors, the cosmic influences that those alchemical philosophers hypothesized. By the use of standardized instruments and standardized methods of research, modern scientists can now establish the non-accidental, permanent nature of important phenomena – and this, please note, in respect of phenomena not first detected or even 'explained' by them.

Let us see the relation that modern scientific research, but notably *modern scientific instrumentation,* has established between the 'crank theories' of Baron Karl von Reichenbach, discoverer of creosote, and the 'Kirlian Effect', result of thirty years' experimentation by the Russian biologists, Semyon and Valentina Kirlian.

A century and a quarter ago the eminent German chemist, von Reichenbach, reported that he had detected 'a sort of energy or luminescence radiating from humans, plants and animals.' Von Reichenbach, after he had himself detected this radiant energy, gathered about him a group of 'sensitives' who affirmed that they, too, could see what von Reichenbach had detected. These 'sensitives' could, in a pitch-dark room, 'see' a force of unknown character emanating from crystals and other substances. 'There is a blue pole', they told the Baron, 'which feels cool and pleasant to the hand; there is an orange-red pole which is warm, with a loathsome tepidity.' Von Reichenbach, seeking a name for this newly perceived emanation, called it 'the odic force',

Von Reichenbach had the misfortune to collect his evidence and present his conclusions at a period when 'the irregular' demanded attention in the face of a good deal of competition. It was an age of new theories, and as some – many, indeed – of these theories partook of the nature of the mystic, of the occult, of the supernatural, almost all the theories, in their totality, engaged the animosity of those 'who couldn't be bothered with such rubbish'. The trouble was that even the educated confused 'the charlatan', Daniel Dunglass Home (subject of Browning's bitter attack in *Mr Sludge, the Medium),* and his dilettante-mystic patrons, such as Lord Lytton, with serious investigators of the 'new' phenomena, such as Sir William Crookes, Sir Oliver Lodge, Lord Adare and Lord Rayleigh – the confusion being not at all ended when Crookes, Lodge and the other scientists appeared to 'believe in' the 'wild' theories of von Reichenbach and his like.

Looking back at the century which separates us from the investigators of the phenomena of 'radiation', 'emission', 'emanation' – the names varied, but the phenomena were all of a 'family' – one is struck by a fact which is once again apparent: if the phenomena could be detected and registered by instruments of mahogany and ebonite and silk-bound copper wire and lacquered brass, they could be, and generally were, 'believable',

All these scientific findings, reported fully throughout the popular 'technical' press, were eagerly debated by all classes of Victorian society, and, provided that they were reported by the right sort of journals, implicitly believed. But any phenomena reported by the 'wrong sort' of journals, as, for instance, *Astrology* or *Future*, would be as fervently rejected.

Yet, throughout the world, 'accepted' scientists were proving the existence of invisible intangible radiation which, *ordinarily* imperceptible to the human senses, could yet be detected and controlled by instruments of special design.

When Becquerel placed a lump of pitchblende in a cupboard already containing some undeveloped photographic plates in their light-proof wrappings, and, removing the wrappings later, discovered that the plates had been 'exposed', he found that he had discovered, by accident, the phenomenon of radioactivity – a phenomenon to be investigated, with literally world-shattering results, by the Curies.

But the perception of some form of radiation had been suspected by 'sensitives', and those who watched them, for centuries. The idea that there are levels of perception, as imagined, for instance, by the 'weird' novelist and short story writer, Sheridan le Fanu, invariably implies a theory of levels of 'attention-calling'.

Le Fanu had been struck by the fact that the 'hallucinations' seen by drunkards in their alcohol-induced delirium seemed to share a remarkable similarity; and this despite the widely differing temperaments and backgrounds, domestic, religious and educational, of the unhappy subjects of alcoholic delirium.

Le Fanu was not the first to notice this fact; every attendant in a drunks' home knows, and knew, it. Indeed, it was from a physician specializing in the treatment of alcoholism that le Fanu first learned of it; but le Fanu was the first to ask himself why? Why should men and women so varied all see the same things – the bugs, the rats, the 'faces', the pink elephants? Why should they feel the same things: best-known of all, the so-called 'arachnation syndrome': the feeling that face and hands are covered with spiders' webs? Why should they smell the same things, from

49

violets at one tolerable end of the scale to unnameable filth at the other? Why should all these 'hallucinations' follow the same pattern? Le Fanu asked himself, and then suggested his own answer: perhaps similar causes produce similar effects? In other words, the 'hallucinations' may not be subjective at all, but completely objective, having a reality perceptible only to senses having their visual, tactile, auditory, gustatory and osmic 'spectra' vastly widened by the *purely physical* effects of alcohol. It occurred to le Fanu that all such powerful stimulants – not only alcohol, but hashish, opium and the delirifacients mentioned in the witch trials of the sixteenth- and seventeenth-centuries – might each have its specialized power of 'perception-heightening'; each drug, as it were, having the power to reach (or reach for the observer) its own allotted and distinct level of perception. Le Fanu was a contemporary and friend of the most famous drug-taker of a generation of drug-takers: Thomas de Quincey, author of the *Confessions of an English Opium Eater*. From both de Quincey's book and from the author himself, le Fanu found that, with opium as with alcohol, the 'hallucinations' tended to conform to a traditional pattern, irrespective of the temperament, education, personal desires and fears of the subject. It was as though, when one threw back the blinds, the person invited to look through a window saw what any other person would have seen.

It offends many that 'officially godless' Russia should be investigating, with what the technical advertising copywriters call 'the most sophisticated electronic equipment', the dark mysteries of that dimension into which only, so far, the hysterics, the ecstatics, the drunkards, the drug-takers, the small children and the very old, the travellers on a lonely road, and the fevered and the starving, have strayed for a moment.

For centuries, men have used the 'psychic' powers of the man with the divining rod to find things – water, oil, metals. The provincial government of British Columbia, Canada, seeking metals, called in Miss Evelyn Penrose, noted lady 'diviner'; and several companies in both Britain and in the United States manufacture divining rods of copper and aluminium for use by the public utility companies which have regularly employed them for many years.[8]

It really doesn't matter that Soviet scientists feel happier in searching the properties of 'dowsing' or 'divining' if they rename 'dowsing' the Biophysical Effects Method (BPE). What does matter is that careful research first enabled the Russian professor Dr Nicolai Sochevanov (himself an expert dowser) to redesign the traditional Russian 'wizard's rod' of wood as a U-shaped rod of steel, which has the advantage of being operable in all seasons and climates; something that the traditional rod of live wood is not.

Now, with dowsing renamed and promoted to official scientific status, the Soviets are, as they would affirm, making dowsing pay. Delegates to the All-Union Astro-Geodesic Society's meeting of 31 October 1966 reported that 'the biophysical effects method is being used to search for water in the Soviet Union's many deserts, for ore deposits in the Central Asian Soviet Republic, and was being extensively studied in field and laboratory by Leningrad and Moscow geology institutes.'[9]

Once we have overcome our distaste for the 'mechanization of the mystic', we have honestly to admit that, once

---

[8] See my article: 'Still it Twitches,' in the British journal *Underground Services*.

[9] Sheila Ostrander and Lynn Schroeder, PSI – *Psychic Discoveries Behind the Iron Curtain (see Bibliography)*.

they are permitted to examine any phenomenon with 'sophisticated electronic equipment of the most advanced design', the Russian investigators are not inhibited by religious or political prejudice from examining anything and *everything*.

In Europe and North America 'thought-readers' do their tricks in variety theatres and circuses; in Russia and in Russia's nearer colonies they do them in the blinding light of white enamelled laboratories, wired up to machines which record their pulse rate, blood pressure, respiration, perspiration, skin and body temperature and so on.

Telepathy is a well-known phenomenon – strictly incredible, of course, to those who have never encountered it. Wolf Messing, a telepath who escaped from Hitler-occupied Poland to the USSR, is today a sort of superstar known to all levels of society, a legendary figure for more than a quarter of a century. Messing is a household name even to celebrated scientists. Soviet Nobel Prize-winning chemist, Dr Nicolai Semyonov, Vice-president of the Academy of Sciences of the USSR, said in *Science and Religion,* in September 1966, 'It is very important to study scientifically the psychic phenomena of sensitives like Wolf Messing.'

A century ago, in an atmosphere of incredulity and hostility, Baron Karl von Reichenbach was examining *his* 'sensitives' and publishing their experiences to an unbelieving world. Now, in the USSR, those experiments have been repeated by a husband-and-wife team of scientists – and what they have found not only completely vindicates von Reichenbach, but brings us, I think, nearer to the solution of that mystery of which this book principally treats.

5

THE KILNER EFFECT
AND THE KIRLIAN EFFECT

Roughly halfway in time between the 'amateur science' of Karl von Reichenbach and the consciously 'super-scientific' researches of Soviet investigators of the paranormal comes the significant figure of Dr Walter Kilner, of St Thomas's Hospital, London. Kilner is not only significant in that he announced experimental findings which, he claimed, supported von Reichenbach's discoveries of 'odic' auras, but he also did more: he bestowed on his own Reichenbach-supporting results the valuable prestige that mention of any chemical conferred on scientific experiments in the immediate post-1900 period.

Dr Kilner anticipated − and checkmated − the critics by explaining that he hadn't merely looked 'sensitively' at this object and that, trying to discern its aura he had looked, first of all through glass, and, much more importantly, through glass stained with dicyanin − a blue dye.

Having paid his tribute to 'rational physics', by using a chemical, Dr Kilner deserved to be believed. He wasn't altogether believed, but he got more credence than had von Reichenbach − and what Kilner reported to have seen when he viewed the human body through a screen of dicyanin was well remembered when, in 1939, Semyon Davidovitch Kirlian, Russian-Armenian electrician, took the first photograph of the 'Kilner effect'. (Jung would have found it 'only natural' that 'Kirlian' − especially as pronounced in Russia − is almost an anagram of 'Kilner'.)

What Kilner said that he saw was the aura surrounding the human body: 'a cloud of radiation extending out about six to eight inches, and showing distinct colours.' These colours, Kilner noticed, would alter, and the aura itself change in size, according to whether the patient was vigorous or fatigued; healthy or ill; happy or depressed. The aura, Kilner noted, was also highly sensitive to the external influences of magnetism and electricity, and to the external-internal stimuli of hypnotism.

On the basis of his observations, Dr Kilner erected an elaborate medical philosophy of 'aura-diagnosis', which gained many followers, has still its supporters to-day, and may expect to gather very many more recruits as the results of the Kirlian research become more widely known.

The aura surrounding not only the human body but all other living things had been 'known' since earliest times, and though we do not as yet understand the subtle differences between the *ka* and the *ba* of the Egyptians (both being some life force beyond and above ordinary vitality), we may suppose that one – or perhaps both – may correspond to what has since come to be called 'the astral body'. The existence of this extra-corporeal and super-corporeal force was taken for granted until the very end of the middle ages, and it is represented in Christian religious art by the 'nimbus' or 'glory' in which God the Father and Christ, and sometimes lesser divinities, are represented as standing or sitting. A 'lesser aura' is the halo which surrounds the heads of all holy persons, Christ and the saints alike.

What is so interesting is that the 'glories' – especially the irridescent, rainbow 'glories' surrounding either God the Father or Christ – have striking similarities to the auras not only seen by von Reichenbach's 'sensitives' and by Dr Kilner through his dicyanin-dyed glass plates, but also photographed by the severely down-to-Soviet-earth Semyon Kirlian and his wife.

What Dr Walter Kilner had done was this: he had found a *mechanical* means of seeing and observing *at any time* the human aura which, before, had been visible only to persons of highly specialized vision, and to them only in certain abnormal psychosomatic conditions. With the Kilner dicyanin-dyed glass, mankind had been provided, for the first time, with an 'aura-detector' which operated independently of the 'psychic content' of the observer. In 1939 the first Kirlian experiment was to take all the mystical hit-and-miss out of the study of the aura of the living organism – but let us not forget that, in making scientifically acceptable what von Reichenbach's 'sensitives' had seen and reported, the Kirlians vindicated all those who had been seeing auras since there were auras to be seen.

'Our birth', said Wordsworth, 'is but a sleep and a forgetting.' Man's progress since he became 'civilized' has been a progressive loss of powers of perception once the common property of mankind, which are now the rare and chance-met talent of a few.

The reason for the loss of such 'normal' abilities as telepathy, telekinesis, levitation, mind-bending, 'shape-changing', invisibility-at-will is that these abilities do not agree with the conditions necessary to the organization of man into 'society'. But the reader could find a support for my argument in the fact that such vestiges of mankind's lost 'paranormal' (once completely normal) powers are to be found more in those whose life tends to the primitive and less in those whose lifestyle conforms rigidly to the urban and the civic.

If we knew when we were to die, would we undertake new enterprises? Would we invest for a time when we would not be around to reap the material benefit of our investment? City life, the social pattern, would not survive such dangerous knowledge. We have traded our sensitivity for the advantages not so much that our belonging to modern society gives us, but for what a less debilitating and degenerating association of men promised our remote ancestors.

Now, with such researchers as the Kirlians, these lost powers are about to be replaced mechanically. And if, in remedying the loss of our primal powers by the products of the laboratory technician and the scientific machinist and electrician, such researchers as the Kirlians have taken some of the romance out of the 'paranormal', let us admit that they've taken out much of the hit-and-miss, too. And now, what exactly did Semyon and Valentina Kirlian find?

In 1939 Kirlian was called into a research laboratory in Krasnodar, capital of the Kuban, to do a routine repair job. He did the repair, and on the way out of the institute he happened to see that a patient was about to receive electro-therapeutic treatment from a high-frequency generator of new design. Attracted to the demonstration by his profess-ional interest in electricity (and not, he afterwards said, by the medical aspects of the case), Kirlian noticed that, as the glass electrodes were being moved against the patient's body, there was a momentary flash of light.

Kirlian discovered afterwards that this 'flash' had often been noticed before; but he also discovered that he was the first to be interested in it, and decidedly the first to wonder if it could not be photographed.

There were difficulties in this plan. With the existing glass electrodes, the photographic plate would be ruined by exposure before the current could be switched on; metal electrodes would be satisfactory, but metal electrodes would also be dangerous. None the less, Kirlian decided to go ahead with the use of metal electrodes.

The machine was switched on. Kirlian's hand, under the metal electrode, was burning. He was in agony, but the dedication of the self-dedicated investigator persisted through the pain. For a full three seconds his hand burned.

56

Then, with the current switched off, he rushed his plates over to the dark-room. As they developed, one of the strangest photographs ever to be taken by man both excited and shocked the pioneer. 'I studied the picture with pain, excitement and hope all combined. Had I made a discovery? Had I invented something? It wasn't clear yet what I'd done.'

This new field of research demanded, Kirlian saw at once, an entirely new technology. Established modes of photography were useless for the achievement of his aim. So Kirlian, master electrician, set to work to design an entirely new high-frequency spark-generator giving from 75,000 to 200,000 oscillations per second. The photograph which had come out of that first vital experiment had not been a recognizable 'picture' as such, only a kind of luminous cloud, shaped like his own hand. But already, despite his assertion that 'it wasn't clear yet *what* I'd done', Kirlian was intuitively half-aware of what he had found and half-aware of the nature of the phenomenon that he had, by chance, investigated. But it was now with something more than mere half-knowledge that he designed his special high-frequency oscillator.

In the now forty years since that first experiment, Kirlian and his wife have 'photographed' almost the whole range of the animal and plant kingdom. I put the word 'photo-graphed' in quotation marks because no camera is needed; the high-frequency field causes the object or material to be studied to radiate what is still an unclassified and un-explained radiation or luminescence; and the image of this radiating object can be transferred directly to photographic sensitized paper.

The Kirlians' first 'photographs' were of a leaf. Placed within the field of the high-frequency oscillator, the leaf 'revealed a world of myriad dots of energy. Around the edges of the leaf there were turquoise and reddish-yellow patterns of flares coming out of specific channels of the leaf. A human finger placed in the high-frequency field and photographed showed up like a complex topographical map. There were lines, points, craters of light and flares. Some parts of the finger looked like a carved jack-o'-lantern with a glowing light inside.'[10]

'. . . myriad dots of energy . . . lines, points, craters of light and flares . . . a carved jack-o'-lantern with a glowing light inside . . .' Is not all this familiar from long before the Kirlians began to investigate the Reichenbach-Kilner 'auras' with their special high-frequency oscillator? Are not these the 'hallucinations', not only of opium-smokers and of drunkards, but also of the fevered and even of the desperately fatigued, who, seeking sleep, close their eyes only to see the kaleidoscopic swirls, the fireworks displays of 'lines, points, craters of light and flares'?

And while we are on the subject of the Kirlians' first 'photographs' of a luminescent leaf, with its 'myriad dots of energy', let me call the reader's attention to the *patterns* pricked or *dotted* into the halos of mediaeval saints, notably in the strange other-world frescoes of Giotto.

Who taught the mediaeval religious painters that the auras of holy men – *abstracted* men, men in another dimension – were dotted with myriad points of energy? Or did the painters of the dawn of the Renaissance see those auras for themselves?

Discontented with an ability to 'photograph' the luminescence only of the immobile, Kirlian devised a technique by which a living, *moving* subject might be placed within the high-frequency field. In the first important experiments he used his own hand.

---

[10] Sheila Ostrander and Lynn Schroeder, op. cit.

And then, a fantastic world of the unseen opened before the husband and wife team.

The hand itself looked like the Milky Way in a starry sky. Against a background of blue and gold, something was taking place in the hand that looked like a fireworks display. Multi-coloured flares lit up, then sparks, twinkles, flashes. Some lights glowed steadily like Roman candles, others flashed out then dimmed. Still others sparkled at intervals. In parts of his hand there were little dim clouds. Certain glittering flares meandered along sparkling labyrinths like spaceships travelling to other galaxies.

What did these flares mean? What were they illuminating? The pulsating sparks weren't playing some game of chance. The game seemed to have rules, but what were they?[11]

This is very well said, but it is not the excellent description which impresses so much as the sense of familiarity; not only with all these phenomena of 'hallucination', all faithfully recorded by some painter somewhere in the world's artistic history, as with the verbal echoes of what the Kirlians saw as Semyon Kirlian's hand began to 'luminesce' within the high-frequency field. In the mediaeval and post-mediaeval mystics, Christian and Moslem and Jewish, in the eclectic twelfth- to seventeenth-century mysticism of Paracelsus and Albertus Magnus, of Boehme and Spinoza and Glanvil and Sir Thomas Browne, no less than in the vastly more ancient Chinese and Japanese poet-philosophers, we find echoed in words what mystics have always claimed to know and to see, and what the very high-frequency field of Kirlian permitted, eventually, to be photographed.

Here, at last, evidenced in permanent visual form on 'fixed' photographic paper, was the quasi-corporeal, 'astral' body of Paracelsus' theorizing: that second body, second

---

[11]   Sheila Ostrander and Lynn Schroeder, op. cit.

persona; not quite spirit and not quite flesh; sharing equally the qualities of the material and of the immaterial; living within the flesh, and pervading it; but extending itself far beyond the earthy confines of the flesh. The 'mirror-image' of the material body: the 'fact' which lies behind every tale of the haunting 'double', from the German legend of the *Doppelgänger* to Poe's strange story of William Wilson.

The Kirlians had found – and had photographed – what seemed to be the unseen energy locked up within every living organism.

They took a leaf and placed it within the vhf field: again there was that coruscating blaze of primal energies, the triumphant fireworks display of the Creative Will.

But now they went back, away from bursting life to the foreshadow of death. This time the leaf that they placed within the field was half withered. 'It looked like a great metropolis turning out its lights for the night. They tried an almost completely withered leaf. There were almost no flames and sparks and 'clouds' scarcely moved. As they watched, the leaf seemed to be dying before their eyes and its death was reflected in the picture of energy impulses . . . ' *We appeared to be seeing the very life activities of the leaf itself*', the Kirlians said. 'Intense, dynamic energy in the healthy leaf, less in the withered leaf, nothing in the dead leaf.' '[12]

Over the years of unremitting research, the husband-and-wife team examined the 'life-pattern' of every available substance, finding – as they had half-suspected from the very beginning of their tireless experimentation – that the

---

[12] My italics. This quotation is from Sheila Ostrander and Lynn Schroeder, op cit. I have followed in the main the account of the Kirlian experiments as given in this extremely valuable book, to whose authors I would like here to acknowledge my deep indebtedness. MH.

life-pattern, the energy-pattern, of every substance was as individual as the fingerprints of a human hand. And that this individuality extended not merely to species and genera, but to the separate items or organisms within the species or genera. Leaves not only differed from, say, leather, but *each* leaf, *each* piece of leather, differed from all other leaves, all other pieces of leather. There was always energy, but that the human mind had never been at fault in distinguishing 'the quick' from 'the dead' was dramatically demonstrated when the Kirlians put a living leaf and a 'dead' metal coin beneath their high-frequency microscope, and compared the energy-patterns of the two. For, while the leaf's energy-pattern sparkled and coruscated, the energy-pattern of the coin showed only as a glow evenly encircling the disk of metal. The Kirlians reported:

> What we saw in the panorama through the microscope and our other optical instruments seemed like the control board of a huge computer. Here and there lights brightened and dimmed. If something's wrong inside or conditions need adjustment, the engineer at the control board can read the signals in the lights.
>
> In living things, we see the signals of the inner state of the organism reflected in the brightness, dimness and colours of the flares – as, indeed, Kilner had noted forty years earlier. The inner life-activities of the human being are written in these luminescent hieroglyphs. We've created an apparatus to write these hieroglyphs. But to read them we're going to need help.

The 'hieroglyphs' were read sooner than the Kirlians had hoped – and, as it happened, it was the Kirlian team which read them. They were already famous throughout the Soviet Union – it was now ten years since they had begun the study of 'energy-patterns', using their own hf 'microscope' – when the director of a major state research institute brought Semyon Kirlian two fresh leaves, taken from the

61

plant at the same time. The director asked Semyon to put them under the 'microscope' and see what was to be seen.

Now the two leaves should have given off, not *identical* but strikingly *similar,* patterns – being near-identical leaves removed at the same time.

But they differed greatly – and continued to differ greatly through many successive viewings. 'The luminescence from one leaf showed roundish, spherical flares scattered symmetrically over the entire image of the leaf. The second leaf showed tiny geometrical dark figures grouped sparsely here and there on the leaf's image.'

Working throughout the night to account for the wide divergences in the energy-patterns of two 'identical' leaves, the Kirlians, on the following morning, met the director with their worry showing plainly on their tired faces.

But the director was happy – and satisfied. 'His face lit up with delight. 'You've found it!' he said excitedly.

The explanation was simple – and, literally, epoch-making.

'Both leaves', said the director of the botanical research institute, 'were torn from the same species of plant all right. But one of these plants had already been contaminated with a serious plant disease. You've found this out immediately! There is absolutely nothing on the plant or this leaf to indicate that it has been infected and will soon die. No tests on the actual plant or the leaf show anything wrong with it. With high-frequency photography, you've diagnosed illness in the plant *ahead of time!'*

In the years which followed, the Kirlians learnt many more unexpected things about their 'aura-detector'. They were asked to examine living organisms – particularly plants – from all over the Soviet Union; and their conclusions can best be summed up in Semyon Kirlian's review of the implications of his discoveries. What, perhaps, did not surprise him so much was that, the more he and his wife discovered, the more it seemed that the 'mystical' and non-mystical philosophers and experimenters of the past, from Paracelsus, through Baron Karl von Reichenbach, to Walter Kilner, had anticipated the Kirlians' every finding.

It is astonishing how the careful definition by the Kirlians of what they have seen and deduced with their specially devised apparatus reproduces not only the theories of the old-time 'mystics', *but their very phrasing also.* When Semyon Kirlian affirmed that the 'energy-body' is not merely a radiation from the normally visible and tangible body, but appeared to be a discrete entity which 'mirrored' the visible body, we find ourselves hearing again the words of Paracelsus, 'the zenith and rising sun of all the alchymists' (1493-1541), in which he described the paraphysical 'other body'.

And again, when the Kirlians inform us that the activity, colour and dimensions of the aura reflect accurately the physical state of the object or material studied under the hf 'microscope'; that the paraphysical 'body' reflects, 'mirrors' – sometimes in advance of event – the changes in the physical body, do we not recall what Dr Walter Kilner found: that the aura was always affected by ill-health, fatigue, depression of the spirits, and that 'various patches of disturbed patterns in the colours indicated diseased areas'?

Indeed, in his book *The Human Aura,* Kilner, with his simple 'detectors' of dicyanin-dyed glass, discovered the basic principles that the Kirlians' more refined instruments have endorsed and verified.

All the basic principles? Well, there is one that Kilner did not detect – and this, to my mind, is one of the most important.

One day, the Kirlians, long after they had become famous – at least throughout Soviet academic circles – were awaiting the arrival of two distinguished scientists from a Moscow state institute. In preparation for the visit Kirlian gave his instrument a trial run, when, to both his astonishment and his alarm, the instrument refused to function. The instrument was disassembled and put together; again it refused to work. Once more the instrument was dismantled, but, as the parts were lying at random all over the workbench, Semyon began to feel faint and dizzy. It was an attack of a trouble that had affected him for years; he would have to go to bed. This he did, too ill to care about the visiting Moscow scientists, and merely hoping half-heartedly that Valentina would be able to reassemble the scattered parts in time for the demonstration.

Valentina Kirlian quietly set about the task of bringing the pieces of the instrument together, and when the scientists arrived the demonstration that she gave them went through without a hitch. Only late that same evening, when Semyon had partly recovered from his attack, did he understand: *it was his own physical breakdown which had caused the instrument to refuse to function.*

Here, in the functioning of this instrument, was a phenomenon familiar from the world of mechanics: *the feedback.* Not only did the physical body cause its own malfunctioning to be 'mirrored' in the paraphysical 'self', but also the intensely powerful *duality* of physical and paraphysical, that duality which makes up and completes the totality of mundane *being,* exerted its imperious influence on the very instruments which were perceiving, measuring and recording its own existence.

Obviously, then, the mechanized metaphysics of this new scientific age are revealing once more what we have already known – perhaps many times. We have forgotten – or made ourselves forget - and now, with new instruments, are being forced to look at it boldly, as the truth.

And what is this truth? No one this side perfection can ever know completely. But, as we read of such findings as those of the Kirlians, we find something more than half-familiar in the accounts – a feeling almost of *déjà vu* (that sensation as universal as it is disturbing of 'I have been here before'; 'I have experienced all this before . . .').

What we gropingly see now is something of the inter-dependence of those parts, great and small, which make up the *balanced* totality of the universe, of all creation. We see, too, that there may be – indeed, there must be – many aspects of fact invisible to the normal eye; that the *ba*, the *ka*, of the ancient Egyptians; the 'astral body' of the six-teenth-century Hermetics and Rosicrucians; the 'etheric', 'fluidic', 'Beta', 'counterpart', 'pre-physical' and other 'parallel' bodies of nineteenth- and twentieth-century 'cranks' appear to be merely the many names for that 'mirror-body' which was perceived by the vastly extended vision of the 'mystics' thousands of years before Kilner made his simple, and the Kirlians their complex, detectors.

We may recognize, too, in the new findings, the fact that these same mystics described, though in most 'unscientific' terms, many of the truths now being revealed through the instruments of the most scientific researchers.

If we look beyond the 'loading' which inevitably affects all words and phrases habitually used in certain 'closed' contexts, we must see, in the Judaic, Moslem and Christian concept of the 'guardian angel', an 'unscientific' (or shall we say 'pre-scientific'?) statement of the 'parallel body' of the Kirlian findings. And, since we are considering 'old beliefs', what of, if not the immortality of the soul, the continuance of life after death? There are 'post-Kirlian' findings which have, for the purely materialist, some highly disturbing implications.

In a different laboratory from that of the Kirlians, some of their disciples went further into their pursuit of the energy-pattern of a leaf, and the photographs taken during these 'para-Kirlian' experiments are thought-provoking indeed.

First there is the 'standard' picture of a living leaf, familiar now to the world of science through the Kirlian experiments. Then there is another picture of the same leaf, but with what appears to be a line drawn down the middle of the right-hand part of the leaf. There is a difference, too, in respect of the flashing background of the aura: in the second photograph 'the sparkling outline and veins seemed airier, the background fluffier.'

The explanation of the difference is that in the *second* photograph we are looking at the 'Kirlianograph' of the leaf photographed in the first picture, but now with *one-third* of its bulk removed – yet the energy-pattern of the entire leaf remained to be photographed.

The Soviet scientists admit that the energy thus photographed is not confidently to be classified with the 'ordinary' aspects of energy – electrical, magnetic, electromagnetic, gravitic, etc. – familiar to modern science. They talk hopefully of referring this energy-pattern to the new – and fashionable – 'fourth state of matter': plasma.

But while science is waiting to classify the type of energy whose manifestations – or, at least, some of them – are made visible by the Kirlian instrumentation, certain valid inferences may already be drawn from the experiments' results.

In the first place, there is the extraordinarily significant fact that, with only two-thirds of the living leaf remaining, its aura, its 'etheric body' – call it what you will – is still virtually intact; only when all the leaf has been cut away or has died does the 'etheric' counterpart vanish. In other words, the energy-pattern of the *whole* living organism survives, even though a part of the physical 'half' has been removed.

This, then, can mean only that the well-known 'phantom limb' effect in amputees – the effect in which itching or pain in the amputated member is completely 'real' to the patient – is a reality, not simply something imagined by the patient.

Nor, indeed, does common medical opinion think that the phenomenon of the 'phantom limb' is simply something imagined by the patient; if the pain or mere itching be 'real' to the patient, it is no less 'real' to medical opinion. The theory here is that, when the limb was still functionally attached to the body, a pattern of communication was established between brain and limb, and that the message-pattern, impressed into the nervous system, survives the amputation of the limb with which, once, the brain was in communication contact. That, at any rate, is the commonly given medical profession's opinion. There is no reason why we should not accept this explanation of the 'phantom limb'.

With this comment: that it is not the amputated *physical* limb which is itching or aching, but the counterpart of that limb in the paraphysical body – *a body from which no member has been amputated.* No fact could make clearer the complete interdependence, indeed the complete integration, of the two 'bodies', so that injury to one will cause pain in the other, and persistent pain in one must mean that remedial measures (amputation and so on) must, to be effective, be applied to both bodies.

The *ka* and *ba* of the Egyptians, the 'astral' (or 'mirror') body of Paracelsus, the *auras* of Baron Karl von Reichenbach and Dr Walter Kilner, the 'etheric' body of the noted English medium, Geraldine Cummins, and the 'double' of Mrs Eileen Garrett, president of the New York Parapsychology Foundation, have now, through the work and the discoveries of the Kirlians, been officially admitted to the Soviet corpus of 'recognized fact'.

In 1968, on behalf of Soviet science, the dogma was solemnly pronounced, *urbi et orbi*, by Drs. V. Inyushin, V. Grishchenko, N. Vorobev, N. Shouiski, N. Federova and F.

Gibadulin: 'All living things – plants, animals and humans – not only have a physical body made of atoms and molecules, *but also a counterpart body of energy.*'

A new name was also found for an old fact: the 'biological plasma body'.

The findings of the six Soviet doctors are given in their joint paper, 'The Biological Essence of the Kirlian Effect', published by the Kazakhstan State University at Alma-Ata. Says the paper: 'The bio-luminescence visible in the Kirlian pictures is caused by the bio-plasma, not by the electrical state of the organism.'

These energy-patterns to be detected in all living things have, say the scientists, their own 'specific spatial organization' (a remark which might imply that they have their own time-pattern). The pattern, they say, has shape, but, more, the processes detected within the energy pattern have their distinctive 'labyrinthine motion', completely unlike the energy-patterns in the physical body. The 'bio-plasmic' body, they affirm, is also polarized: 'The biological plasma of the energy body is specific for every organism, tissue and possibly bio-molecule. The specificity determines the form of the organism.'

Which must mean – if it means anything at all – that the physical organism is a product of, or, at least, a development from, the paraphysical; a conclusion which returns us, in thinking, to the most ancient religious speculations of the East – that is, if we slightly antiquate the phrasing, and say that 'the soul and its energy-pattern antedate and control the organization and energy-pattern of the body.' Brahmin and Buddhist would certainly agree with that.

6

FROM SODOM
TO SYDENHAM

The strange tale of the inhabitants of Sodom and Gomorrah is told in Genesis 19.

23. The sun was risen upon the earth when Lot entered into Zoar.
24. Then the LORD rained upon Sodom and upon Gomorrah brimstone and fire from the LORD out of heaven;
25. And he overthrew those cities, and all the plain, and all the inhabitants of the cities, and that which grew upon the ground.
26. But his wife looked back from behind him, and she became a pillar of salt.
27. And Abraham gat up early in the morning to a place where he stood before the LORD;
28. And he looked toward Sodom and Gomorrah, and toward all the land of the plain, and beheld, and, lo, the smoke of the country went up as the smoke of a furnace.

It is the fashion to suggest 'modern' explanations of this ancient tale: were Sodom and Gomorrah blotted out, with all their inhabitants, by a 'super-bomb' (uranium-236, deuterium oxide, lithium hydride or cobalt)?

Sydenham, in 1922, was still a quiet and highly 'respectable' suburb of London, one of the several districts of varying social standing, which, originating in the spas of this hilly south-eastern part of the capital, now seemed to be grouped about the Crystal Palace, and the adjacent railway stations, hotels, restaurants and shops.

Of course by 1922, after the first shattering of the social order, Sydenham had inevitably 'come down a bit'. There were no longer servants to manage the big houses of the City merchants, and so the houses had been converted into flats.

Mrs Euphemia Johnson, sixty-eight, a widow, lived by herself in one of the now shabby ex-mansions of Sydenham. She had lost her husband in the Boer War. She was not fat, though neighbours afterwards described her as 'comfortable'; somewhat above the middle height for a woman, she probably weighed about 170 pounds. It was not established that she drank to excess.

On a summer's afternoon – 1922 had a very hot and prolonged summer – Mrs Johnson returned from shopping in Sydenham. She filled a kettle at the corner sink, put the kettle to boil on the small gas-stove, and, with the windows open on the still lush gardens of Sydenham, sat down to wait for the water to boil, so that she could make her tea.

She made her tea, and brought a cup to the table which stood between the two windows, the table being covered with a large piece of washable oilcloth.

She drank a little of her tea; the rest she left – for she suddenly no longer had a need for tea, nor, indeed, any ability to drink it.

When they found her – or, rather, what was left of her – she was 'consumed so by fire that on the floor of her room there was only a pile of calcinated bones . . . The fire, *if in an ordinary sense it was fire,* must have been of the intensity of a furnace. . . '[13]

But note some of the very odd points which so disturbed the coroner.

---

[13] Quoted from *Lo!,* by Charles Fort *(see Bibliography).*

70

She had certainly blazed in some heat which rivalled in intensity that of a furnace, but the burning had been so swift that her 'calcinated bones' were lying within her *unburned* clothes. In falling, she had upset the chair on which she had been sitting to drink her tea; but though she had burned to a cinder within inches of the overturned chair, only a slight bubbling of the varnish showed that the chair had been exposed to any heat. More, the tablecloth – or a corner of it, rather – hung down to within nine inches of the 'utterly consumed' body; but again, apart from a slight yellowing of the treated fabric, it was quite unburned. The linoleum under 'the pile of calcinated bones' was slightly – but only slightly – charred. Whatever, or whoever, had come with his fiery flaming sword had come on the wings of light; had struck within a heartbeat; and had gone as quickly as it – he – had come: his specialized victim a mass of cinders, the rest of the room (even the victim's clothing) of no interest to the Spirit of Flame . . . and so untouched by his momentary passing.

But it is mandatory in all English inquests to 'discover' and name 'the source of heat'. It was at the height of summer when Mrs Johnson was struck by the Fire from Heaven. It is true that she had a small gas-stove in the room, but she had turned off the gas even as she had poured the boiling water into the heated pot.

It is also true that there was a fireplace in the room; but no fire burned – no fire had been laid – on that warm summer's day.

Into the design of the royal tombs of Ancient Egypt are incorporated 'doors' which, though complete with jambs, lintel and entablature, are not merely blocked up; they were never made for the passage of anyone or anything physical.

The same sort of doors are to be found in the larger tombs and even larger necropolises of Etruria, Greece and Rome. These doors, impassable to living humans, are 'spirit doors' – doors through which the immaterial entities may freely pass.

To the 'spirit', which may pass through any material obstacle, just as may cosmic, x-ray, radio and other waves, the 'door', because it has been made to look like a 'real' door, is perfectly passable. What the 'spirit' requires to lead him to this type of door is that it shall look like the 'real' door that he knew in what we had better call his physical existence.

If, then, 'token' doors serve, for the world of the spirit, as 'real' doors do in the physical/material world, what function then have the non-working grate, gas-stove, electric heater, lamp, box of matches, cigar lighter and so on? If the blocked-up doors of the Egyptian and other tombs 'work for' non-physical entities, may not the 'turned off' gas-stove, the unlit grate, be *always* aflame in other dimensions than ours?

You remember that, when the living leaf was cut, its 'parallel' form suffered little or no diminution? You recall what I said on page 68: not only that the 'etheric body' possessed by all living organisms (including the human) had its own energy-pattern, 'completely unlike the energy-patterns in the physical body'; and that I ventured to suggest that these 'parallel' bodies not only had their own energy-patterns, but also had their being *in a time different from ours.*

If time, as a dimension, is different in the parallel world, the world of our 'etheric body', then perhaps, to 'beings of incendiary appetite',[14] the grate is *not* cold, the gas-stove *not* unlit. Perhaps that point in time when the grate was glowing, the stove burning is, to be Being, not only to-day but, it may well be, a 'time' in which it is eternally 'to-day.'

---

[14] Charles Fort.

72

The absence – or small dimensions – of a fire are always disturbing questions to a coroner.

Cutting from *Lloyd's Weekly News*, London, 5 February 1905:

MYSTERIOUS BUSINESS

Ashton Clodd, 75, died in Louth Hospital. The deceased had fallen into the grate, whilst putting coals in it, and then, for some reason, probably rheumatism, had been unable to rise, and had been fatally burned.

The 'mysterious business' was not that the late Mr Clodd had been fatally burned after having fallen into the grate, but that the extensive burning of his body did not seem at all commensurate with the amount of fire available to burn him. As the principal witness told the inquest: *'If there was a fire* in the fireplace, it was a very little one.'

In other words, there was considerable doubt that there had been a fire at all; but any evidence casting doubt on the presence of 'source of combustion' was – and is to-day – always passed over without comment by the coroner in advising the jury how to arrive at their verdict. The statutory 'reasoning' of all coroners goes like this: 'We have here a body which has been burned. Burning implies, as a necessity, some form of heat. *Ergo,* there must have been some form of heat.' (And why trouble the jury's heads with a search for some exotic form of heat when we have a fireplace – albeit cold – in the room where the victim was found?)

If Mr Ashton Clodd, seventy-five, who was not a plump, elderly female given to drink, really died of extensive burning – and there is no reason to think that he did not – there is much reason for thinking that the fire wasn't started by anything in his fireplace. Clodd's fellow-roomer never saw this 'causative' fire, and I think it highly unlikely that poor Clodd did either.

We may now ask the question: is there any connection between the mass-destruction by fire of the cities of Sodom and of Gomorrah and the individual destruction, equally by fire and equally complete, of Mrs Euphemia Johnson, sixty-eight, of Sydenham? Is there some causative link, extending over some thousands of years, between Sodom and Sydenham?

Well, there may be no traceable link between the deaths of those perverse Sodomites and Mrs Johnson, but there does seem to me to be a 'moral' link. The inhabitants of Sodom and Gomorrah were punished by Fire from Heaven because they had 'sinned', and – according to the medical evidence – the 'average' victim of spontaneous combustion is an alcoholic. In other words, public opinion, over the millennia, has been disposed to accept the hypothesis that 'Fire from Heaven' is a 'Punishment' necessarily following an infraction of some 'moral' rule. In the case of those of Sodom and Gomorrah, their infraction of the rule was sexual; in the case of more modern victims, they had been punished for having 'put an enemy in their mouths, to steal away their brains'.

Now, rejecting such a loaded word as 'moral', one might adopt some less prejudiced phrasing as, say, 'irregular' or 'contrary to rule'.

If a suicide strips off his clothes, jumps into a filled bathtub, and plunges a switched-on electric heater into the bath-water, he will probably die. If a person, with no thought of suicide, gets into the bathtub, and, by accident, pulls in a switched-on electric heater, he, too, will probably die. Here intention has nothing to do with the result of 'irregularity'.

If we accept a 'moral' link between the mass-destruction of the Sodomites and the death of Mrs Johnson, we must accept that, in both cases, death by Fire from Heaven resulted from some 'infringement of the rules', for the doctrine that 'ignorance of the law is no excuse for wrong-doing' applies more strictly in heavenly than even in earthly tribunals. So, for *what*, for *which*, specific infringement of which specific cosmic rule were both the Sodomites and Mrs Johnson 'punished'?

Let us return for a moment to the Kirlian experiments and their results, determined by modern instruments, recorded by the most modern methods of scientific notation.

The point that we should always bear in mind is this: the truth, as the prophet said, is a *constant*, which *cannot* change.[15]

What does change, in relation to the unchanging and unchangeable truth, is this: proof changes in fashion. Each age, each generation even, desires proof in a different form. What impresses the present generation as proof – the type of fashionable proof that modern scientists know so well how to supply – would have been unacceptable to earlier generations, as, indeed, it may be unacceptable to generations which are to come.

We must bear in mind that it is never the *truth* which changes. We must bear in mind, however, that the arguments by which truth is demonstrated change very much; that they always have changed, are changing now, and will change to the end of time. We must bear in mind, too, that those who are constantly – from generation to generation – arguing old truths with modern arguments *always* reward themselves by convincing even themselves that they have not merely invented new arguments, new proofs, but new truths also.

---

[15] Esdras 4,41: *Magna est veritas, et praevalet.*

This is not so. The Kirlians did not discover the 'etheric body'; they merely demonstrated, to the convincing of *this* age, that what our remotest ancestors believed to be true was, in fact, the truth.

7

MEN ONLY –
PARTIAL AND TOTAL COMBUSTION

Despite the protestations of those who like to affirm the contrary, men, as well as 'elderly females of corpulent habit, addicted to drink', *are* struck by the Fire from Heaven. I have already described the case of Father Bertholi, who, found enveloped in a blue flame, mortified horribly before dying.

The conspiracy of silence regarding cases of spontaneous combustion is more marked in respect of male victims even than in respect of female. It may be that this silence in regard to men victims is a prejudice surviving from more religious times than ours; for *non-fatal* luminosities of one sort or another – anything from an opalescent 'halo' to a cloak of harmless blue flame – have frequently been the outward signs by which the faithful might recognize the inward grace of a saint. And, if spontaneous combustion has some unsavory touch of moral obliquity about it, then it would hardly do to risk the confusion of the 'irregular' spontaneous combustion with the 'saintly' emission of luminosity or blue flames.

The fact seems to be that, in most of the cases of *male* burning, the victims were not being punished for any gross irregularity of conduct. Some drank, of course, but few to excess, and if 'to work is to pray', then all were well on the way to being good, since most of the victims not only were in regular employment, but were struck down either at or just after work.

As with the women victims, men appear to suffer from partial or total burning – with this singular difference, that, generally speaking, the combustion of the male body seems to generate far more heat than is evident in a female burning.

Let us now examine some cases in which the males have not been either immediately or completely burned.

A fortunate man was the victim described in 'a case of partial spontaneous combustion' reported by John Overton, MD, in the *Transactions of the Medical Society of Tennessee* for the year 1835, and in two other American medical journals.[16]

Mr 'H.'[17] was at the time professor of mathematics at the University of Nashville, and on a very cold Monday, 5 January 1835, he walked home from the university – a distance of about three-quarters of a mile. Some forty minutes after his arrival home he was checking the hygrometer which hung outside the house when he felt a sharp pain in his left leg – 'a steady pain like a hornet sting, accompanied by a sensation of heat'.

Looking down, Mr 'H.' saw that a bright flame, several inches in length, 'about the size of a dime in diameter, and somewhat flattened at the top', was spouting, like a lighted gas-jet, from his leg.

He slapped at the flame several times, but, as it did not go out, he tackled it by 'scientific' means, cupping his hands around it to cut off the supply of oxygen so as to reduce the combustion. The level-headed Mr 'H.' may or may not

_____

[16] Quoted by Vincent H. Gaddis, in *Mysterious Fires and Lights* (see *Bibliography*).

[17] I discovered that Mr 'H.' was Mr James Hamilton. (Information kindly given by Dr J. E. Windrow, George Peabody College for Teachers, Nashville, Tennessee.)

have known afterwards how lucky he had been. Only three years after his mishap, T. R. and J. B. Beck, in their *Elements of Medical Jurisprudence* (1838), pointed to the 'well-known fact' that water, far from extinguishing the fire of spontaneous combustion, 'aggravated it, and that spontaneous combustion has been recorded in all seasons and in both northern and southern countries.'

The French medico-legal writer, A. Devergie, is one of the few who have written on spontaneous combustion after having been one of the extremely rare witnesses of the Fire's outbreak. He writes: 'Spontaneous combustion commences by a bluish flame seen to extend itself, little by little, with an extreme rapidity, over all the parts of the body. This always persists until the parts are blackened, and generally until they are burned to a cinder. *Many times attempts have been made to extinguish the flame with water, but without success. . .*'[18]

This escape of Mr 'H.' seems to me to have attracted far too little notice.

However abnormally the fire involved in spontaneous combustion behaves, most noticeably in it being concentrated at 'the point of impact', and not radiating its heat (so that materials and objects in close proximity to the flame go even unscorched), it obviously has this in common with all 'ordinary' flames: it is dependent upon a supply of oxygen.

Another point arising from this conclusion, which might be more closely examined, is that, if water 'rather aggravates than extinguishes the flame', the fire of spontaneous combustion is the product of a *very* rapid oxidization; so very rapid, in fact, that the flame absorbs the oxygen from

---

[18] From the *Texas Register*, 7 November 1835, quoted by Vincent H. Gaddis, op. cit.

the water, leaving free hydrogen, which, in turn, steps up the rate of combustion. (Or so it would seem.)

The Nashville professor put out the flame, but the pain in his leg seemed to go far deeper than any ordinary burn. He went indoors, took off his pants and underpants, and examined the wound. 'On the surface of the outer and upper part of his leg was an injury that resembled an abrasion, about three-fourths of an inch in length, very livid in appearance. It extended from the femoral end of the fibula in an oblique direction towards the upper portion of the gastrocnemii muscles. The wound was extremely dry, and the scar tissue had gathered in a roll at the lower edge of the abraded surface.'[19]

The wound, abnormally caused as it had been, presented some unusual features to the examining physician. At the point of egress, a small hole had been burned in the underpants (though without any scorching around the tiny hole), and the pants were not burned at all. However, inside the pants, on the inside of the cloth facing the hole in the underpants, was 'a thin frostwork of a dark yellow hue which did not penetrate through the broadcloth'. This Mr 'H.' scraped off without harming the material.

The wound took longer to heal than usual; it 'did not attain cicatrization until thirty-two days after the infliction of the injury' – and muscular soreness persisted for some time. But the wound did heal, and, according to Dr Overton, the patient enjoyed good health. The Fire from Heaven never struck him again . . .

Not so fortunate were Carl C. Blocker, forty-four, and Jack Larber, some thirty years older. Both were found in flames before the combustion had had time to consume

---

[19] Vincent H. Gaddis, op. cit.

their bodies; both received hospital treatment; both died – and neither was able to tell what had happened.

Blocker was seen by a passing motorist on the evening of Thursday, 3 May 1951, in a ditch running alongside the main highway near Wabash, Indiana. As the motorist pulled up, he saw that, not only were Blocker's clothes aflame, but that he had already been extensively burned. Help was called, and the injured man was rushed to hospital. It was too late; he died without regaining consciousness.

The burned man's car was standing on the curb of the road; examination showed that in this case, as in others, damage to the vehicle was minimal, and confined to the small area around the driver's seat. However, 'the heat had been so intense that it had started to melt the metal on the dash-board.'

Again, as in *all* the car cases recorded to date, this heat, though intense enough to burn up a human body, failed to ignite the highly volatile gasoline in the nearby tank.

As usual, the coroner sought some 'rational explanation' of what was, and always is, a decidedly 'irrational' affair. As Blocker and his wife owned some 'high-class dress shops', the coroner suggested to the widow that the deceased might have been carrying some cleaning fluid in the car. Mrs Blocker said that it had never been her husband's practice to do so – though how the ignition of cleaning fluid could burn car and man only around the driver's seat, and begin to melt metal, the coroner prudently did not attempt to explain. The verdict followed a time-honoured pattern: an open verdict of death 'from third-degree burns'.

Jack Larber was an elderly male patient in the Laguna Honda Home, San Francisco. He was not an alcoholic. The Fire struck him as he was drinking the glass of milk that Sylvester Ellis, a male nurse, had just given him. Only five minutes later, as Ellis was passing the open door of Larber's room, he saw that the patient was enveloped in flames. And here again was the mystery of the 'heatless environment': Larber did not smoke, so that there were not even matches to take the blame for the fire.

'So baffled were the police and fire department investigators', says Vincent H. Gaddis, in reporting this very typical case, 'that one officer suggested that someone might have drenched the old man with lighter fluid and set him on fire. But Larber had no enemies, and the theory was not substantiated.

Mr Gaddis might have added 'and there was no smell of gasoline, either'. As we shall see, the absence *of any odour whatever* in a number of these cases is not the least of all the mysteries surrounding them.

Even in the bizarre annals of spontaneous combustion, the death of Glen B. Denney, forty-six, is unique. There is, in this case, the element of 'punishment' that I mentioned earlier. For Mr Denney was not only about to commit suicide when the Fire struck him – he may, though he was alive when found, be said to have committed suicide already.

Owner of a reasonably prosperous foundry at nearby Gretna, in Louisiana, Denney had been depressed over matters in his private life, a despondency which had led him to, and been increased by, too much indulgence in drink. In this case, if not a confirmed alcoholic, the victim was temporarily very much 'under the influence'. It was testified that, seen for the last time, Denney had had the shakes.

Mrs Stalios Cousins, a neighbour, noticed that smoke was coming from the apartment above her own, and telephoned the fire department; the firemen, getting no answer from their hammerings on the door of Mr Denney's apartment, broke down the door. The owner, possibly not yet dead, was burning. The firemen put out the flames with a blanket. Even they, who are used to a variety of fires, saw that this fire had most unusual qualities.

Said Lieutenant Louis Wattigney: 'The man was lying on the floor behind the door, and he was a mass of flames. Not another blessed thing in the room was burning . . . I don't know what caused the fire to burn so hot. He could have been saturated with some oil. *I did not smell anything, however* [my italics – MH]. In all my experience, I never saw anything to beat this.'

There were no matches, used or unused; all the windows were closed and, though 18 September 1952 was a grey, rainy day in Louisiana, it was not a cold one. The central heating was off.

There was blood on the kitchen floor – Denney had been burning on the *bedroom* floor.

That the fire had enveloped him while he was still alive as indicated by the large amount of carbon in his trachea and lungs. A writer, intent on solving the problem of Denney's strange death, approached the coroner, who was 'most reticent in giving out information'; but finally 'admitted' that Denney had cut his arteries and then cremated himself with burning kerosene.

What the persistent writer Otto Burma failed to get from the coroner was a simple explanation of how Denney managed to cut his arteries, pour kerosene over himself, strike a match with oil-soaked fingers over which the arterial blood was pumping – and then, in flames, manage to hide the kerosene can and the used and unused matches. (To this day, the hoped-for explanation has not been forthcoming; as Lieutenant Wattigney said: '. . . he was a mass of flames. Not another blessed thing in the room was burning. . . ')

No kerosene had burned Mr Denney up. Otto Burma wrote afterwards: 'In [my] mind, there is no doubt that Denney did, in fact, attempt suicide. But while in the process of carrying out this act, his body caught fire, due to some unknown cause . . . [20]

Now, that there is 'punishment' here, in the ordinary sense of the word, is unlikely; *who* would 'punish' – and for *what?*

But that the decision to disturb and destroy, not merely the physical body, but also the energy-pattern of the 'etheric' body, might well set up stresses which find their most dramatic and final expression in what is called spontaneous combustion, is not impossible.

For Mr Denney's was not the only suicide in which spontaneous combustion has 'taken over.' There was the case of Billy Thomas Peterson, a suicide, who was found burning in his car. A passing motorist had seen smoke coming out of Billy's garage, had raised the alarm, and had led firemen and police to where Billy sat smouldering. They took him off to Pontiac General Hospital, where he was pronounced dead.

Billy had died, said the doctors, of carbon-monoxide poisoning, for he had coupled a flexible pipe with the car's exhaust. There is no doubt that he intended to do away with himself, even though he had just left his mother, whom he had been visiting. Billy, a welder on sick leave from General Motors, was suffering from a serious kidney ailment. But where did the fire which burned him so badly come from? 'His left arm was so badly burned that the skin peeled off. His genitals had been charred to a crisp. His nose, mouth and ears were burned.'

---

[20] *Fate* magazine, May 1953; quoted by Vincent H. Gaddis, op. cit.

There was also the fact that 'the hairs on his body, his eyebrows, and the top of his head were all unsinged. Even though burned body hairs protruded unharmed.'[21]

Even more mysteriously, *all* Billy's clothing remained unscorched and undamaged in a fire so hot that it had burned his genitals to a crisp and melted a plastic religious statue on the dashboard.

Of course, those equally mysterious but always prompt-to-appear inhabitants of the journalists' imagination, 'The Secret Six', obligingly made their appearance – as they always will when something needs explaining. On the following day, Monday, 14 December 1959, the *Detroit Free Press* carried this headline on its front page: *Possible Torture Killing*

The theory to account for the fact that Billy had been badly burned, his clothes not at all, held that Billy had first been stripped then tortured, then put back into his clothes and into his car, to die of carbon-monoxide poisoning. Even the police rejected this attractive theory.

And while *They* were burning the naked Billy, why should there have been a fire in the car of such intensity that the plastic religious statue was melted? Who introduced heat of such intensity into the car? – and why? And how . . . ? And why was it heat of such a curious type that it did not ignite the gas tank, melted plastic, but confined itself to the area around the driver's seat (just as in the case of Carl Blocker and many others)?

The medical director of the Pontiac General Hospital, Dr John Marra, who was also a deputy coroner for the district, issued this report on the death of Billy Thomas Peterson:

---

[21] *Cf* the unburned candle wicks in two other cases of spontaneous combustion.

A conclusion was reached as to the appearance of the burns on Mr Peterson's body. It was determined that these were caused by intensive *[sic]* heat in his car which resulted from the exhaust pipe's being connected to the front seat, causing a fire in the upholstery. His blue jeans became so heated that superficial burns of the skin resulted.

So that the gases from the exhaust, led into the car, heated Billy's jeans so much that they burned Billy 'to a crisp', but not enough that they themselves were in the slightest degree scorched.

This ability on the part of the authorities to make pronouncements which ignore the insistent claims even of the common-sense accessible to a low-grade moron is a *consistent* aspect of the mysterious, the unexplained.

The official explanations in the case of Billy Peterson being obviously unacceptable, I decided to do some checking of my own. Estimating that the length of a flexible pipe sufficient to connect the exhaust outlet with the driver's seat would be about ten feet, I arranged with an interested garage owner I know to put a ten-foot pipe on the end of the exhaust. We then found an old but undamaged car seat and tried to set fire to it with the fumes from the exhaust. Nothing. The vinyl covering was not even discoloured. 'Perhaps in the Billy Peterson case', I suggested, 'the seats had leather covers.' We tried the experiment on a leather-covered seat. Perhaps, thought I, the seat having been inside the car when Billy Peterson received his fatal injuries, and the pipe having been curved to return from exhaust to driver's seat, may have . . . We tried that, too. The seats still did not ignite; they did not even scorch.

Then it occurred to me that the covering of the seats – were it vinyl or were it leather – might have split, and that the stuffing might have been in direct contact with the hot gases from the exhaust. We split the covering of our two

86

experimental seats, and played the exhaust gases over the stuffing. It was not even scorched.

Then I put my hand in front of the pipe's end. The gases coming through were warm, still, but not so warm as to hurt me; certainly not so warm as to burn me . . . or anything else. Not a car seat, not Billy Peterson's jeans; most certainly not Billy; and, even more certainly, not the plastic religious statue on Billy's dashboard.

Now, this foolish 'explanation' of Billy's death had come from, of all places, Detroit, home of the U.S. automobile industry. Was there no one in Detroit sufficiently informed or sufficiently interested to blow this preposterous story of Dr John Marra's to smithereens? One feels, with Charles Fort and Vincent Gaddis, that not only do we *always* have the convenient and willing 'explainer' to 'account for' (and so dismiss) the various incidences of the unexplained, but that, in such glib and irrational 'explanations', even the commonsense of the public is willingly set aside so that the public may enter into the conspiracy of silencing with the silencers.

I must note here some information which came to me after the above words were written. Whether or not the fact that I am about to mention had any bearing, not only upon Peterson's death, but on the singular strangeness of that death, I do not know; but in an enquiry in which every known fact – relevant or irrelevant – was dragged in to 'explain' the death, this additional fact, of which I learned only recently, ought to have been produced alongside all the others. As I say, it may have had nothing to do with Peterson's death by the Fire; on the other hand, in our nightmare search for the truth about the Fire, we find that we have been taken, almost without our being aware of the transition, from the solid realities of our everyday world, into 'another dimensional' cosmography, where the laws seem illogical, irrational and even insane. This appears to be a world in which topsy-turvydom rules, dominated by a Fire which always behaves in a contradictory manner: here burning men and not their clothing; here burning clothing and not their wearers; burning a sleeper but not her bedding; burning the bedding but leaving the sleeper still sleeping . . .

As we cannot know which facts are relevant to our enquiry, as we still may only guess at the nature of the Fire, *all* facts become relevant – *all* facts ought to be considered, since, one of these days, one of these facts may yield us the master clue to the truth. The fact that I learned was this: the nature of that 'plastic religious statue', mentioned at the inquest on Peterson as being the only thing, apart from Billy, to be affected by the Fire. It was a 'religious' statue, indeed; but no one mentioned that the statue was of distinctly unusual type.

It is sold attached to a piece of card, printed with blue, gold and white on a background of blue and white. Above the plastic statue of the Infant Jesus, the Blessed Virgin and St. Joseph (all within its transparent cover) is the word *new,* and to the side, in three languages: *Magnetic Auto Statue,* a legend 'decorated' with the conventional 'lightning flashes' by which commercial artists traditionally convey the fact that electrical energy is involved. Beneath this legend is an explanatory one, though in one language only – English: *Sticks Securely to the Surface.*

Well, we know at least one surface to which the statue securely stuck, and – like the sentry at Pompeii – stuck there in the face of all-consuming heat: the surface of Billy Peterson's dashboard . . .

As I said, the presence of the statue may have had nothing to do with the sudden onset of the Fire; but then, again, it may have had everything to do with it. To those who believe in what such (to the unbeliever, trumpery) statues symbolize, they are powerful symbols indeed – and one may recall here the significant words that Herman Wouk, in his wholly memorable *The 'Caine' Mutiny*, puts into the mouth of one of his characters: '. . . the test of the validity of any symbol is the extent to which it's rooted in reality.'

Because as children we play with magnets, because the standard 'experiments' with a magnet and some iron filings is part of the basic science curriculum at school, because refrigerators are fitted with simple pot magnet closers, we have failed to understand that magnetism is no less a mystery and a wonder than the Fire. We can magnetize iron, we can control that magnetism, put it to industrial uses – but ask any manufacturer of industrial magnetic clamps 'how magnetism works', and – if he is an honest man – he will confess that he doesn't know.

And so, because we don't know the least thing about the nature of magnetism, we do not know how little or how much the presence of even a small bar magnet, such as attached the plastic statue to Billy Peterson's dashboard, might count among the factors whose combined influence brought down the Fire from Heaven. Until we shall have discovered what the Fire is, and how it comes, we cannot say what is important here and what is not.

But, to persons of strong religious belief, the force of which religious art provides its many symbols is a powerful force indeed. I mention Billy Peterson's religious statue here because it was not mentioned (save as having melted in the heat) at the inquest, and we are not yet in a position to say whether or not its presence in Peterson's car was a fact relevant to his death.

So much for the male victims who have been found by neighbours or passers-by before the Fire has been able to effect total consumption of the burning body. What of the others struck down, found only when beyond all hope of saving? Here again there are alcoholics and abstainers, fat men and thin, the dissipated and ascetics, the young and old.

On Christmas Eve 1885, Patrick Rooney and his wife, of Seneca, Illinois, died from the effects of combustion, Rooney's death occupying a unique position in the records of death from fire: he was asphyxiated by the fumes from Mrs Rooney's funeral pyre.

There is no doubt that the Rooneys, all of them, were drunk; and drunk in the classical Irish fashion. Farmer Rooney had brought a jug of whisky from nearby Seneca, and all the family, Rooney, Mrs Rooney, son John and John Larson, the hired man, sat around the kitchen table, in the true Christmas spirit. Larson had two drinks, 'to be sociable', then went upstairs to his bed on the first floor. At some time long after Larson had gone to bed, the Rooneys' son, John, left for his own farm, a mile or so distant.

On the morning of Christmas Day, Larson, rising early, went down to the kitchen; his first intimation that something unusual had happened came with his inability to strike a match on the iron stove; its surface was covered with a greasy film. However, striking the match on his thumbnail, and so being able to light the lamp, Larson soon discovered what was wrong: Rooney sitting dead in a chair – and no Mrs Rooney to respond to Larson's frightened shouts. The hired man saddled a horse and rode hell for leather to John Rooney's farm.

Mrs Rooney was a buxom woman, weighing, in life, over 190 pounds. When John Rooney and Larson found her remains they weighed nothing like that: what was left of her – no more than 'a calcined skull, part of a vertebra, a foot and a mound of ashes' – was lying at the bottom of a hole in the floorboards, which had been charred through by her furiously burning body.

Obviously, as Dr Floyd Clemens, the coroner, tried to point out to the bewildered jury, it was a classic case of spontaneous combustion: the absence of any signs of fire apart from the hole in the floor, a slight – a very slight – scorching of the tablecloth immediately above the hole, and, of course, the completely consumed body of the late Mrs Rooney made that evident beyond a doubt. But the jury, never having heard of spontaneous combustion, and not recognizing it when they saw it, could not reach a verdict, save in respect of Mr Rooney's death. They found that he had died, as the medical evidence testified, of asphyxia – choked by the dense, greasy smoke from his wife's mysteriously burning body.

In their *Anomalies and Curiosities of Medicine*, G. M. Gould and W. L. Pyle, the authors, quote the sweeping conclusions of a Dr Jacobs with regard to the 'essential preconditions' of spontaneous combustion. To the classic imperatives – 'the victim is always corpulent or intemperate', and so forth – Dr Jacobs adds his own contribution: the victims 'all led an idle life'. This is yet one more example – had there not been so impressively many – in which medical 'observation' has seen what it felt ought to be seen, and not actually what the record showed.

Certainly John Greeley, helmsman of the SS *Ulrich*, led no idle life; he was, in fact, in the course of steering the ship when something – or someone – stopped him in the middle of his duty, and the ship began to yaw. Alarmed, the second mate, P. F. Phillips, ran to the pilot-house, where all that he found of the helmsman was 'a human cinder'.

'Burned to a crisp', the unfortunate Greeley was; but why did nothing else in the small pilot-house show even the slightest signs of heat? The compass, the varnished wooden wheel – even the scrubbed floor on which the man was lying – all these were unscorched. Other seamen had been constantly passing the pilot-house with its large windows. No one had heard Greeley cry out.

Asked to account for the unaccountable, the doctors, who had not been on the ship when Greeley died, suggested 'a freak lightning bolt'; but those who *had* been on the ship recalled that Greeley had died in the sunshine in a cloudless afternoon. I shall have reason later to return to this mysterious death of the helmsman; I mention it first here in order to begin a brief series of deaths in which the occupation of every victim firmly rebuts Dr Jacob's contention that the victims of spontaneous combustion 'all led an idle life'.

Carl Blocker, the motorist whom I have already mentioned as having been seen in a ditch on the highway, fatally burned, was no idler either. Blocker was in partnership with his wife in running 'several high-class dress shops'; and it was to visit one of these that Blocker was driving on the evening of 3 May 1951.

Nor, indeed, was Peter Vesey – victim of one of the more mysterious of these Fires from Heaven – an idler; he was a hardworking freelance author, who contributed astrological fiction to *American Astrology*. In stories which circulated after Vesey's death there were hints that 'he went in for the occult rituals of mediaeval magicians'. In this case there was a fire in the room, but a small one, in a fireplace of modest dimensions, and, what is more, nothing between the almost completely calcined body of Vesey and the grate had been burned or even scorched.

The fire-blasted suicide, whose case was considered on page 82, was not an idler. He was the owner-manager of a successful foundry at Gretna, Louisiana.

George Turner was driving a truck when, at Upton-by-Chester, in England, the truck stopped and rolled into a ditch. It was 7 April 1938, the day that John Greeley died in the pilot-house of the SS *Ulrich;* a connection in time, if not in place, that I shall consider carefully later.

Police, called to the scene of the accident, opened the door of the driver's cab, and found that George Turner was as lifeless and charred as John Greeley had been in the pilot-house and, as with the fittings of the pilot-house, nothing in the cab had been damaged; even a grease stain on the passenger's seat had not ignited. As in all the cases of car deaths so far considered, the gasoline tank was undamaged. It is a consistent mystery within the greater mystery that a highly volatile spirit seems to lose its inflammability in the presence of the Fire from Heaven. Again the expected verdict was reached by the coroner's jury. 'Accidental death by fire of unknown origin.'

We sense, too, in this death of George Turner's within his driver's cab, the impression of a *pattern* – too vague an impression, at the moment, to be more than sensed – but the definite impression that there *is* a pattern, nonetheless.

It is this: George Turner was not the only truck driver to die in precisely the same way – A. F. Smith also burst into flames within his driver's cab; but the sense of a pattern's presence comes from the fact that *both Smith and Turner* came from Birkenhead. What precisely should be deduced from this fact, I cannot at present say, but, from this and other 'clusters' of deaths by spontaneous combustion, it would seem that *location* may be one of the elements of 'predisposition' which ought to be considered in the search for the Fire's cause.

No idler, either, was Mr G. A. Shepherdson, a prosperous building contractor whose strange death was reported at length – though without editorial comment – in the responsible *Sheffield Independent*. Mr Shepherdson, too, died in a car; and so swiftly did the Fire strike *him* that he had hardly returned his gaze to the road, after waving to some workmen, when he 'turned into a human torch', his car, as in the other cases of like nature, remaining untouched.

93

A tendency to leap to unproven – and, it seems to me, unprovable, certainly unsupportable – conclusions marks the 'considered medical opinion' of the past three centuries, and its apparent irresponsibility appears to increase as we approach the present. So that I must be wary of adding one more 'invariable' to the list of factors making up the 'average' spontaneous combustion. All the same, though victims of this strange fate are not all elderly, idle, corpulent, alcoholic females, living alone, they do seem to me to be excluded, generally speaking, from the higher social classes. It is true that numbered among the victims are the Countess di Bandi, the Countess von Görlitz and Mrs Thomas Cochrane, of Falkirk, a member of the ancient Scottish family of Cochrane, Earls of Dundonald, and some others of gentle blood; but between these members of what we may call 'the upper class' and the rank-and-file members of spontaneous combustibility, there appear to stretch many untenanted social levels. Of the twenty-eight cases listed by Plouquet in his *Literatura Medica*, none is of higher social grade than clerk. Dr Trotter's well-known essay on drunkenness gives many examples of spontaneous combustion, without taking any out of the class of small artisan; though here the insistence on pointing a moral may have forced a certain selectivity on the doctor. The same must be said, I suppose, for the socially not very elevated persons mentioned in Pierre Lair's *Essai sur les combustions humaines, produites par l'abus des liqueurs spiritueuses* (1808).

All the same, making allowance for the 'loaded' evidence of the last two classic observations, it must be admitted that death by spontaneous combustion is not – or, more precisely, has not been until now – an occupational hazard of the upper classes. How the upper-classes acquired and developed what seems to be a *class* resistance to this fatal disorder, I cannot, at present, tell.

But a clue may lie in Dr Jacob's insistence that *all* victims of spontaneous combustion 'led an idle life'. Perhaps we should look more closely, not at the word 'idle', but at the concept to be conveyed by that word. Is it idleness of the body or idleness of the *mind* that Dr Jacobs would have us believe is a fault common to all victims of spontaneous combustion? We have seen that he is wrong, so far as day-labour is concerned: the employed classes have supplied more victims than have the unemployed. But, in the practical meaning of the phrase, are the upper classes so idle – are they, in fact, 'idle' at all?

Generally speaking, it was true until after the Second World War that the upper classes were superior, intellectually, to the classes socially inferior. There was no 'divine dispensation' in this fact – and it *was* a fact. The upper classes received a superior education, both at school and university, and at home; they grew up in an educated environment, and the development of the intellect was cultivated as much by their domestic and social environment as by the progress of their formal education. In short, they learned to 'use their brains', and with such the moments of (not 'idleness', but) physical inactivity rarely leave the *mind* unoccupied. The better, in short, the education, the less likely is a truly idle mind able to develop.

If I say that the number of well-educated persons who fall into ''second childhood', save when they do so through the malignant effect of disease, are fewer than those not so well-educated, I am not advancing any theory based only on 'class prejudice' – I am stating what may be seen as a fact. A better education implies the availability of more money, and the availability of more money makes leisure available, too – leisure to develop and train the mind. The educated person has generally an active mind; a mind trained by experience not to panic in emergencies, to imagine a way out of even unprecedented difficulties.

Let us reconsider the case of Mr Hamilton, professor of Mathematics at Nashville University, one of the few persons of superior class to have been recorded as a victim.

After walking home from lectures, Mr Hamilton saw a blue flame jet out from his leg. If we may believe the detailed description given by A. Devergie at the beginning of the last century (see page 79), all cases of spontaneous combustion of the human body begin with the appearance of 'a bluish flame', a flame being 'seen to extend itself little by little, with an extreme rapidity, over all the parts of the body affected.'

With the majority of the victims, they must have found that they could not quench this jet of flame, and, paralyzed in the despair of horror, have submitted to the 'extremely rapid' seizure by the Fire.

Nashville's professor of mathematics responded quite differently.

Not for him any abject abandon to the 'hopelessness' of the situation. From the very commencement of his unnerving experience (save that it did not unnerve *him!*), he kept his head. He must have realized that what he was seeing was, however unusual, however unprecedented, a *fact* – that a blue flame was spurting out of his left leg, against all *reason*, but not, the intelligent man told himself, against all *observation*. Experimenting in the most natural way, he sought to extinguish the flame with his bare hands; and realized at once that this method of damping the flame would not work.

He was not a chemist, he was a professor of mathematics, but he was an educated man. He knew that combustion could not subsist without oxygen to fuel the flame. So calmly, *intelligently*, he cupped his hands to cut off the oxygen which supplied the flame. The gas-jet died down – the flame was extinguished. Mr Hamilton, the intelligent, educated man, had, by his own education, his own trained intelligence, survived the Fire from Heaven by his own self-possession, his own calm reasoning in the face of terrifying danger. He deserved to escape. He did escape . . .

Continuing with the theory that there may be some protection against the Fire in human intelligence itself, I shall now investigate two 'typical' cases of death by spontaneous combustion – those of Carl C. Blocker (see page 80) and George Turner (see page 92), both originating within a motor vehicle; Blocker in a private car, Turner in a truck. There are some striking differences in the two deaths. Both men died, of course, but Blocker did not die within his car: he was found in a ditch nearby, to which he had run or crawled, and though frightfully injured, he lay there, still alive, until he was found and taken to hospital, where he died.

When the police opened the door of George Turner's cab they found his 'incinerated remains' in the driver's seat.

Now it is possible that, in the case of Blocker, he was given more time than Turner; with Blocker, the onset of the Fire was slower; with Turner, it came on swiftly and fiercely.

But consider what we know of the domestic and business environment of the two men, united only in the manner of their strange deaths. George Turner was doubtless a competent truck driver – but he was no more. Carl Blocker, on the contrary, had acquired some commercial (and doubtless social) standing in his community as the owner, with his wife, of a chain of 'high-class dress-shops'. This man had made something of himself; he could have done that only by the use of his intelligence. The Fire had overtaken him, as it had overtaken George Turner; but whereas we may assume that Turner had been too scared, too paralyzed with terror, to move, Blocker – like Hamilton – had not surrendered without a fight. He had exercised the privilege of 'brains', and had attempted to defy the Fire to save himself.

8

THE LADIES **ARE** FOR BURNING

As with the male victims of spontaneous combustion, female victims are rarely to be found in the higher ranks of society.

Once we have noticed the strange (and horrible) death of the Countess di Bandi and the few other ladies of rank, we have to descend several strata in the social scale before we encounter what may be called the 'main body' of combustibility. Indeed, generally speaking, women who perish by spontaneous combustion are rarely as high, 'socially', as are the men – and, as we have seen, the men rarely come within nodding distance of the 'socially prominent'. A difference, too, between male and female deaths in this specific way is that female victims can be of far lower ages, compared with men. It is rare to find a male victim even so young as Willem ten Bruik – probably about eighteen. It is not at all rare to find a female victim of pubescent age – though here, it will be noted, the Fire attacks in a distinctive way.

There is another aspect of female susceptibility to spontaneous combustion which should be mentioned here: though it is rather the femininity than the susceptibility which calls for comment. Perhaps matters have improved to-day – but two generations ago the very femininity of women made them the natural and easy prey of coroners determined, at all costs, to impose the doctrine that spontaneous combustion was a non-fact.

Take the case of Margaret Dewar, retired schoolteacher, who lived with her also-retired schoolteacher sister, Wilhelmina, at Whitley Bay, Northumberland, in England.

One evening in 1908 Margaret Dewar came back to the house that she shared with her sister; called out on entering, received no answer, and walked upstairs to the bedroom. On the *unscorched* bed was lying the terribly burned body of Wilhelmina.

One does not need to be a member of Women's Lib to feel angry at the treatment accorded to the wretched Margaret Dewar. In addition to the shock that she must have undergone in finding her sister so mysteriously and horribly burned, Margaret had to endure the vicious denunciation of the coroner, and, inspired by him, the conspiracy of attack by her neighbours. The case of 'The Coroner versus Margaret Dewar' may well stand as the classic example of the prosecution of a witness by an officious nobody, with all the lunatic power of the Law behind him.

Basing his 'arguments' on the 'fact' that bodies are *not* found burned on unburned beds, the coroner flatly rejected Miss Dewar's tearful (and truthful) evidence; reminded her – in stating bluntly that she was a liar – that she was speaking under oath; and that the penalties for wilful perjury were severe; and (to 'give you a chance to come to this court and tell us the truth') adjourned the inquest.

Who 'got at' Miss Dewar? Margaret Dewar was sent home, to get the neighbours to work on her. By the time that the inquest was recalled, Margaret would have testified to anything.

She 'admitted' that she had *not* found Wilhelmina lying burned on her bed. The 'truth' was that Margaret had found her sister on fire on the ground floor; had put out the flames, and had then helped Wilhelmina upstairs to her bedroom, where, *on the unscorched bed,* she had died.

Margaret Dewar, telling this carefully 're-regulated' story, was not even rebuked for her having 'lied' at the first hearing of the inquest – certainly she was not committed for perjury.

She had endured the active opposition of the neighbours to her 'lies'; the local newspapers had attacked her story; she had been threatened by the coroner, with prosecution for perjury. She did well to listen to police 'guidance' on the revision of her memory.

What Gaddis[22] does not mention here – but which may be assumed from the *tone* of the newspaper accounts of March 1908 – is that the 'highly respectable' ex-school-teachers neither drank nor smoked. The newspapers make no mention of Wilhelmina's weight; so that we cannot say whether or not she was a 'corpulent' elderly female – but she was certainly not an alcoholic.

In these deaths by spontaneous combustion, where women are involved, the same odd pattern is seen – if, indeed, it be a pattern – which alternates in the burning and the sparing of the victim's clothing. When Thomas Morphey, proprietor of the Lake Denmark Hotel, Dover, New Jersey, found his housekeeper, Lillian Green, burned and dying, the Fire had consumed her clothing, but had not done more to the carpet beneath her than slightly scorch it.

Miss Green was one of the rare type of victim: the 'partial'. They managed to get her, still alive, to hospital; but, though she could still speak, she was unable, as was Ashton Clodd, to say what had happened.

As this book has already made clear, there are, within the general pattern of the Fire, countless variations of type, both as regards the victims and as regards the manifestations of the Fire. But there is one apparently invariable rule, to which, so far, I have found not one exception: that when the attack of the Fire is less than fatal, and the victim may be questioned, he or she is never able to explain what occurred. No clue to the nature of the Fire or the con-

---

[22] Vincent H. Gaddis, op. cit.

ditions in which it may attack has ever been elucidated through the questioning of a victim still able to talk – and I doubt that it ever will. I am not the only student of the Fire to have remarked and commented upon this fact.

The inability to 'explain' is, as Harry Price, Vincent Gaddis, and other students of the Fire have pointed out, a *consistent* quality of those cases in which the victims have been found before the actual supervening of death. They *always* 'can't say what happened' – indeed, in two cases of the burning of young girls (by a fire which spouted out of their backs), the victims were unaware that they had been attacked.

In his *Poltergeist over England*, the late Harry Price, probably the most famous investigator of the 'psychic' that Britain has produced, tells of the mysterious burning of Mrs Madge Knight, who woke the household *with her screams* early in the morning of 19 November 1943 – during, I would ask the reader to note, 'the worst year' of the Second World War.

Mrs Knight lived in Sussex with her husband and sister; and those who remember the year 1943 will recall the acute tension that the varying fortunes of the war induced in the minds of most. Mrs Knight *screamed*. That in itself is unusual: the victims of the Fire rarely scream.

What had happened to Mrs Knight was this: she was lying in her bed; none of the bed-linen was burned or even scorched. But Mrs Knight's back was so badly burned that the physician, hastily called, had to anaesthetize her before he could touch the burns. 'There were', he said, 'extensive burns over the whole of her back; but there was no smell of burning.' The absence of the characteristic smell, it will be remembered, is frequent in cases of burning by spontaneous combustion.

A specialist was called in, to identify the burns as burns. Asked to 'account for' her injuries, Mrs Knight said that she

101

'had no idea'. Removed to Chichester Hospital, she died there, of 'toxaemia', on 6 December 1943.

Even for inquests in a case of spontaneous combustion, the inquest held on Mrs Knight's body was rife with the challenging paradoxes always encountered on such occasions. In addition to the medical man who presided as coroner,[23] there were four doctors present, all giving the sort of meaningless 'evidence' expected on such occasions.

The 'suggestion' was advanced that 'the burns might have been caused by some corrosive fluid' – a 'suggestion' notably half-witted even for this type of evidence, since anything which would corrode human skin would also corrode bed-linen. To this intelligent 'suggestion' was added the contradictory evidence that 'the hands, head, hair, bed-sheets, and Mrs Knight's clothing showed no signs whatever of burning or scorching; and the police found no evidence in the house of burnt or stained floors, and no bottles that had contained acids.' There was also testimony that all heaters in the house were electric, and none was in operation at the time of Mrs Knight's death.

Edgar Allan Poe talks in one of his stories of a book 'which dare not be read'. In even the most superficial examination of spontaneous combustion, one cannot but be struck by the fact that – at least, so far as coroners are concerned – spontaneous combustion is a fact 'which dare not be admitted'.

It is true that the 1922 edition of Dixon Mann's *Forensic Medicine*, while still describing in detail 'the remains of a woman . . . a heap of calcined bones', only three feet from an unscorched tablecloth, dismisses the victims of the Fire as 'gin-sodden old women', and that in the March-April 1952

---

[23] In England the appointment of a coroner is for life; but he must have both legal and medical qualifications.

issue of the *Journal of Criminal Law, Criminology and Police Science* (North-Western University) Dr Lester Adelson, a forensic pathologist of Cleveland, Ohio, dismisses the concept of spontaneous combustion as 'a monument to bygone days'. But it is also true that in the revised edition of Taylor's *Principles and Practice of Medical Jurisprudence,* Vol. I, Professor Keith Simpson, M.D. has – while not admitting the *fact* of 'spontaneous' combustion – at least admitted that there are features of this type of burning not easily explained by reference to accepted experience.

There is something subtle about the Fire: usually it attacks by stealth, cutting off (so quickly does it attack) even the victim's cry of horror. But sometimes the Fire – and especially if we may personify it – seems to take to itself an irresponsible exhibitionism. It not only *is* seen in operation, it *wishes* to be seen.

As in the case of Phyllis Newcombe, who blazed, enveloped in 'bluish flames', as she waltzed on the dance floor. Phyllis Newcombe was twenty-two, an enthusiastic and practised dancer. She suddenly glowed with blue flames, and, while the horrified and (as it seems) momentarily paralyzed fellow-dancers looked helplessly on, was 'within minutes a blackened mass of ash'.

This tragic case, that took place at Chelmsford Shire Hall on 27 August 1938, presented more problems to the coroner, L. F. Beccles, than the actual fire itself. The headlines in the *Daily Telegraph* of 20 September – three weeks after the death of Miss Newcombe – carried as much of the story as the public could be expected to know:

GIRL BURNED IN BALL DRESS
A Coroner: 'Most Mysterious Case'
Town in Need of Official Ambulance

At midnight on Saturday, 27 August 1938, Phyllis New-combe was leaving the dance-floor with her fiancé, Henry McAusland, of Romford – the 'weekly hop' at the Shire Hall was over. Twenty-two-year-old Phyllis, happy to have been dancing all the evening with her young man, stepped lightly off the floor – and, within a minute or two, died.

She was wearing what was described in court as 'a dress modelled on an old-fashioned crinoline' – a description which was eagerly pounced on by authority as providing a 'reason' why the dress should have flared up – as Henry McAusland testified – 'in seconds'. Phyllis screamed; Henry tried to beat the flames out with his bare hands; and badly, indeed, fatally, burned, Phyllis was taken off to the manager's office – there to await an ambulance which did not turn up.

Immediately after the 'accident', the manager of the Shire Hall telephoned the police – it was then only a minute or two after midnight. Not until 12.35 a.m. did the ambulance turn up, St. John Inspector Parrott 'explaining' that the police – having no ambulance of their own – had 'passed on the call' to the St. John Ambulance Brigade; but, as the ambulance (their only one in a city of some 25,000 people!) was 'out on a call', Inspector Parrott had had to wait until its return before redirecting it to the Shire Hall.

The ball gown 'modelled on an old-fashioned crinoline' was too good to miss – and the coroner surmised that, as the sides of this 'old-fashioned' dress stuck out, the light from a cigarette may 'inadvertently' have touched it – upon which ('inevitably') the dress flamed up, 'with the tragic results that we have heard'.

Now this case would have gone the convenient way of all well-handled inquests had not Miss Newcombe had a father of enquiring mind. He asked – and was given – permission to speak; and what he had to say caused the

Coroner to declare: 'In all my experience I have never con
across a case as mysterious as this.'

Producing a piece of the material of which his dead
daughter's dress had been made, Mr Newcombe invited the
coroner to try its inflammable properties. 'Begin with this
lighter', said Mr Newcombe. The material flared up. 'Now
let me light a cigarette', said Mr Newcombe; 'and let us try
that . . . ' A lighted cigarette would not ignite the material
– and, recalled, all the witnesses swore that no one had
even produced a lighter at midnight in the Shire Hall, let
alone a flaming one . . .

Even if we subdivide the occurrence of spontaneous
combustion into many classes, none of these classes is
unique. An almost precisely similar case to that of Miss
Newcombe is described by Emile Schurmacher in his *Strange
Mysteries,* and quoted by Colin Wilson in *The Occult.*

Again we have a young woman dancing – that is, *moving
rhythmically with rotary movements* (a potent source of
power, according to 'primitive' belief) – in a place in which
there were no open flames: it was the large room of a Soho,
London, nightclub.

Nineteen-year-old Maybelle Andrews was dancing with
her friend, Billy Clifford, 'when flames suddenly burst from
her back, chest and shoulders, igniting her hair. She died
on the way to hospital. Her boyfriend, who was badly
burned trying to help her, explained that there were no
open flames in the room – the flames seemed to come from
the girl herself.'

In the fact that Maybelle was dancing with her male
companion, her case most closely resembles that of Phyllis
Newcombe; but in the fact that the flames seemed to come
from her back and chest, rather than from her dress, her
case bears a strong resemblance to the several cases quoted
in this book, from Ayer, Massachusetts, to Binbrook, Norfolk,
of the fire-from-the-vertebrae phenomenon. But, as I have

said, even with the minutest sub-classification, no case of spontaneous combustion appears to be unique – apart from the main classification of Spontaneous Combustion, it will share at least one feature with some other case.

No less lacking in privacy was the sudden death by the Fire of Mrs Mary Carpenter, who perished while holidaying in a cabin-cruiser off Norfolk on 29 July 1938. As with Phyllis Newcombe, on the Chelmsford dance-floor, the Norfolk holiday-maker 'was engulfed in flames and reduced to a charred corpse'. In this case, the presence of a volatile fuel on board ship should have provided the authorities with a ready-made excuse; but, with rare honesty, they ignored the tempting fact of gasoline or diesel oil, and admitted the inexplicable nature of the tragedy. 'I suppose her clothes caught fire, but I can't understand how it happened . . .' Honest, if not altogether explanatory.

A report of Mrs Madge Knight's death (see page 101), in the *West Sussex Gazette* of 23 December 1943, calls it 'one of the most baffling combinations of circumstances which a coroner could have to investigate'.

But how less mysterious was the death by fire of Mrs Ellen K. Coutres, fifty-three, six years later and four thousand miles distant? Just as much mystery here at Manchester, New Hampshire – but a good deal more honesty in the face of the inexplicable. Mrs Coutres was found in her home, burned to death – in a room where no fire had been lit in the fireplace. And in that room only Mrs Coutres's frightfully disfigured body bore the signs of fire: 'There was no other sign of fire, and although . . . the woman must have been a human torch, flames had not ignited the wooden structure [of the frame house].' There was no discoverable source of fire. . .

Deaths by spontaneous combustion which take place in easy-chairs are frequent in mishaps of this class; but it may be doubted that the type of chair is a causative factor, save in the sense that it induces sleep – and sleep does seem, in many cases, to be a predisposing state; many victims obviously have been asleep at the onset of the Fire.

The Kileys, it will be remembered, had been sitting in large, comfortable chairs of the 'saddle-bag' type; and in such a chair had Mrs Esther Dulin been sitting when, in May 1953, the Fire struck her, so that she was burned to death. The death by spontaneous combustion of Mrs Dulin, of Los Angeles, raises some interesting points which have not, in my opinion, been given their due consideration.

In the first place, Mrs Dulin was only thirty – one of the youngest victims of spontaneous combustion whose death has been recorded. In the second, her death belongs to that class of combustion in which the intense heat is obvious. As in the case of Mrs Rooney, the fire attacking Mrs Dulin was of such intensity that her body was 'virtually consumed', and – again as in the case of Mrs Rooney – the flames ate their way through the carpet, floorboards, scantlings and plaster ceiling into the room below. But, and once more we have the 'sign-manual' of the veritable Fire, 'no other rooms or objects in the house were damaged'.

Mrs Dulin died in a chair; death after death is reported in the world's press of those who have died in chairs or beds which have been 'set alight by a cigarette'. I knew two such cases: middle-aged men in each case, who had awakened to find themselves in (not a smouldering, but) a *blazing* bed; one being very badly burned – he was sixty at the time – the other not so seriously injured. Both had awakened almost, it would seem, as they were about to be killed; both had been drinking heavily; and both accepted as fact that the fire had been caused by a cigarette, since each admitted that he did, indeed, smoke in bed.

In a detailed analysis of the *circumstances* in which victims of SHC die or are more or less gravely injured – an analysis which (though I have not yet had the time to undertake it) must be made before we may hope to determine the nature of the Fire – it will be apparent that the armchair stands high in the list of common fire death circumstances. In fifteen cases of the Fire, of which the circumstances have been reported, and which have come to my notice since writing this book, I have noted that the cases fall within the following categories:

Dressing-room	Bedroom/Mattress	Armchair	'Fire-prone'
D. Boote (1974)	P. Seaton (1939)	Mrs M. Hogan	Boy at Bath (1975)
	R. Davies (1974)	(1970)	Mrs Boley (1975)
	Hotel guest (1974)	Miss E. Thompson	Van Reenans(1975)
	Mrs E. Steers (1974)	(1972)	D. Webb (1976)
	T. Nelson (1974)	W. Cashmore	
	Mrs E. Cooks (1975)	(1975)	
	W. Seale (1976)		

From my list, admittedly far from a complete record of the injuries or deaths by SHC which must have happened all over the world, the armchair deaths total just over 50 % of the bed/mattress deaths, since two of those who found themselves lying on a fiercely burning mattress – Roland Davies of Corby, Northamptonshire (26 August 1974), and Terry Nelson, 33, of Digby Street, Scunthorpe, Lincolnshire (18 October 1974) – were not killed by the flames, but made a slow and painful recovery in hospital (both, of course, unable to explain 'what had happened').

The case of William Cashmore is curious, not on account of his age – 82 – but because there died, with him, his dog and budgie. When Mr Cashmore was found dead, the only signs of fire in his home at Autumn Close, High Heath, Walsall, were on his clothing and on a chair in which he had been sitting when the Fire struck. Public utility officials found nothing wrong with the gas and electricity fittings, and Mr Cashmore had been a non-smoker. At the inquest, no even imaginary 'case of fire' was tendered in evidence.

To get back to the ladies with whom this chapter is primarily concerned, the SHC deaths in my new list maintain their now traditional pattern, in which the only certain fact is the death.

Miss Edith Thompson, 75, was found dead – and charred – in her flat in Littlewood Road, Cheslyn Hay, Staffordshire, on 16 February 1972. An 'armchair death' by SHC, Miss Thompson's burning manifested one of the most consistent signs of SHC: only her armchair had suffered damage. According to the evidence at the inquest, Miss Thompson 'had apparently been lighting a fire' – *but had not succeeded in doing so,* a fact which was glossed over in the verdict of 'Death by Misadventure'. To many readers, the name 'Edith Thompson' may well be unfamiliar; but, just after the First World War, when another Edith and her young lover, Frederick Bywaters, were hanged in Britain for the murder of Mr Thompson, 'Edith Thompson' was a notorious name indeed. Now consider: Miss Edith Thompson, who died of SHC on 14 February – note the month and the day! – 1972, died on St. Valentine's Day, the day of lovers, exactly fifty years after wretched Mrs Edith Thompson had been dragged, screaming, to the gallows. 'Our' Edith Thompson, seventy-five in 1972, would have been only twenty-five when her romantically foolish, rather than calculatingly murderous, namesake was hanged. Does one imagine that Miss Edith Thompson's name did not become then, and remained so for many years after, a cause for idle or malicious jest . . . ? She was and remained an unmarried woman; she died unmarried. Why . . . ? Did the jokes about the Thompson-Bywaters murder drive her from social life; induce her to seek that lonely but unharming solitude which ended in a small apartment in a small Staffordshire town, where, dead from the Fire, she was found only through the curiosity of a neighbour? Fort, as I have said elsewhere in this book, called attention to the psychic conditions apparent in many cases of SHC – almost one might say, to the psychic 'preconditioning' of the victims. He specially mentions the high incidence of SHC among 'the desperate'. Might not a lifetime of being offended, even merely bored, by silly jokes about Mrs Thompson and Bywaters have put Miss Edith Thompson into the psychic condition in which the Fire struck, not merely a likely victim, but a willing one?

Mrs Ellen Steers, 79, of Stoney Lane, Shaw, Berkshire, might well have been sufficienfly desperate to have got herself included in any Fortean list of probable 'SHC-prones'.

The inquest stressed that Mrs Steers, who 'regularly smoked in bed', had done so 'despite warnings from friends of the danger' – a piece of 'evidence' so typically irrelevant that one feels that one could encounter it only in the record of a coroner's inquest. For no evidence was adduced that the fire in which Mrs Steers perished – not burnt, but asphyxiated behind the bathroom door – had been caused by a cigarette . . . *or by anything else;* though the absence of evidence on this important point was attributed to the fierceness of a fire which had seriously damaged a bedroom (but not the rest of the house). On the previous day, Mrs Steers ('who had a history of hypochondria') had lost her husband, though, the doctor testified, she had not seemed 'unduly stressed' – an option of that conventional vagueness to which one may attach as great or as little importance as one wishes.

It is a curious case, not altogether unmatched in the record; but distinctly unusual in that the fierceness of the Fire's attack would seem to have been directed against the bed (which was completely consumed) and only secondarily, if at all, against the bed's occupant. When, at the end of this book, I shall sum up the evidence and the conclusions to be drawn from that evidence, we shall see the implications of the Fire – what it is, and where it appears to originate.

But here we may mention that strange 'mirror phenomenon' which sometimes alters the accepted pattern of the Fire: where the clothes and not the wearer burn; where the bed and not the sleeper catches fire.

With men, as with women, the ignition of the mattress comes often during sleep, and in one of the more recent cases – it involved an unnamed guest, staying at the Air Terminal Hotel, South Kensington, London, on 12 September 1974 – makes one wonder if, sometimes, the target of the Fire is not the mattress rather than the sleeper; and whether or not the Fire sets up defences against interruption. (It is as though, through some error in the programming, the Fire is given erroneous orders.)

Smoke was seen coming from a bedroom of the hotel, and, when the alarm was being given, firemen rushed into the room. It was not a large fire, and was easily put out. Doctors examined the guest who was unhurt and hotel staff changed the bed-linen, *while the man slept soundly* throughout alarm and commotion, to say nothing of the Fire. Have we here a case of SHC which was halted halfway (as was the case of Mr Hamilton)? Was the near-trance in which the guest slept through the Fire a commonplace of SHC, never seen because the Fire has consumed the body, but seen here because the alarm was given and the firemen arrived in time to save the sleeping man?

There is, apparently, another way in which the Fire guards against 'outside interference': by a heat far greater than that to be accounted for in some of the actual burnings. In case after case – see that of little Peter Seaton on page 10 and that of 65-year-old William Seale on page 360 – firemen and other would-be rescuers have been driven back by intense heat. 'It seemed as if I had opened the door of a furnace'; '. . . beaten back by terrific heat.' Is the Fire trying to keep those away who would prevent it from carrying out its appointed task . . .?

Then, as I speculated in the similar cases of Turner and Smith (page 93), are there focuses of Fire-influence, in which people more easily succumb to its menace? For, in Miami, Florida, on 12 January 1975, Mrs Esther Cooks died as mysteriously of unaccountable burns and other injuries as did Mrs Mary Reeser in July 1951, as will be described later. The point to bear in mind here is that Miami, where Mrs Cooks died, and St Petersburg, where Mrs Reeser's fatal experience provided what is still the 'all-time classic' of SHC, are not only both in the state of Florida, but very near each other. And, in that part of the book where I note the 'fire-raising' abilities of certain persons, I shall remark on the fact that one of the seven fires associated with the presence of Mrs Booley, a cook with a self-confessed 'temper', and described in the London *News of the World* for 19 October 1975, took place at Bath, Somerset, the same town in which a boy was charged anonymously before the juvenile court with having 'raised fires'. Lightning does quite often strike twice in the same spot – sometimes more than twice – and the Fire can hit more than once in the same place.

The case of Mrs Margaret Hogan, an 89-year-old widow, of Prussia Street, Dublin, Ireland, is remarkable in that the city coroner, Dr P. J. Bofin, permitted himself to add, after having 'found' that Mrs Hogan died of burning: 'The circumstances of the burning are unusual, and would conform to what is called Spontaneous Combustion'. In saying that 'the circumstances of the burning are unusual', Dr Bofin of course meant that they would be unusual were they associated with an ordinary fire; but, in fact, the circumstances were not unusual for a fire of the SHC type. The only damage in the room in which Mrs Hogan was charred to a cinder was the burning of the armchair in which she had been sitting and a scorching of the linoleum directly beneath the chair. This absence of 'unnecessary' burning is, as we have already seen, one of the most characteristic 'signatures' of an SHC visitation. The case of Mrs Hogan was reported in full in *The Irish Times* of Tuesday, 12 May 1970.

I continue to find the phenomenon of the *blazing* – not merely *smouldering* – mattress one of the most mysterious, as well as the most striking, of the many lesser phenomena within the one important and all-embracing phenomenon of the Fire itself. For – and I speak from an experience that thousands of people must share with me – mattresses simply don't blaze. They smoulder. The hardest thing to burn, as one burns paper or wood, is anything which is stuffed – a cushion, an armchair, a mattress; and it matters little what the stuffing is made of – wool, kapok, horsehair, foam-rubber . . . Unless one pours on some volatile spirit or other inflammable substance, the mattress will not 'blaze' – it is the most difficult task to get it even to light.

No one – least of all firemen, police officials, coroners and other medico-legal experts – has commented upon the *unusualness* of a *blazing* mattress, even when that *blazing* mattress (as in the Air Terminal Hotel, South Kensington, on 12 September, 1974) left the sleeper not only unharmed, but even unawakened. On page 86, I described experiments that I made in attempting to ignite something very similar to a mattress: the upholstered seat of a car. The reader will remember how I failed to ignite a car-seat with the hot exhaust fumes; a cigarette or dropped match will not set a mattress ablaze any more easily.

Now I have, at one time or another, had friends stay with me; they were all men in the cases that I am about to discuss, who not only smoked, but smoked carelessly. One let a cigarette burn its way down through the arm of a well-stuffed chair; one was found by me, fast asleep in another well-stuffed chair, with the remains of a cigarette attached to his limp fingertips, where it had burnt itself out on a new Axminster rug; two others had managed to make a lighted

113

cigarette burn its way through a pillow and some inches through blanket, sheet and mattress; while a fifth, who had laid down to rest on a bed in his bathrobe, had let the cigarette burn its way through the thick double-collar of the robe. In no case was there a fire, as such; in every case the cigarette, though maintaining an obstinate reluctance to go out, had been extinguished at last – and that without setting fire to mattress, chair, bathrobe, and so forth. One must ask oneself: what *additional* circumstances are required to convert this smouldering cigarette into a fire source of such intensity that it will utterly consume the human body? Or must we accept the conclusion that many a spontaneous combustion hides tactfully behind the fiction of 'fire from a dropped cigarette'?

An oddity, in this catalogue of oddities, was the death of Mrs Martin, on 18 May 1957. Her son, a West Philadelphia fireman, came home to find what little was left of his widowed mother's charred body. Mrs Martin had been burnt rather differently from the usual. In her case the extremities had been totally consumed, while the torso remained fairly intact. Again differing in detail from the (assumed) 'average', was the fact that Mrs Martin was found lying on her stomach. This is unusual. However, her shoes, as in the 'average' burning, were intact.

Not altogether 'abnormal', but certainly different from the 'average', was the intensity of the heat which had consumed her. Despite the fact that 'a stack of newspapers and several cardboard cartons, alongside a pile of mail-order catalogues . . . within two feet of the body . . . were not even scorched', the Chief Medical Examiner, Dr Joseph W. Spelman, giving testimony at the inquest, stated that only a fire of some 1700 to 2000 °F would have been able to effect the damage to the victim's body. As Gaddis, quoting *Fate*

Calcined remains of Mrs E.M., a widow, aged 69; found dead of 'preternatural combustibility', at Hammersmith, West London, 29 January 1958. *Photograph by courtesy of Dr Gavin Thurston, MRCP, DCH, DMJ, barrister-at-law, HM Coroner, Inner West London* (through Contrad Research Library).

Desiccated remains of 'an old soldier', found dead, on Sunday, 19 February 1888, of 'so-called "spontaneous combustion" ', in the immediate proximity of 'dry woodwork and hay, loose and in bundles', none of which was even charred. *Photograph by courtesy of the Royal Society of Medicine* (through Contrad Research Library).

The old (no longer existing) University of Nashville, Tennessee, from which, on Monday, 5 January 1835, Mr James Hamilton, Professor of Mathematics and Natural Philosophy, walked home to a triumphant struggle with the 'Fire from Heaven'. *Print by courtesy of Dr J. E. Windrow, George Peabody College for Teachers, Nashville* (through Contrad Research Library).

The subconscious, instinctive, elemental and irresistible attraction towards Fire. An early nineteenth-century (after George Cruickshank) of children, at Christmas, burning their fingers at snapdragon. *Print: Contrad Research Library.*

magazine,[24] remarks: 'A stain about four feet square lay over the floor around the body. It was not oil, as it first appeared to be, but residue from the consumed body. So puzzled were detectives that they wondered if an intruder had murdered the woman and then had set fire to her body. However, there was no evidence of forced entry or signs of a struggle.' And, even so, the question remained: What caused the fire to burn with such tremendous intensity? And since it obviously had, why didn't it spread and at least scorch the paper only two feet away, and the joists above? Chief Inspector John J. Kelly, who investigated, later stated: 'It's one of our most mysterious cases.'

We may find ourselves wrongly reasoning: Fire of the 'spontaneous combustion type' may be recognized by its *selective* nature – in that it seems to choose its victim and destroy him, her, or it, thoroughly, but to the exclusion of objects not designated as victims. This is wrong reasoning because we do not know that the Fire from Heaven will 'burn only selected objects', and will refrain from burning surrounding property. Who is to say that there have not been extensive fires, involving perhaps whole cities (the *epidemic* of fires which, in 1871, burnt Old Chicago may have been such) which, in their origin, were as 'inexplicable' as that which killed Mrs Martin? A reference to the reports of any Fire Chief, anywhere in the world, will show that the entry 'arson', under the heading 'Suspected Cause of Fire', is common indeed – and is little more precise that the less common entry, 'Spontaneous Combustion'. (They may, indeed, be no more than variants of the same entry.)

The plain truth is that we – even the 'experts', particularly the 'experts' – know very little about fire, as we know very little about electricity, and even less about

---

[24] September 1957; June 1958.

gravitation. In a later chapter, I shall suggest a link between gravitation and a possible explanation of the Fire from Heaven. But what we must do now is to consider the 'cosmic link' joining all catastrophes; a link which was seen and noted ages ago, but which, dismissed as 'old wives' tales' in the age of scientific reason, was studied anew by that pioneer thinker, the late Charles Fort, and, after Fort's death, by the English science-fiction writer, Eric Frank Russell. These two clear-minded researchers deserve a chapter to themselves.

9

THE 'COSMIC' ELEMENT
IN CATASTROPHE

I put my hand out to the bookshelf in front of me, and take out *The European Magazine and London Review,* Volume 75, which covers the six months from January to June 1819. I take out this book because I looked into it last week, and there was something in it which reminded me of Charles Fort.

On page 414 of the volume in question there is a long correspondence on the subject of the 'crimson-coloured snow' reported by Captain Ross, RN, on his 'late voyage of discovery, for the purpose of exploring Baffin's Bay, in the expectation of finding a north-west passage, through the ice, to Behring's Strait.' This 'crimson snow' was seen by Captain Ross and his crew in 1818.

On page 157 of the same volume, under the heading, 'Chronological Sketch of the Most Remarkable Events for the Year 1818', I find this:

July 23
At Salisbury, the thermometer was 121°F. in the sun, at three o'clock, pm; at eight o'clock it was at 80°F.; and at half-past ten at 73°F.
July 25
The average of six thermometers in the sun, at two o'clock, was 114°F. – *two degrees above fever heat* [my italics – MH]. In the shade it was, at Northern aspect, at 87°F, and in South, at 88°F. The oppressive heat of the weather everywhere complained of.

The harvest commenced under the most happy auspices everywhere.

Charles Fort, a New York journalist who dedicated himself to the study of the Odd, was not the first man to have observed that such happenings do not come singly. He argued that, *somehow,* the incidence of these oddities had a causal connection. Our ancestors had known this for a fact; but when Fort bent his inquisitive mind to the regaining of that forgotten truth, a worldwide press clipping service was at his disposal. From every country he collected newspaper stories of odd happenings – spontaneous combustions, a rain of fish, 'manna' falling in a desert, red rain (red falls everywhere, not only visible to Captain Ross in Baffin's Bay), the incredible and unnecessary proliferation of birds, insects, small mammals.

Fort saw that what *appeared* to be aberrations of the natural order of things happened in 'batches'; that if, say, there was a death by spontaneous combustion, it was never (or rarely) alone; and that these odd deaths were always accompanied – according to the newspaper reports – by happenings equally 'abnormal'.

For instance, Fort was particularly impressed, as a student of the Odd, by the widespread 'abnormalities' of the year 1904-5, especially in Great Britain. To turn up the newspaper files of that time is to realize, first, how 'seriously' even the newspapers took the onset of oddity in the winter of 1904-5, and, second, how short the public memory is which could forget the facts behind a *Liverpool Echo* headline of 18 January 1905; 'Wales in the Grip of Supernatural Forces'.

With a rare sense of what was 'right', the Liberal *Daily News* sent, to investigate the phenomena of the odd in Wales, a Welshman, B. G. Evans, who had an eye which, if sympathetic, could still be critical.

The focus of the Welsh 'disturbances' was the small town of Egryn, and within Egryn the 'personal focus' was a Mrs Mary Jones, on whom – or on whose fervid preachings – brightly luminous clouds or 'balls of reddish fire' concentrated in a 'hovering, dipping' manner that some found uplifting and more found gravely disturbing. The *Daily News* sent Evans to Wales because the representatives of two professionally cynical papers, the *Daily Mail* and the *Daily Mirror,* had been sending back distinctly untypical reports. They wrote of the appearance of brilliant lights over the meetings, in chapels and conference-halls, of the Revivalists; and they reported, too, that these lights, as though they were luminous presences of intelligence, 'inspected' a meeting, and then drifted slowly away to the next.

Evans's first report from Wales appeared in the *Daily News* of 9 February 1905. He made it clear that, whatever he had expected to find in Wales, he had come up against the inexplicably mysterious, and he claimed the right of any consciously objective observer to report what he had seen. In all truth, it was odd enough.

He *had* seen the lights over Mrs Mary Jones's meetings.

The first light resembled a brilliant star emitting sparklets. All saw this. The next two were as clearly subjective, being seen only by Mrs Jones and me, though the five of us walked abreast. Three bars of clear white light crossed the road in front, from left to right, climbing up the stone wall to the right. A blood-red light, about a foot from the ground in the middle of the roadway . . . was the next manifestation.

This was Revival. Britain, especially Wales had known it before; and so, indeed, had North America – especially the United States. But nothing like this had been seen in the earlier manifestations of Revival; not, that is, unless one went back two hundred years, to the extraordinary activities of Father Hell and his Parisian *convulsionnaires* – and even

119

there no signs in Heaven appeared to whip up the Revivalist frenzy.

'Enthusiasm', against which our Puritan forefathers so strongly set their faces, took over. From Wales the 'religious' impulse burst powerfully outward. Shop assistants turned away from their customers, clapped hands, and began to chant the praises of the Lord. Parties of enthusiasts invaded churches, to take over the more traditional ceremonies with noisier and more 'liberated' rituals of their own. People entered police stations, to 'confess' to wrongdoings of which the police were to prove them guiltless. Mobs of the 'liberated' gathered outside theatres and football stadiums and bars, menacing, in the belief that they were 'persuading' the would-be patrons not to enter the haunts of sin. The mobs even poured into police stations, seeking to 'convert' the officers.

Smaller groups, inflamed with mob authority, now took over. Cabs and private carriages were stopped, and the passengers forced to alight, to join in Revivalist street meetings. And then private violence became, once again, mob violence, and sectarian prejudice took over from a generalized 'religious' sentiment.

In Scotland Road, Liverpool, the liberated turned on the Roman Catholics, and, as Gaddis points out, 'One man, taking a biblical passage literally, chopped his right hand off; another led a procession every night, towing his coffin behind him. "When you see one of these processions", a Liverpool magistrate advised, "run from it as you would from a mad bull." '

If all this had happened three- or even two-hundred years before, men would not have been astonished that the world seemed to have gone mad in other ways: the public would have expected it. But between, say, 1604 and 1904 three centuries of rational and rationalistic science had managed to convince the public that there was no such thing as a linked coincidence; that two catastrophes happening at the same time had no causal bond.

That – as in 1904 – there was nothing 'in reason' to connect the improbabilities of Mrs Mary Jones's preaching the Word in a Welsh tin chapel under a blazing (and wandering) luminescence and the deaths of several people, by burning, in circumstances which, said each relevant coroner, were 'hard to explain'.

I mentioned Mrs Thomas Cochrane, widow, who died on 16 December. Mrs Cochrane, of Rosehill, Falkirk, England, was discovered seated in a chair which had been 'stuffed' with pillows and cushions. Mrs Cochrane had been 'burned beyond recognition'. Neither pillows nor chair had been burned. No one had heard the victim cry out. *There was no fire in the grate.*

A week later another elderly female, Elizabeth Clark, died in the same mysterious way. Mrs Cochrane had been wealthy. Mrs Clark was a pensioner of the Trinity Almshouse at Hull, nearly two hundred miles away. Mrs Clark belongs to the type of spontaneous combustion victim who is not immediately killed; she was found, terribly burned, but still alive. As in all such cases, she could not give any explanation of her injuries. And, as in the case of Mrs Cochrane, the bedding on which she was lying was not scorched; and, again as in Mrs Cochrane's case, the neighbours heard no cry.

There were many such cases in a winter which saw 'aerial carriages' flying at a tremendous rate, blazing with light, throughout the British skies; which saw inexplicable cattle maimings; an alarmingly high incidence of suicides – and a really extraordinary number of mental breakdowns, especially among prominent people.

Charles Fort quotes from *Lloyd's Weekly News* of 5 February 1905, which, under the heading 'Mysterious Business', reported the fact that 'a coroner had expressed his inability to understand . . . The coroner had said that a cinder might have shot from the grate, igniting the woman's clothes, but that she had been sitting, *facing the fire,* and that the *burns were on her back*'.

It was a fatal case, of course, otherwise the coroner would not have needed to try to reconcile what he saw with what he thought he ought to have seen. It was reported on 5 February; twenty-three days later, the death of Barbara Bell, seventy-seven, offered no better explanation to the coroner. She had been found by neighbours, lying on an unscorched sofa, 'fearfully charred . . . as if, for a long time, [her body] had been in the midst of intense flames.'

What neither Fort nor Gaddis has observed in this case is that it took place on 28 February, at Blyth, Northumberland, and that it was at Whitley Bay, six or seven miles from Blyth, that Margaret Dewar found her sister, Wilhelmina, burned in her unburned bed, three years later.

Unlike fireballs, the Fire which consumes, not merely threatens, seems to hit the same spot, the same house, rarely; though, as we shall see, like lightning, it can hit the same person more than once. The fact that it should have killed both Wilhelmina Dewar and Barbara Bell within seven miles and three years of each other is a matter for remark and for possible future investigation.

On 4 March in that same 'disturbed' year the elderly couple, the Kileys, whose case was described on page 41, died at Butlock's Heath, near Southampton. Their case was remarkable (it may be unique) in that the 'scratching sound' which drew neighbours to the house occurred hours after the Kileys had suffered their joint burning.

Once we begin, after the widest examination of the spontaneous combustion phenomenon, to generalize about it, we find that, though there is the most striking *type-resemblance* uniting all the cases of burning into a common pattern, no two cases are *exactly* alike; and that, between two cases selected at random, there may be the widest divergences. We have a comparable condition in the human fingerprint; no two sets of prints precisely match, yet all fingerprints obviously conform to a common type of skin-pattern.

Owing to the suppression of evidence in what we may well believe to be the majority of the cases of spontaneous combustion − 'tactful' suppression by relatives; 'rational' suppression by coroners; the covering-up of the facts by more 'acceptable' pseudo-facts; 'smoking in bed', 'faulty electric wiring', etc. − it is impossible at present to treat this subject statistically. And until we can begin to record *every* case of Spontaneous Combustion we cannot possibly extract from such evidence as is available more than the pattern of a pattern.

Still, even the hints tell us much; and, as was said before, the keen observation of two men − Charles Fort and Eric Frank Russell − detected and demonstrated the existence of parallel phenomena, phenomena different from, but seemingly linked with, the phenomenon of spontaneous combustion.

It was Fort who pointed out, from the evidence of press clippings collected over a period of forty years from every part of the world, that all 'irrational' phenomena are linked in the still uninvestigated, and still unexplained, Odd.

Eric Frank Russell is more statistically-minded than Fort was. Whereas Fort collected oddities in quantity, Russell detected, as, indeed, Fort had done, a pattern of happening; but with Russell this pattern was not merely expressed in the remark that 'Oddity manifests itself in an infinite number of forms'. With Russell it seemed that there was some *mathematical* pattern in all this. Could it be coincidence − *could* it? − that, on the same day, and almost at the same time, the Fire from Heaven struck three men down, each being hundreds of miles distant from either of the other two?

The day was 7 April 1938; the time, a still afternoon. Two of the men I have already noted. They were John Greeley, helmsman of the SS *Ulrich,* and George Turner, truck driver. The third was Willem ten Bruik, an eighteen-year-old Dutchman, who died at the wheel of his car near Nijmegen in Holland. All were 'burned beyond recognition'. All were charred with little or no damage to their surroundings.

On 13 March 1966 Michael McDougall, a journalist, retelling the story first noticed and noted by Eric Frank Russell in 1939, wrote in the *Newark Sunday Star-Ledger*: 'It was as if a galactic being of unimaginable size had probed earth with a three-tined fork: three fingers of fire, which burned only flesh.'

Only the phrasing is exaggerated: the facts are precisely as stated – *'three fingers of fire, which burned only flesh.'*

Now, in asking ourselves what connection, if any, there might have been among the three men burnt so mysteriously and so completely on that April afternoon just before the outbreak of the Second World War, we may remind ourselves that neither the science-fiction writer, Mr Russell, nor the feature-writer, Mr McDougall, appears to have looked for any. Mr Russell, a dedicated collector of spontaneous combustions – he found nineteen, of which six involved men, in going through the newspapers of 1938 alone – was simply struck by the fact of the three-pronged attack by the Fire; Mr McDougall, three decades later, simply retold the story.

One would have expected that Mr Russell, at least, would have taken out a large-scale map of Europe, and seen exactly how the three deaths of Greeley, Turner and ten Bruik related to each other *topographically.* I think that he would have been considerably interested in what he might have found – and what I *did* find.

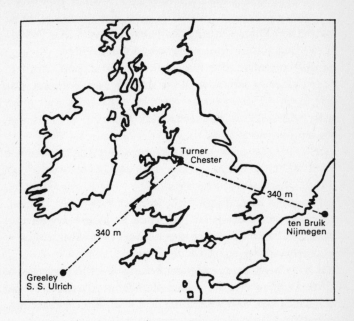

On 7 April 1938 the triple strike took three men. Greeley, helmsman of the SS *Ulrich*, who was exactly as far from Turner, the truck driver, as ten Bruik, the Dutch student, was from Turner.

Now, at the present time, I cannot explain them, but these are the facts.

The SS *Ulrich* was steaming east, bound for Liverpool. As she was passing along the 50th parallel of north latitude, she reached a point south-by-west of, and some 120 miles from, Cape Clear. At this point, the SS *Ulrich* and helmsman

John Greeley were 340 miles from where George Turner, driving his truck at Upton-by-Chester was making for the SS *Ulrich's* (and John Greeley's) home port of Liverpool.

And at precisely that moment, too, Willem ten Bruik, driving into Ubbergen, near Nijmegen, was precisely as far from the Birkenhead truck driver, George Turner, as George was to find himself from helmsman John Greeley.

At that moment, the Fire struck – three men, dead in perhaps as many minutes. Did it strike *because* George was at the apex of an isosceles triangle, with sides 340 miles long – and Greeley and ten Bruik were at each of that triangle's base angles?

If the suggestion sounds ludicrous, let the reader ask himself what we know of the Fire and its causes; of its mode of action; of what triggers it.

Many years ago, following a hint in a book on numerology, I collected sufficient evidence to assure myself that there is, indeed, a close connection between the names of the actors and the times of their acts.

There *is* another connection linking the three victims of 7 April 1938; there are some sounds in common – and Greeley is linked with something odd in another connection. The reader is here reminded that sound, no less than heat, light and the invisible forms of radiation, is an outpouring of energy – energy seemingly on a lower scale of force; but energy, and powerful energy, for all that. For example, the ancient knowledge that sound, no less than light, could effect radical changes in energy-patterns is shown in:

GENESIS I.

2. And the earth was without form, and void; and darkness was upon the face of the deep. And the Spirit of God moved upon the face of the waters.
3. And God said, Let there be light: and there was light.
4. And God saw the light, that it was good. And God divided by His word the light from the darkness.

JOHN I.

1.   In the beginning was the Word, and the Word was with God, and the Word was God.

2.   The same was in the beginning with God.

3.   All things were made by him; and without him [and His Word] was not any thing made that was made.

From the Egyptian belief in 'the Word of power', which could 'do all things', to the Hebrew belief that the true name of God, *if ever pronounced,* could, and would, effect unimaginable things;[25] from the tale of the rock door which swung back to the command, 'Open, Sesame!' (a 'sonar lock'?) to the demon-compelling powers attributed to the *sounds* of wizards' and witches' conjurations; ancient knowledge observed and acknowledged the power of the energy manifested in *sound.*

Let the reader bear these things in mind . . .

There is, indeed, a curious factor linking those three strange deaths, already linked by their having taken place, many miles apart, on the afternoon of 7 April 1938. There is an initial sound common to all three deaths – the sound of U. For consider:

John Greeley was helmsman of the ship	*Ulrich*
George Turner, truck driver, died at	*Upton*
Willem ten Bruik burned to death at	*Ubbergen*

Greeley was further linked with the odd in a personal fashion; he was steering the SS *Ulrich,* and the patron saint of fishermen and sailors bears the same name.

---

[25]Using this theme, *The Eight Billion Names of God*, by Arthur C. Clarke, is one of the best six short stories ever written.

The difficulty in establishing links of this sort – links whose significance I do not pretend to explain – is that the researcher has necessarily to work on extremely limited evidence.

There must be many other such links: perhaps of a 'star sign' shared in common; perhaps a common heredity; maybe a common religious belief; possibly even a common type of pigmentation. Who knows? But if we are to explain in detail the *results,* we must know everything of *causes* – and this we may know only by collecting every detail, however 'irrelevant', concerning the oddities that we wish to examine and explain.

I have retained the above four paragraphs, not *despite* the fact that they aroused the derision of Mr Robert Rickard, Editor of *The Fortean Times,* but *because* they did. I quote the relevant comment of Mr Rickard:

> Harrison . . . also suggests [that] the sights *[sic,* but *sc. sites]* are linked by the sound/vibration of the initial 'U' – laughable when you realize it's two 'oo's' and an 'uh'.

– the last being the sound with which Mr Rickard supposes the name, 'Upton', commences. But George Turner, of Upton-by-Chester, did not pronounce the name, 'Upton', as a Londoner pronounces it; he would have given the name its local pronunciation, which may be represented phonetically as 'Oopton' – beginning then, with the same 'oo' sound with which both 'Ulrich' and 'Ubbergen' commence.

Mr Rickard then goes on to ask sarcastically why I did not note the sound-similarities of 'Wright, Knight and White' or 'Bartholi, Bertillon and Bartholin'? The answer should have been self-evident: only 'Ulrich, Upton and Ubbergen' are linked by the fact of *simultaneous happening:* three deaths, by a common means, at the same time.

As I said above, and as I have said elsewhere in this book (notably in relation to the 'religious plastic statue' in Billy Peterson's car), facts associated with the Fire-deaths are adduced, not because we think that they are important factors in establishing the 'right conditions' for the manifestation of the Fire, but because we don't know which factors are important and which are not. So that, as far as we are able, we give all the facts, leaving it to later research to include what is significant and to jettison the rest. I don't know whether or not a concordance of sound has anything to do with the Fire; but it would be remiss, when we do see these concordances, to omit the fact from our record. And a very curious and striking concordance *did* emerge from the additional facts about the Fire.

I have collected fifteen well-attested subjects to include in the record of Fire-manifestations. Here they are, in chronological order.

---

1. Seaton, Peckham Rye, London (1939)	*death*
2. Hogan, Dublin (1970)	*death*
3. Thompson, Cheslyn Hay, Staffs. (1972)	*death*
4. Watt, Walker, Newcastle-on-Tyne (1974)	*death*
5. Davies, Corby, Northamptonshire (1974)	*injury*
6. Anonymous, Air Terminal Hotel, South Kensington (1974)	*no injury to person*
7. Steers, Stoney Lane, Shaw, Berks. (1974)	*death*
8. Boote, BBC TV Studio, Cardiff (1974)	*injury*
9. Nelson, Scunthorpe, Lincolnshire (1974)	*injury*
10. Cooke, Miami, Florida (1975)	*death*
11. Cashmore, Walsall, Staffordshire (1975)	*death*
12. Anonymous boy, Bath, Somerset (1975)	*no injury to person*
13.*	
Booley, Stone, Gloucestershire	*no injury to person*
Booley, St. Hilda's School, Bridgwater, Somerset	
	no injury to person
Booley, High School, Bath, Somerset	*no injury to person*
Booley, Swan Hotel, Tewkesbury, Glos.	*no injury to person*

Booley, Swan Hotel, Tewkesbury, Glos.	*no injury to person*
Booley, Swan Hotel, Tewkesbury, Glos.	*no injury to person*
Booley, Torbay Hotel, Sidmouth, Devon	*no injury to person*
14. Van Reenan, Plettenberg, South Africa (1975)	
	no injury to person
15. Webb, Paddington, West London (1975)	*no injury to person*

* August 1971-October 1975

In twenty-one manifestations of the Fire, the letter S appears as an initial, either in the name of subject or name of place, no fewer than nineteen times – this in a list which has not been arranged to yield any special quality; this is simply the list of SC fires.

According to the commonly received order of frequencies, S is by no means the most frequent letter of the English alphabet, and what its abnormal frequency in this list shows, I cannot say. It may mean something; it may mean nothing. But until we know the value of the facts as we perceive them,

1. we are not entitled to reject *any* fact as being 'irrelevant';
2. we are not entitled to accord a relevant value to any fact.

Our duty is to deduce from the evidence; and the value of the facts will be assessed only from their *totality* – we cannot know which are essential to an understanding of the truth until all (or, at least, the principal) shall have been collected.

It is idle at this moment to ask 'But why the letter S? What's that got to do with it? What's the connection between the manifestation of the Fire and the letter S?'

I, for one, cannot say. There may be a connection; there may be none.

The death of Krook by 'spontaneous combustion'. The original illustration by 'Phiz' (Hablôt K. Browne) from Charles Dickens's *Bleak House*, 1853. *Photograph: Contrad Research Library.*

The Kirlian Effect. Leaf of the dead-nettle plant in actual growth, shewing its regular and brilliant corona. From *Science and Life*, August 1974, by courtesy of the editor. *Photograph: Novosti Press Agency (APN), Moscow.*

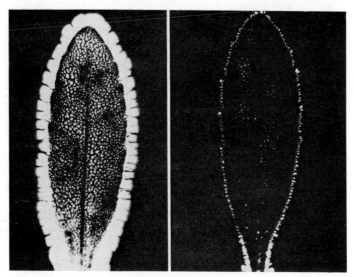

The Kirlian Effect. How Life and electro-magnetic Luminescence are fundamentally linked. Left. Though the leaf has now been separated from the living plant, the brilliance and regularity of the luminescence persist without apparent change. Right. But five hours after the leaf has been picked the almost total eclipse of the luminescence indicates the imminence of death in the electro-magnetic 'parallel body' of the leaf. From *Science and Life*, August 1974, by courtesy of Editor. *Photograph; Novosti Press Agency (APN), Moscow.*

But to dismiss such concordances of sound with the remark that 'there's nothing in it' would be nothing more than unscientific arrogance.

10

SHADRACH, MESHACH, ABEDNEGO
. . . AND MRS REESER

Because they would not bow down and worship the golden idol that Nebuchadnezzar had set up, the King commanded that Shadrach, Meshach and Abednego should be cast into 'the burning fiery furnace'. The story of how these three obdurate believers escaped has made the short (and never very theological) Book of Daniel one of the most popular, and the 'legend' of the Burning Fiery Furnace one of the best remembered.

As popularly told, the story of the three young men has been simplified: King Nebuchadnezzar 'made an image of gold, whose height was three-score cubits, and the breadth thereof six cubits: he set it up in the plan of Dura, in the province of Babylon.' He ordered everyone within his kingly jurisdiction to come to the image and pay it ritual homage; Shadrach, Meshach and Abednego refused. They were cast into the burning fiery furnace; preserved there by the personal intervention of the Most High − and released to rebuke and shame the tyrannical king.

The popular version omits some points which seem to me to be significant.

One of the principal points is that Nebuchadnezzar threatened the three young men with the burning fiery furnace if they refused further to worship his idol; adding, sarcastically, 'and who is that God that shall deliver you out of my hands?'

Another − and certainly even more significant − point is that the three accepted the ironic challenge literally, and offered to enter the burning fiery furnace in the sure and certain expectation that they would be 'delivered' – that is, they assured Nebuchadnezzar that they would not be burned.

A further important omission from the popular version of the tale is the detailed description, in Daniel, of the preparation of the furnace for the reception of the three.

Enraged by the defiant attitude of Shadrach and his two companions, the King ordered that the furnace be heated 'one seven times more than it was wont to be heated'.

This implies not only some precise heat-regulating mechanism, but also an equally precise heat-measuring (thermometric) instrumentation. 'One seven times . . .'

Again the Biblical narrative goes into details which are almost always omitted from the popular version. The King 'commanded the most mighty men that were in his army to bind Shadrach, Meshach and Abednego, and to cast them into the burning fiery furnace'. Why 'the most mighty men' if the three had already volunteered to enter the furnace, to demonstrate to Nebuchadnezzar the superiority of their own God? Does the next verse in Daniel cast any light on the problem?

Verse 21 of Daniel 3 becomes curiously detailed.

Then these men were bound in their coats, their hosen, and their hats, and their other garments, and were cast into the midst of the burning fiery furnace . . .

Upon which, the heat of the furnace burnt up the men who had cast the three into the flames.

Before we go on to examine the details of the rescue of the three from the furnace, let us see what facts may be concealed under the very non-scientific rendering of the Authorized Version.

Why were the three 'experimental subjects' so elaborately clothed before being bound and put into the furnace – 'their coats, their hosen and their hats, and their other garments'?

And, we may well ask ourselves, were these garments of some special quality? Were they, in fact, fire-proof fire-fighters' outfits, of that asbestos-proofed cloth already discovered by the time of King Nebuchadnezzar II the Great (reigned 605-562 BC), and described by Pliny in his *Natural History* (19:4) some six hundred years later?

Had the God who was to save them in the fire a superior scientific knowledge on which the three relied? Was there a scientific test, not mentioned, because not understood, by the Biblical historian: a test which involved the (relatively) unclothed soldiers and the three dressed in fire-proof garments? So that the soldiers perished in the intense heat, and the three did not?

The end of the strange tale has another point which has helped to earn it the scoffing classification of 'fairy-tale'. Nebuchadnezzar, looking into the mouth of the burning fiery furnace, to see how the daring three were getting on, called out in astonishment that there seemed to be not three persons in the furnace but four:

> . . . Lo, I see four men loose, walking in the middest *(sic)* of the fire, and they have no hurt; and the form of the fourth is like the Son of God.

This expression, 'the Son of God', is hard to explain; but we may well hazard a guess that it refers to some highly abnormal quality of either personal appearance or clearly seen 'supernatural' ability – almost certainly the former, since the references seem always to concern an appearance rather than a more spiritual quality – though, of course, the spiritual abnormality would be inferred from the physical.

In considering how widespread the worship of light in general and of the sun in particular was throughout the ancient cultures we may confidently believe that this abnormality which characterized the 'Sons of God' had to do with light. They were 'golden'; they 'glowed'; they 'shone forth'; they 'blazed' – either momentarily or permanently. The Superior Being with whom Moses talked – from whom Moses received orders – shone with a brightness too strong for mortal eyes to tolerate; Buddha shone, as did Confucius. When Christ, another readily acknowledged 'Son of God', was 'transfigured' before His disciples, He blazed with an unearthly light.

This type of Being, who appears so often throughout the history of the Ancient World that the Biblical historian need give no more detailed description of him than 'Son of God', appears to have a special affinity with fire. The 'chariot' in which the 'Selected Ones' are lifted skywards blazes with 'fire.' And it is in the burning fiery furnace that Nebuchadnezzar is 'astonied', but not altogether surprised, to find another of this mysterious and superior breed, walking with the three whose bonds the Son of God has untied.

Was the Son of God waiting inside the furnace for the three men? – or did he come from some other place (and, perhaps, time?), not so much to 'rescue' them – for one suspects that the 'experimental' fire-proof suits would have put them beyond danger – as to verify the heat-resistant quality of their asbestos overalls?

Tolerance of heat varies in the human being as much as tolerance of cold. The resistance of fire-walkers to temperatures which would gravely injure the untrained is too well known now to merit the least doubt; nor is this cultivated resistance confined to those taking part in the ritual fire-walkings of Hindus, Hawaiians, North and South American Indians and the rest.

'Fire-defying' acts were a popular feature of the vaudeville theaters of the last century, and fire-eating and flame-swallowing are not unknown to-day. Some notable mediums of recent times have demonstrated their ability to resist the normal results of heat in handling very hot or burning materials: among them the best-known medium of the last century, Daniel Dunglass Home, and Mrs Annie Hunter, who carried a blazing log about the room in the presence of a *Daily Express* reporter who 'backed away after his hair was singed.'

Performing before a much larger audience, such fire-resistant persons as 'The Incombustible Lady', the 'Fire Kings', the 'French Salamander' and the rest demonstrated their resistance to fire: licking white-hot pokers, placing shovels of burning coals on their heads, washing out their mouths with boiling lead, letting themselves be shut up for fourteen minutes – this was Martinez – in an oven heated to 338°F.

Extremes of cold seem to have been as readily and easily borne; especially in Tibet, where certain 'adept' lamas have been known to endure temperatures so low that they would have killed others.

Sometimes, this resistance to lethal conditions derives its power from religious persuasion; but this is not always so. Often the most astonishing feats of fire- or cold-defiance come from persons in no way religious: members of no organized cult; partakers in no well-rehearsed ritual. When asked to account for their powers, such persons simply answer that they 'have no idea'.

Nor have they.

Just so might have answered Mrs Mary Hardy Reeser had she been asked, not why she had mastered fire, but why – and how – fire had taken her off in so terrible and mysterious a way.

The death of Mrs Reeser, sixty-seven, on the night of 1 July 1951, falls obviously within the classification of 'death by spontaneous combustion'. However, the detailed and lengthy treatment that Gaddis gives to this death is justified by some features unusual in deaths of this type, not the least unusual of the features being the presence in the case of the FBI.

The other unusual features included the relatively high social standing of the victim. She was the widow and mother of qualified physicians in good practice; she was also, though a widow, not of the 'lonely' type so prominent in medical histories of spontaneous combustion. There is no evidence that she drank to excess; though she was mildly addicted to sleeping pills – one of the barbiturates marketed under the trade name of Seconal.

The points to bear in mind at the beginning of this record are that Mrs Reeser was an elderly – but not too elderly – widow, apparently in good health, whose deprivation of companionship by the death of her husband was offset to a large extent by the friendly attentions of her son Richard and his wife.

The widow's son had served in the U.S. Army Medical Corps during the Second World War, and was now building up his private practice in St Petersburg, on the west coast of Florida. Mrs Reeser, Senior, had moved to St Petersburg to be near her son; and she now lived within a few hundred yards of her son.

The first day of July 1951 was as sunny as usual in West Florida, and, the evening being hot, Dr Reeser suggested a visit to the beach. His mother, who had spent the day with her son and his family – there were two children – did not wish to go; so Dr and Mrs Richard Reeser, and one child, went to the beach, Mrs Mary Reeser staying behind with the other child. On the Reesers' return from the beach, they found that Mrs Mary Reeser had gone home. The younger

Mrs Richard Reeser then got into her car and set out in the hope of catching up with her mother-in-law, so as to take her by car the rest of her journey.

It happened that Mrs Mary Reeser had already arrived at her Cherry Street apartment by the time her daughter-in-law had caught up with her. A few friendly words were exchanged before young Mrs Reeser returned to her family. She had seen nothing in the older woman's appearance or manner to cause her the least concern. When, however, Dr Reeser visited his mother later that same evening he saw that she was mildly depressed, though this 'depression' seemed to have no deep-seated cause.

Mrs Reeser had already turned back the covers on her bed by the time her son left at about 8:30 p.m. She told him that she wished to retire early, and would take two Seconal tablets to ensure a good night's sleep.

The last person known to have seen Mrs Reeser alive was her landlady, Mrs Pansy M. Carpenter, who called in to see her about half an hour after Dr Reeser had left; that is, at about 9 p.m. Mrs Reeser had already changed for bed; she was in her nightgown, over which she wore a house-coat. Mrs Carpenter found her tenant sitting in 'an over-stuffed easy-chair', smoking a cigarette.

We must note the presence of two heat sources, the cigarette, and the lightning which was playing over sub-tropical Florida on that warm July evening.

Mrs Carpenter stayed for a few minutes, then left for her own apartment, which was in the same building, but separated from that of Mrs Reeser by two untenanted suites.

Mrs Reeser did not go to bed; she stayed in the easy chair until a strange death overtook her.

Is it altogether meaningless coincidence that in the case of Mrs Reeser – a case which, for one reason or another, has become one of the most famous in the history of spontaneous combustion – the principal witness should be

138

a Mrs *Carpenter?* And that a Mrs *Carpenter* died of spontaneous combustion in 1938?

For, in the last century, the eminent physiologist W. B. *Carpenter*, Fellow of the Royal Society, lecturer in anatomy and physiology at the London Hospital, Professor of Medical Jurisprudence at University College, London, Professor of Physiology at the Royal Institution, and one of the most influential scientists in Victorian England, was also one of those who admitted the phenomenon of spontaneous combustion, in an age when it was fashionable among fashionable medical men to deride the phenomenon as – in George Lewes's phrase – 'a vulgar error.'[26]

A temperance fanatic, Carpenter was one of those who sought to establish a direct causative relation between 'intemperance' and spontaneous combustion.

However, Carpenter was too much of a scientist to be satisfied with this simple explanation, and set out to discover which natural law brought about the 'punishment' of spontaneous combustion.

In his *Principles of General and Comparative Physiology* (London, 1839), pp. 366-7, Carpenter speculates on a possible connection between phosphorus and 'the extraordinary phenomenon of spontaneous combustion', and, as some support for his speculation, relates the case of a friend whose 'troublesome sore, occasioned by the combustion of phosphorus on the hand, twice at distinct intervals emitted a flame which burned the surrounding parts'.

Mrs Carpenter awoke on 2 July 1951 to a smell of smoke; the time, 5 a.m. Attributing the smell to a water-pump which had been overheating, Mrs Carpenter got out of bed, went into her garage, turned the current off, and went back to

---

[26]Echoing, of course, Sir Thomas Browne's *Pseudodoxia Epidemica*.

bed. At 8 a.m. a boy arrived with a telegram for Mrs Reeser. Mrs Carpenter signed for the telegram, and took it to Mrs Reeser's apartment. The smell of burning to which Mrs Carpenter had awakened at 5 a.m. was no longer noticeable, but the doorknob of Mrs Reeser's apartment was hot. So hot that the landlady instinctively shouted for help; a shout which was heard and promptly answered by two decorators working on a building on the other side of the street. The two men, Clements and Delnet, ran to the door that Mrs Carpenter had been too scared to open; Delnet opened it, with a rag to cover the super-heated doorknob, and a blast of hot air gusted through the open doorway. Mrs Carpenter had screamed that her tenant was inside, but, as the two painters moved cautiously into the room, there was no Mrs Reeser. The apartment was a small one: merely a living-room, a small kitchen and a bathroom. It took only a minute or so to be sure that there was no one within the apartment. What was perhaps, at that moment, more curious was that there was no fire either, save for a small flame on the wooden joist over a partition dividing living-room from kitchenette. As the unscorched bed had not been slept in, it was assumed at first that Mrs Reeser had left the apartment. The arrival of the fire truck soon revealed a different set of facts.

Mrs Reeser, or what was left of her, was in the apartment, as completely consumed as any victim in the long history of spontaneous combustion.

Within a blackened circle about four feet in diameter were a number of coiled seat-springs and the remains of a human body.

The remains consisted of a charred liver attached to a piece of backbone, a skull shrunk to the size of a baseball, a foot encased in a black satin slipper but burned down to just above the ankle, and a small pile of blackened ashes.

As in most, though not all, of the other cases of spontaneous combustion, the only evidence of fire was in the immediate vicinity of Mrs Reeser's chair and the aforementioned joist, which was directly above. In all other respects, fire had left the apartment untouched, but there were some effects of heat that students of this peculiar form of death will recognize as familiar from other cases.

The combustion, especially the *total* combustion, of Mrs Reeser's easy chair is uncharacteristic of these cases; but such combustion of the chair is not without established precedent: in the case of the Gräfin von Görlitz (1848; see page 156), the chair from which the dead woman had fallen had been partially burned; and there are other cases in which the furniture has shared, partially or totally, the fate of its owner.

Heat, though, rather than *fire*, was responsible for the buckling and melting of light switches and switch-plates; but what principle governed the location of this heat is not easy to say.

For, at a height of some four feet above the floor, an area of smoke-blackened wall began; below this smoke level everything (with the exception of Mrs Reeser and her easy chair) was untouched; above, the effects of heat were apparent.

Not only were the electric fittings buckled and melted, but candles on a chest of drawers had melted too, though the wicks had not been burned. Even so, this was a curious, and curiously *selective*, kind of heat. It had stopped, but not injured, an electric clock (the clock had stopped at 4:20 a.m.); yet the clock went at once into action when plugged into an undamaged outlet. Two electric fans showed a similar pattern of behaviour. This strange heat had cracked one of three mirrors, all fixed to the wall at about the same height. Why had the heat not cracked the other two?

Now, the survival of unburned wicks from candles melted by the heat generated in spontaneous combustion was an oddity noticed in the death of the Countess Cornelia di Bandi (see page 21); but the soot-blackening of a room above a clearly defined level was a feature of an explosion in which two friends of mine were involved rather more than forty years ago.

Husband and wife, they were two young actors more often 'resting' than acting, and they lived in one of the large, rambling mid-Victorian London houses which had been converted. One of the attractions of the apartment, besides its roominess, had been the many cupboards set high on the corridor walls.

One day I received a telephone call from the husband, telling me that there 'had been a ghastly explosion' at the apartment, and asking me what he should do about suing the landlord and/or the Electric Light and Power Company.

What had happened was this.

His wife had landed a day's work as an extra at Pinewood, a motion picture studio near London, and the work called for the possession of a ballgown. As her dress was in need of cleaning, she decided to clean it herself.

She bought two gallons of benzine, poured in into the bath tub, put her dress into it – it was made of silk, with a net overlay – knelt down on a bath mat, and began to rinse the dress. There was a flash, no bang, and she was hurled backwards; her eyebrows and front hair were singed. There was no fire, but just such a soot-darkening of the upper walls throughout the apartment as the firemen saw when they were called to Mrs Reeser's place.

We had an electrically-minded friend, and brought the problem to him. He pooh-poohed the idea of suing the electric people: 'The static in a silk dress like your wife's should have been enough to blow up half the neighbourhood – what with all that cleaning fluid. And, anyway, what

142

were you thinking of, pouring benzine into a bath tub? Don't you know that it's not only damned dangerous, but illegal? I'd shut up about suing anyone if I were you; and think yourself lucky *they're* not suing you . . .'

I mention this explosion – there was no fire; the dress was not even scorched – because, despite our electrically-minded friend's positive statement that the cleaning fluid had been ignited by the static electricity in the silk dress, its effect on the apartment was so strikingly similar to the staining by smoke of both Mrs Reeser's and the Countess von Görlitz's apartments.

Was it the static in the dress? Or was it a lesser case of spontaneous combustion, 'masked' by a convenient 'explanation'? I have often wondered. And I thought of it recently, when I remembered that *absolutely level line* above which everything had been soot-blackened (as in the case of Mrs Reeser) and how, in my friends' apartment, the soot had penetrated into every cupboard above the 'smoke level', and, within each cupboard, into every box and package, however tightly sealed.

Those who found the ashes of the Countess Cornelia di Bandi remarked upon the presence everywhere of 'moist ash-colored soot, which penetrated the drawers and foul'd the linens . . .' – just as it had penetrated the cupboards and 'foul'd' the contents in my friends' apartment forty-odd years ago.

As in all recorded cases of spontaneous combustion, that of Mrs Reeser had both its 'typical' and its 'untypical' feature.

There was – one almost said 'inevitably' – the modern equivalent of the fireless grate; in this instance, a wall-fixed gas heater, with the gas turned off, not only at the appliance but also at the main. The electric stove and other appliances had been switched off, with the exception of the electric refrigerator, which had not only not been switched off but was still working. No fuses had been blown.

Again on the 'typical' side was the presence of soot on the outside lintels of the open windows – and again one is reminded of the smoke, coming through the windows, which had drawn attention to the fate of Countess Cornelia di Bandi.

More 'typical' was the fact that, though the floor lamp by the easy chair had been almost entirely consumed – entirely, so far as its organic matter was concerned – a pile of old newspapers on top of a radiator less than a foot from the circle marking the total combustion of Mrs Reeser was not even scorched.

Contrasted with these 'typical' features were some other 'untypical' ones: the melting of a plastic tumbler in the bathroom, some distance from where Mrs Reeser had been sitting (though plastic toothbrush handles near by had not been affected). Of a floor lamp by which Mrs Reeser had been reading in her chair, only the metal core remained: wood and shade had both been entirely consumed – it is rare that objects in close proximity to the destroyed body suffer; but, then, it was 'untypical', in any event, that Mrs Reeser's chair should have been consumed as completely as she was. (And it was this 'untypical' fact which brought the FBI into the case.)

But the most 'untypical' feature of Mrs Reeser's death was the inexplicable shrinking of Mrs Reeser's skull. This quite 'untypical' feature hardly balanced such 'typical' features as the survival of a slipper-clad foot, as the absence of any outcry, as the absence of any disagreeable odour – and there may hardly be any odours so disagreeable as that of burning human flesh.

The coroner, Edward T. Silk, signed the death certificate usual from coroners in these cases: 'Accidental death by fire of unknown origin', to which he added, 'pending further investigation'. As he pointed out in instructing the jury to return its verdict: 'It is fantastic to suppose the fire itself could have been an act of suicide. Her death appears to be accidental, and there is nothing to indicate it was anything but accidental . . .'

But what, especially in this important context, does the word 'accidental' mean?

Before the coroner, together with Fire Chief Claude Nesbitt, Police Chief J. R. Reichert, and Detective Lieutenant Cass H. Burgess, issued their report, they had to wait for the finding of the FBI Forensic Laboratory in Washington, D.C., to which Mrs Reeser's remains had been sent 'to determine whether or not a flammable substance or chemical had been involved in the cremation' (which seems a hardly adequate explanation of why the FBI were called in!).

The committee of investigation set up by Police Chief Reichert cast its net wide: not only were the 'arson experts' and criminal investigators, FBI laboratory technicians and weather experts called into the investigation, but also the manufacturers of the 'overstuffed easy chair', to state whether or not the padding had any self-igniting or explosive properties (the manufacturers stated that it had not).

Unasked for *their* 'expert advice', hundreds of members of the public nevertheless gave it – freely and imaginatively. Reading the 'solutions' which poured into either the *Tampa Tribune* or police headquarters, it was evident to the police that many of the 'solvers' were more acquainted with the literature than was the arson expert, Mr Edward S. Davies. For though the literature does not, at least in so many words, suggest that Mrs Reeser swallowed, by accident or design, an 'atomic pill', here again is the phosphorus theory of W. B. Carpenter; the alcoholically-inflammabilized-body-ignited-by-electric-spark theory of Dr James Conolly, the reforming superintendent of Hanwell Lunatic Asylum; the explosive breath theory of Thomas Woolner, the English sculptor – and all the others familiar to the student of medical jurisprudence.

One interesting – if illiterately expressed – theory came on an unsigned postcard addressed to 'Cheif of Detectiffs': 'A ball of fire came through the window and hit her. I seen it happen.'

The message seems more literate than the address; so that the communication may not have been from an illiterate at all; merely from someone who wished to preserve his or her anonymity. Did the writer see a 'ball of fire'? Many others have seen them – and been 'attacked' by them. Many, 'attacked' by a 'ball of fire', have escaped, with grave, mild or no injuries.

In the meanwhile, the FBI technicians prepared their report. It cannot be said to have added anything to what was not already known, and it left many oddities not only unexplained, but even unmentioned.

It 'explained' that a woman weighing 175 lbs, together with the large easy chair in which she had been sitting, as well as a small table and the wooden portions of a floor lamp, say a total of some 240 lbs, had been converted into ash weighing less than 12 lbs.

It is to be presumed that the FBI tested for all those 'solutions' – 'reasonable' and 'unreasonable' – which had been suggested in letters and telephone calls to newspapers and police: suicide by paraffin or gasoline, ignition of accumulated methane in the victim's body, murder by a flame-thrower or oxyacetylene torch, 'atomic pill', magnesium (as used in flash-light photography), phosphorus and . . . yes, indeed! . . . napalm.

As it stands, the FBI report is a masterpiece of the non-factual as well as of the (to be expected) non-committal.

The one supremely important feature – that all the major heat damage occurred within a circle four and a half feet in diameter – was never explained; and the fact that this circular limit existed was noted only indirectly, when it was 'suggested' that the satin-slippered left foot of the dead lady had survived only because, having a 'stiff' left leg, she used, when sitting, to stretch the leg out straight.

Completely negative though the conclusions of the FBI report were, the report itself could claim a sort of positive quality in that, in ruling out probable and improbable causes of the fire which had burned Mrs Reeser, it emphasized the absence of evidence to support the likelihood of their presence.

It pointed out that the characteristic odours of the many suggested substances – gasoline, paraffin, napalm, etc. – were absent, and that, had there been an explosion, or even a blazing fire, the combustion would not, *could not,* have confined itself to a four-and-a-half-foot diameter circle. Most of the inflammable substances suggested, the report pointed out, burned fiercely – true enough – but also burned rapidly: too rapidly, in fact, to have done more than consume the flesh. They would not have consumed the bones.

And that the 'fire' in which Mrs Reeser perished was not a rapid one was demonstrated by the quantity of soot which had been generated. No attempt was made to explain why that soot (and the heat associated with it) was manifested only above the four-foot level. (Nor why, if it ever struck the technicians, *the height of the smoke-level above the floor was equal to the diameter of the circle in which Mrs Reeser and her piece of furniture were utterly consumed.)*

Morally supported, if not exactly enlightened, by the FBI'S report, the coroner and chief of police issued their own 'explanation' of Mrs Reeser's death. The report, dated 8 August 1951, followed, as Gaddis sarcastically points out, 'a logical sequence of events up to a certain point, *and would probably satisfy the unthinking*' [my italics – MH].

Here is this masterpiece of official gobbledegook:

According to her son, Mrs. Reeser habitually *[note the loaded word]* took two sleeping pills before retiring. There is every possibility *[officialese for 'it is absolutely certain that']*, while seated in the overstuffed chair, she became drowsy or fell asleep while smoking a cigarette, thus igniting her clothes. At that time she was clad in a rayon acetate nightgown and a housecoat (according to Dr. Reeser who had visited her the evening of July 1). The nightgown, being highly flammable, could have been ignited by the cigarette, and burst into flame, causing almost immediate death to a person in a semiconscious condition.

When her clothes became afire, they would also set the chair afire, creating intense heat which completely destroyed the body, the chair and a nearby table (nothing was found of the end table which had been beside the chair when Mrs. Reeser was last seen alive). Once the body became ignited, almost complete destruction could have resulted from the burning of its own fatty tissues (Mrs. Reeser was a heavy woman, weighing 175 pounds), an uncommon but entirely possible occurrence.

In this case the absence of any scorch or damage to furniture in the room can only be explained by the theory that heat liberated by the burning body rose to form a layer of hot air which darkened the upper walls and ceiling of the room, but never came in contact with the walls and other objects at a lower level.

This statement contains one untruth which must have been recognized as such by the 'experts' of the fire department. Rayon acetate does not burn, except in special circumstances which could not be possible in this case. It 'flashes', as every woman who has had the misfortune to drop the spark from a cigarette on her rayon acetate stockings knows. The synthetic fibre 'flashes' into a hole at the point of contact with the spark – *and at that point*

148

only. It does not smoulder; it does not (as the report confidently and dishonestly stated) 'burst into flames'.

For the rest, the report should interest students of the language in showing how adroitly tenses may be handled to serve their disingenuous ends. 'Mrs Reeser's nightgown, being highly flammable [it was not] *could have* been ignited . . . burst into flame . . . *when* her clothes became afire . . . intense heat *which completely destroyed* the body . . .' In three shameless lines the hopefully hypothetical becomes the pontifically dogmatic.

All the same, a year later, the investigating detective, Cass Burgess, stated: 'Our investigation has turned up nothing that could be singled out as proving, beyond a doubt, what actually happened. The case is still open. We are still as far from establishing any logical cause for death as we were when we first entered Mrs Reeser's apartment.'

And, privately, Police Chief J. R. Reichert was equally candid: 'As far as logical explanations go, this is one of those things that just couldn't have happened, but it did. The case is not closed and may never be to the satisfaction of all concerned.'

Dr Reeser was permitted to bury his mother's scanty remains in Chestnut Hill Cemetery, Mechanicsburg, Pennsylvania.

How was it known that the few pounds of carbonized animal matter were what remained of Mrs Reeser? By the unburned, satin-slipper-clad foot, of course. As the records of this type of death plainly demonstrate, there is always at least one of the extremities untouched. Whatever variations there may be in the combustion pattern of these strange deaths, where there is some trace of the body there is invariably a survival of a (relatively untouched) foot or hand; in most cases, survival of both feet and hands.

From the eighteenth-century burning of Countess Cornelia di Bandi – 'In the morning, the maid, going to call

149

her, saw her corpse in this deplorable condition. Four feet distant from the bed was a heap of ashes, *her two legs untouch'd,* stockings on, between which lay the head, the brains, half of the back part of the skull, and the whole chin burnt to ashes, among which were three fingers blackn'd' – to recent cases described by Drs D. J. Gee and G. Thurston, one of the extremities has always survived the burning.

In the case of Mrs Reeser, the surviving left foot was recognized as that of Dr Richard Reeser's mother by the satin slipper in which it was still encased. This slipper was recognized, not only by Mrs Pansy Carpenter and Dr Reeser as one that Mrs Reeser had been wearing, but by a store clerk as part of a pair sold to the *vanished* woman.

It must be recognized that this slipper did not constitute the absolute proof required by medical jurisprudence to identify the unidentifiable remains as those of Mrs Mary Reeser. But it should be borne in mind that the surviving foot had the *potential* of valid proof.

Let us put it in this way. Mrs Reeser, respectable widow of a physician enjoying public esteem, had obviously no criminal record, nor, as far as may be gathered, did she serve in the armed forces of the United States. She had, therefore, never been finger-printed. In like manner, her footprints had never been put on official record.

And the same remark seems to apply to all other victims, to date, of spontaneous combustion.

But seeing that in finger-, palm- and footprint lie the certain means of identifying the human being, a means to which may be added a newly theorized means – the longitudinal striation of the nails[27] – does it not strike the reader

---

[27] 'A new Means of identification of the Human Being: The Longitudinal Striation of the Nails', a paper, by Dr F. Thomas and Miss H. Baert, read at a meeting of the Forensic Science Society, King's College Hospital, London on 21 November 1964.

as something beyond the range of mere coincidence that, of all the parts of the human body spared by the Fire, those parts only should be spared in which the certain means of identification resides?

It is as though, in every case, what took the major part of the body almost never did so without leaving those important fragments by which the identity of the dead could be established without doubt. It makes no difference that, since finger- and other prints had not been taken, this means of identification was not available to relatives and officials. The point is here that it is possible to make a certain identification of the dead . . . through the unburned portions of the body spared by the Fire.

I began this chapter with Shadrach, Meshach and Abednego, and we end it with Mrs Reeser. Is there any connection between the burning fiery furnace which consumed Mrs Reeser so utterly, and that which left the three men unharmed?

Is there not something familiar to the reader in the *circle* within which Mrs Reeser was consumed? – a circle of such nature that 'to explain' why her left foot and ankle escaped almost unmarked from the consuming fire, *the investigators thought it might have been extended to a point beyond the fire outside the circle.'*

Why should 'the investigators' have thought any such thing? Why, in recognizing the presence of a circle – of a precisely circular limit to the fire – should they have conceded to this 'circle' such self-restricting powers, such thus-far-and-no-further permission, as to attribute the saving of the foot to the fact that it had, somehow, managed to escape from the deadly ring inside which it was the doom of everything material to burn?

Is there not something at once familiar and unfamiliar in all this? Are we not reminded, in a through-the-looking-glass way, of the magician's circle *within* which deadly powers had no control, and *outside* of which all danger lay?

Have we not, then, in the circle in which Mrs Reeser burned to cinders, both the analogue and the mirror image of the circle within which and from within which, the magician or wizard spoke to the conjured-up demons, raging impotently outside the impenetrable barriers of the protecting circle?

In these strange and disturbing hints, not so much of a topsy-turvy world, as of a topsy-turvydom in the existing cosmos, one senses a striving towards a balance – a striving so intense, so desperate, that errors, blunders, seem constantly to be occurring. One senses that there is experimentation . . . and that, quite often, the experiment goes wrong.

And all the time one senses, too, the tremendous presence, the immanence (as well as the terrifying imminence) of, not so much great truths, as of a Great Truth. And then we begin to feel that it is not so much that men are searching for ways in which to see and define this Great Truth, as that the Great Truth is desperately seeking a way in which, through men's understanding, it may reveal itself.

A skull shrunk to the size of a baseball, a lump of charred liver fused to a few blackened vertebrae, a foot and ankle, ashes and some greasy soot: not much left of a woman weighing over 175 pounds. In some cases the devouring Fire has left even less – the remains of Mrs Patrick Rooney, for instance, were scantier (though even with Mrs Rooney's 'taking', an identifying foot remained) – but may we ask ourselves if there may not be *a totality of Taking: a complete* removal of the human being, not necessarily by the way of fire, to 'some other place', for examination by 'some other people'?

152

Scissors and important letters and railway tickets are not the only things which are for ever 'disappearing'; people disappear, too – and steamships and railroad trains and all sorts of inanimate objects, often quite big ones. And people disappear in their thousands, too: since records have been kept, an average of 5,000 disappearances *a year is* now taken for granted by the police of the Greater London area.

Sometimes people disappear, reappear, disappear, reappear, and then disappear forever. Such was the case with little Eliza Carter, one of the first victims of that ten-year-long 'abduction' of people – 1881-1891 – known as the 'West Ham Disappearances', since most of them occurred in that part of East London. Little Eliza vanished from her home, but turned up later in the street, and even spoke to some schoolgirl friends, who urged her to return to her family. Eliza rather mysteriously – for she confessed to great terror – refused; and after having hung around West Ham for a day or two, finally disappeared, never to be seen again. When I wrote of the West Ham Disappearances in the London *Evening News* some twenty years ago, I had a letter from a very aged lady who had been the last person known to have spoken to Eliza Carter. She added the significant detail that 'Eliza told me, when I said she ought to go home, that she couldn't – that They wouldn't let her.' (I have given the capital letter to 'They'!) Another famous case involving what we may call a 'delayed disappearance' was that of Jerry Irwin, a soldier G.I. in the United States Army, who 'vanished', turned up again (it is recorded that he 'seemed confused'), absented himself – no one could find out where he went; and he was unable to tell – and reappeared once again, to make his final disappearance from this earth on 1 August 1959.

In these 'total' disappearances, unlike the 'partial' disappearances of spontaneous combustion, the victims are selected impartially from all social classes: a Duchess of

Bedford disappeared; so did the Honourable Henry Bathurst, envoy extraordinary from King George III to the Emperor of Austria; diplomats have vanished, as have sailors, servant girls, farmhands. Whoever − or whatever − is examining living human beings obviously wishes to study representatives of each social class.

The importance of Mrs Reeser in connection with the phenomenon of spontaneous combustion is that, though no conclusions were stated in the ludicrous official findings, more investigative work was done − and so more conclusions reached (even though these were not made public) − than in any previous examination of the phenomenon. Excluding the combustibility of the human body − evidently something still to be ascertained, otherwise this book would hardly have been written − the 'intrinsic' combustibility of organic but inanimate substances must have been determined with the precision available to modern laboratory technology. The investigation was helped, too, by factors not present in previous investigations: not only the professional rivalry of 'competing' laboratories and the organizations that they represented, but the rivalry of vested interests, commercial and otherwise.

One may easily imagine with what care the Jacksonville manufacturers of the chair in which Mrs Reeser died would have assembled their evidence to combat the suspicion that it was *their* chair which had done the damage; the care with which the electric and gas companies examined *their* fittings, to absolve them from all blame. And if the FBI turned in a negative report, that can only mean that even the most fanciful suggestion as to the Fire's origin had been examined and found wanting. In its paradoxical fashion, all this 'inconclusive' work led plainly to one inescapable conclusion: that the Fire which burned Mrs Reeser had no detectable origin − which is but another way of saying that the combustion in which she perished was what, up to this time, we have called either 'spontaneous' or 'preternatural', two completely non-explanatory words to indicate that we have, as yet, no explanation.

11

DARMSTADT AND THE TRIUMPH OF DOUBT

Darmstadt in 1847 was one of the most elegant of Germany's smaller cities, and for centuries the von Görlitz family had maintained a splendid mansion there, near the Luisenplatz. It was to this mansion that Count von Görlitz was returning on the very warm night of 13 July 1847.

It will not be irrelevant to recall that the period was, especially in Germany, one of extreme unrest. Revolution was brewing in most of the German states, and violence would break out in the following year.

In the blazing summer of 1847 the sense of impending doom seemed to weigh on the human spirit more heavily than usual; and it was in no lighthearted mood that Count von Görlitz drove from the grand-ducal palace to his house by the Luisenplatz.

To say that a surprise awaited him would be to commit the gravest of understatements: what awaited him was that most shattering of all shocks – the horror which outwits belief.

On returning home, the Count was informed that the Countess had retired for the night. He took a little light refreshment, and went upstairs to the bedroom that he shared with his wife.

It should be explained that this large bedroom was divided into two halves, each with its own dressing room; the Count's curtained bed being in one half, the Countess's in the other. It was not until the Count had washed and changed into his night attire that he went into that half of the large room in which the Countess slept. There he found

156

his wife's badly charred body lying 'grotesquely' on the floor, near to some still burning pieces of furniture. She had fallen down, and, prostrate on the Aubusson rug, had turned into cinders.

The Count, though horrified, retained possession of his presence of mind; he ran through the door to the top of the staircase, shouting for a footman:

'Call Dr Graff! Send for Dr Graff immediately!'

In the opinion of Dr Graff, the cause of the Countess von Görlitz's death was obvious: the family physician had seen such cases before, rare – and still inexplicable – though they were. He would, he told the Count, have no hesitation in giving a certificate stating the cause of death: spontaneous combustion.

But within an hour the police had arrived, and the Inspector of Grand-Ducal police had all the mistrust of 'unusual' explanations which characterized official thinking then, as it still does. The inspector preferred to see in the Countess's death the evidence of a crime – and promptly arrested the nearest and most arrestable 'suspect' to hand, a footman named Stauff, on the grounds that one of his duties was to attend to the stove in the Countess's bedroom. Loudly and indignantly protesting his innocence, the unlucky Stauff was taken away to the town gaol.

But Count von Görlitz was dissatisfied with the snap decisions both of the family physician and of the local police inspector, and he asked Dr Graff to call in a second opinion. When the second opinion, Dr Stegmayer, professed himself unable to give a positive opinion (he was one of those to whom spontaneous combustion was 'an old wives' tale'), a third opinion, Dr Siebold, was consulted, and as he proved to be in complete agreement with Dr Graff, the manservant Stauff was released, 'cleared of the murder charge'.

157

Now, that should have been the end of the matter. In fact, it was the beginning of a case which was to have its medico-legal repercussions throughout Europe and America.

The Darmstadt police had never been satisfied that the Countess von Görlitz had died by natural means, or that Stauff was as innocent as the opinion of Drs Graff and Siebold had made him out to be. What strengthened the hand of the police in their efforts to have the case re-opened was that some tactful questioning of Dr Graff seemed to show that the doctor had suffered a change of mind; and that he had come to be not at all as sure of his opinion as when he stated the 'obvious' cause of the Countess's death.

The police also took note of the fact that, despite Dr Graff's certainty, it had taken him and Dr Siebold all of nine months – from 13 July 1847 to 12 April 1848 – to prepare and sign the memoir in which the Countess's death was explained, and the innocence of Stauff 'demonstrated'.

Realizing now that, if Dr Graff might not be exactly a confident witness for the prosecution, he must turn out a weak witness for the defense, the police brought pressure to bear on the Medical College of Hesse, whose rector, in turn, brought pressure to bear on Dr Graff. The result was that on 11 July 1848 almost exactly a year after the death of the Countess von Görlitz, the members of the Medical College, in a memorial signed by Dr Graff with all the other members, requested the exhumation of the dead Countess, as preliminary to a forensic examination of her remains.

This examination was carried out by three associated but still distinct interests, each of which appointed its own medical representative at the autopsy, which was performed in the Medical College. The verdict of the assembled doctors was that the Countess's death was the result of 'a deliberate act of incendiarism' – Stauff was immediately re-arrested.

However, the prisoner now found an even more powerful, though completely unexpected, champion: the panel of the Assize Court. Not at all satisfied that they had heard the last word on the subject of Stauff's guilt, the Assize Court called in, as expert witnesses, two leading chemists – the Baron Justus Von Liebig and Herr Doktor Theodor Bischof – who were invited to express their opinions on the possibility or otherwise of the phenomenon commonly called 'spontaneous combustion'. Von Liebig was the more eminent of the two: he had isolated titanium, discovered chloral and was at that time engaged in research which would give the world 'meat extracts'. But it was, one feels, primarily because he was a native-born son of Darmstadt that the Assize Court lent so respectful an ear to his theories.

Apart from the eminence of the expert witnesses, and the interest that the case aroused throughout the West – *The Times* of London of 18 April 1850 (nearly three years after the Countess von Görlitz had died) carried a very full report; the reports being even more lengthy in the reputable medical journals, such as *The Lancet* and *The London Medical Gazette* – this case is of unique importance in the history of spontaneous combustion, in that it was the first judicial inquiry into this phenomenon in which experimental attempts to reproduce the phenomenon under controlled laboratory conditions were first undertaken.

Between them, von Liebig and Bischof succeeded in demonstrating that, even in a laboratory, the human body could not be ignited as that of the Countess had been ignited – a conclusion which, backed as it was by the immense authority of these two master chemists, would inevitably have secured Stauff his freedom – except that Stauff, as Margaret Dewar was to do fifty-eight years later, *made a full confession.*

The fact, as von Liebig and Bischof had demonstrated, that Stauff could not have burnt up the Countess, *as he confessed to have done,* weighed for little with the police or, apparently, the Assize Court. In some extraordinary fashion, this confession, against all probability, against all possibility, was accepted in the face of the Liebig-Bischof contradictory evidence.

Did the Assize Court believe Stauff? Well, the punishment for wilful murder – especially the murder of a *hochwohlgeborene* Countess in the still feudal Hesse of 1850 – was death. But Stauff did not go to the gallows; he was sentenced only to life imprisonment – and after having served a token sentence, he was released on parole. No-one seems to have protested against his sentence, either on the grounds of its injustice or on the grounds of its mildness. Von Liebig and Bischof pocketed their fees and went back to their laboratories.

A century and a quarter have passed since von Liebig and Bischof tried to reproduce in their laboratory the conditions in which a human body had been almost totally consumed – and in those special circumstances in which the burning of the body had not burned the house in which the human combustion had taken place.

In the case of the Countess von Görlitz, it is true that some pieces of furniture adjacent to the body had been set on fire, but we may be sure that so careful a researcher as von Liebig would have read all the available evidence on spontaneous combustion, and thus made himself familiar with the fact that, in the majority of the cases, circumjacent objects and materials are left untouched by the Fire. By 1847-8, there already existed a respectable body of writings on this subject: the two chemists would have been 'well up' on the subject.

With the unsupported – and, indeed, unsupportable – dogmatism without which such seedy 'liberals' as George

Lewes cannot express an opinion, Lewes wrote to Dickens that '. . . I believe you will find no one eminent organic chemist of our day who credits Spontaneous Combustion'. There were, in fact, many such in contemporary Europe and America, one of whom at least should have been known to the toad-eating snob Lewes: Justus von Liebig.

As the title of their then famous paper makes clear – 'Rélation médico-légale de l'assassinat de la comtesse de Goerlitz . . .' – A. Tardieu and X. Rota, writing in 1850 and 1851, held resolutely to the murder theory, as did many others. But not von Liebig, whose attitude, despite mis-representation since, seems to me to be beyond dispute.

Had the case of the Countess not been so abruptly closed by the odd 'confession' of Stauff, the findings of both Bischof and von Liebig would have been against the supposition that Stauff could have killed the Countess, and in favour of the proposition that all the evidence tended to support the probability of spontaneous combustion.

As historical evidence of the *fact* of this phenomenon, von Liebig, in his *Letters on Chemistry*, quoted the following case from the then previous century:

1749: reported by a priest, Boineau.
A woman of 80, who for some time had been drinking nothing but brandy, was seated in a chair when she began to burn – and continued to burn, although water was poured on her – until all her flesh was consumed, the skeleton remaining 'sitting' in the chair.

The narrator was a Priest, and did not see the flame; the story plainly indicates a good intention on his part – that of inoculating his flock with a wholesome terror of brandy-drinking.

This quotation has been cited as proof that von Liebig did not accept the fact of spontaneous combustion; on the contrary, he accepted the fact of the old woman's death by spontaneous combustion, but firmly rejected the theory (current even to-day) that indulgence in alcohol was a predisposing factor in cases of spontaneous combustion.

Since no-one yet, in or out of a laboratory, has succeeded in duplicating the Fire, one may well ask what is it that the scientists are seeking to reproduce? In reading the accounts of the various experiments, one comes as a matter of course upon the statement that the experimenters have succeeded in setting fire to the (dead) human body; have set it on fire so that it gradually burns away 'in the candle-effect'.

One of the most conscientious researchers in this field is the aforementioned Dr D. J. Gee, lecturer in Forensic Medicine at the University of Leeds. Dr Gee's interest in this phenomenon sprang from – or was heightened by – the fact that he was the medical officer called in by the police to examine a corpse charred to cinders by the fire.

Yet, at the beginning of his paper, Dr Gee presents the case as 'of some interest' *because* 'I have only been able to find one other instance reported in this country in the present century' (he is writing in 1965 of a death in November 1963). There seems to be something about this subject which prevents even the most honest researcher or historian from being precise about it. Spontaneous combustion is, as Dr Gee says, 'apparently extremely infrequent', but not all *that* infrequent. We have seen how, from the newspapers alone, the English science-fiction writer, Eric Frank Russell, picked out nineteen cases in 1938-39 with the cases at Chelmsford, Upton-by-Chester and on the Norfolk Broads in England, which are large inland bodies of water much used for pleasure boating. All these cases occurred in 1938 and were widely publicized because of the comments of the *coroners* involved. Dr Gee maintains this fiction of the phenomenon's extreme rarity by making the perfectly unsupportable statement that 'A similar case was described by Dr Gavin Thurston in 1961, the autopsy being performed by Dr Donald Teare, *and this appears to be the only other case recorded in Britain during the present century* [my italics – MH].'

What makes Dr Gee's statement on the rarity of the phenomenon so hard to accept is that the paper in which he makes – twice – his statement that spontaneous combustion is of extreme rarity also takes account of a discussion which followed the reading of the paper, and mentions, with commendable honesty, a startlingly different opinion:

> During the discussion following this paper, Dr George Manning described his experience of several similar cases, and indicated that this phenomenon *was certainly not as rare as might be supposed from the literature.* This view was supported by Dr David Price, who said that *he met with this phenomenon approximately once in every four years* [my italics – MH].

which, if Dr Price's experience may be taken as average (I would suggest that it cannot), would imply the incidence of some fifteen cases since the start of the century. (He was speaking in 1965.)

It would certainly be incorrect to interpret Dr Price's statement as meaning that each British doctor in general practice encounters this phenomenon once every four years – Dr Gee's own experience shows that *every* doctor does not, cannot, have this experience. Yet, as Dr George Manning and Dr David Price affirmed, the phenomenon is by no means so rare as some would make out.

The knowledge that, from 1849, scientists in the field of forensic medicine have been trying to reproduce the phenomenon of spontaneous combustion in their laboratories induces at least this historian to ask, first, what have they been trying to reproduce, and, second, how far have they succeeded?

Perhaps it would be better to take the second question first, and let Dr D. J. Gee tell us, in his own words, to what

163

extent he has succeeded, experimentally, in 'reconstructing' the Fire from Heaven.

In his article,[28] Dr Thurston gives a comprehensive review of the literature, over several centuries, and comes to certain conclusions, among them:

1. That under certain conditions a body will burn in its own fat with little or no damage to surrounding objects.
2. The combustion is not spontaneous, but started by an external source of heat.
3. This has occurred where the body has been in the draft up a chimney from a lighted fire. Oxygenation is good and the pull of the flue prevents outward spread of fire.

To test this theory, we have made a few simple experiments.

Human body fat, melted in a crucible, will only burn when at a temperature somewhere about 250°C. However, a cloth wick in liquid fat will burn, like a lamp, even when the temperature of the fat has fallen as low as 24°C.

Next a rough model was constructed, composed of a test tube, to provide firmness, enveloped in a layer of human fat, the whole enclosed by several layers of thin cloth, producing a roll about 8 inches long. One end was ignited by a Bunsen flame, the fat catching fire after about a minute. Although the Bunsen was removed at this point, combustion of the fat *and cloth* [my italics – MH] proceeded slowly along the length of the roll, with a smoky yellow flame and much production of soot, the entire roll being consumed after about one hour.

This experiment was modified by sewing a covering of skin over the layer of fat, before enclosing the whole in cloth, and combustion proceeded just as effectively as before. In both these experiments the draft of air from an extractor fan was arranged so that combustion proceeded in a direction opposite to the flow of air.

Obviously these simple experiments are by no means conclusive, but they do appear to support the theory put forward by Dr Thurston,

---

[28] Thurston, Gavin, *Medico-Legal Journal* (see *Bibliography*).

which seems the most reasonable explanation for the occurrence of these curious phenomena.

If Dr Gee maintains that these 'simple experiments' prove anything more than that the human body will, in certain circumstances, burn – a fact known for countless thousands of years – then the causes of his self-satisfaction are beyond this writer's recognition.

How, in his opinion, does the production of the 'candle-effect' (as Dr Firth, of the British Home Office Laboratory Service, named it) explain the terrific heat generated in such fiery deaths as those of Mrs Rooney, whose body burnt its way into the room below; of Mrs Martin, of West Philadelphia, of whom only the frightfully charred torso remained in the fire which consumed her on 18 May 1957; or of Mrs Mary Reeser, so totally consumed, with all her circumjacent furniture, that only her shrunken skull, a piece of charred liver attached to a few vertebrae and the mandatory surviving extremity (in her case, a satin-shod foot) remained of a 175 pound woman, her overstuffed easy chair, lamp and a chairside table?

Experiments performed by other forensic scientists have generated far less complacency. Inspired by the early theory, warmly preached by Dr James Conolly, and many other medical writers of the last century, that addiction to alcohol was a strongly predisposing factor in inducing spontaneous combustion ('. . . the human body', Conolly wrote, 'admits of being reduced by alcohol to a highly inflammable state'), several experimenters tested the inflammable properties of alcohol-soaked flesh. In one experiment, Gaddis recalls, a rat was soaked in pure alcohol for over a year. 'When ignited, it burned until the outer skin was charred, and then the fire went out. The tissues beneath the skin were undamaged.'

A modern scientist who has experimented for many years with a view to reproducing, in his laboratory, the phenomenon of spontaneous combustion, is Dr Wilton M. Krogman, Professor of Physical Anthropology at the School of Medicine, University of Pennsylvania. Dr Krogman is one of the scientists on whose help the laboratory technicians of the FBI have often relied.

His special talent lies in the identification of human bodies 'burned beyond recognition' – a phrase which has often been encountered in the course of this narrative.

Dr Krogman's experiments have been far more varied, as well as far more ambitious, than any reported from British forensic laboratories:

> Dr Krogman has burned cadavers with gasoline, coal, oil, acetylene, and various types of wood; bones encased in flesh, or stripped, both moist and dry. He has performed his experiments in combustion equipment ranging from pressurized crematoriums and electric furnaces to outdoor pyres. His knowledge of exactly what happens to bodies in all types of fires under varied conditions is probably unequalled.

Yet, called in to pronounce on the Reeser death, Dr Krogman confessed himself unable to put forward even the most fanciful explanation. Though he produced a theory later:

> I have posed the problem to myself again and again of why Mrs Reeser could have been so thoroughly destroyed, even to the bones, and yet leave nearby objects materially unaffected... But I always end up rejecting it in theory but facing it in apparent fact.[29]

---

[29] Vincent H. Gaddis, op. cit.

166

Not for Dr Krogman to be satisfied with the low temperatures of the 'fully explanatory' Gee experiments. Indeed, it was the generation of *intense* heat that Dr Krogman found inexplicable – at least, out of his own wide experience and knowledge. He called attention to the great heat needed to effect the total consumption by burning of a human body; and told how he had watched a body burn for eight hours in a crematorium at over 2000°F, 'yet at the end of that time there was scarcely a bone that was not present and completely recognizable as a human bone. The bones were calcined, but they were not ashes and powder, as in the case of Mrs Reeser and numerous other deaths by spontaneous combustion.'

> Only at 3000 degrees Fahrenheit, plus, have I seen bone fuse or melt so that it ran and became volatile . . . These are very great heats – they would sear, char, scorch, or otherwise mar or affect anything and everything within a considerable radius . . . They say that truth often is stranger than fiction, and this case proves it.

One may sympathize then with the verdict of the Darmstadt Assize Court that 'spontaneous combustion is absolutely contrary to the natural law'; and understand the regret with which Justus von Liebig recorded, in his *Letters on Chemistry,* that 'no one was ever present during the combustion of the Countess von Görlitz, or ascertained exactly what preceded it'.

Two other pecularities of the Reeser burning also caught Dr Krogman's enquiring attention; one not unknown to the record, the other so far unique. He was struck by the absence of the odour of burning human flesh, though this absence has been fairly frequentiy noted in other cases. But the shrinking of Mrs Reeser's skull to 'the size of a baseball' Dr Krogman found 'absolutely contrary to natural law'.

Never have I seen a human skull shrunk by intense heat. The opposite has always been true. The skulls either have been abnormally swollen or have virtually exploded into many pieces. . . . I have experimented, using cadaver heads, and have never known an exception to this rule.[30]

In an article by Allan W. Eckert in *True*, issue of May 1964, Dr Krogman is quoted as saying of the Reeser case:

I regard it as the most amazing thing I've ever seen. As I review it, the short hairs of my neck bristle with vague fear. Were I living in the Middle Ages, I'd mutter something about black magic.

It is reassuring to find a scientist who tries to find the truth and fails, and then confesses his inability to explain, not so much the inexplicable as the as-yet-unexplained.

However, Dr Krogman was not content for long to remain unable to come up with an 'explanation', for, as he admits, the Reeser case had challenged him to provide a solution. And Dr Krogman worked assiduously and commendably to find a 'rational' explanation for what he had already echoed the scientists of Darmstadt in describing as 'absolutely contrary to natural law'.

However, many students of the Fire may not be altogether satisfied that the solution Dr Krogman offers for our acceptance answers all the questions that the phenomenon of spontaneous combustion raises.

In *Today*, a supplement of *The Philadelphia Enquirer*, issue of 15 June 1973, there was printed an article entitled 'The Case of the Cinder Woman', which deals, not so much with the case of Mrs Mary Reeser (who is not named, but

---

[30] Quoted by Vincent H. Gaddis, op. cit.

presented anonymously as 'the Cinder Woman') as with the opinions of Dr Wilton M. Krogman on this most baffling of all deaths.

The article raises so important a question in regard to 'official' opinion – for Dr Krogman is a well-known and greatly respected professor of physical anthropology – that this book would be incomplete without a précis of *Today's* article and a careful examination of Dr Krogman's theories regarding Mrs Reeser's death.

The article begins, in a typical journalistic manner:

> Krogman's most celebrated case . . . was never actually solved. Thinking about it even today, Krogman says, still causes 'the hairs on the back of my neck to bristle' with a vague fear. The FBI has called the case 'improbable'.

The facts of Mrs Reeser's death, as already given by me, are set out briefly and correctly. Then, after the phrase, 'This, according to Krogman's earlier account, is what [the two painters] saw', are listed the eleven principal oddities in Mrs Reeser's apartment, beginning with, '1. The walls, from a level about four feet above the floor, and the ceiling, were festooned with a greasy soot, *which gave off a peculiar odor.' – and ending with '11. There is no record, during the night, of any smoke, any heat crackle, or any. . . unusual odor. . .*'[31]

Again at point 10 the facts are importantly misreported:

---

[31] My italics – MH. It was at about 5 a.m. on the morning of 2 July 1951 that Mrs Carpenter was awakened by a smell of burning; we know that she was mistaken in attributing this smell to an overheating water-pump. If the theory of Dr Krogman were correct, *what* could have been burning at 5 a.m.?

10. While great heat was reported, *there was no flame, no embers* [my italics – MH], no collection of sticky or of viscous material . . .

In fact, the wooden beam over the partition *was* on fire when the firemen arrived, and though the flame was reported as 'small', it was still a flame and, as for embers, much of the beam had been badly charred.

All the same, these are relatively minor errors; it is when we get further into the article that far more surprising statements are encountered. Describing how Krogman 'was aware of only one other recorded instance of such an occurrence, and that was in a work of fiction, Charles Dickens' *Bleak House*', the writer of the article goes on to tell how 'Krogman researched the cases' mentioned by Dickens, and adds: 'Krogman doesn't believe any of it' – and *why* he 'doesn't believe any of it' is because, 'as part of his experiments, he has burned, under laboratory conditions, dozens of corpses to examine the effects of different types of fire . . .' – and hasn't yet been able to achieve the totality of Mrs Reeser's combustion.

But it is when that tricky concept of 'experience' is introduced that the surprising statements begin to come thick and fast. The article reports Dr Krogman's observing that 'at no time has he seen that the body itself, which is basically a bag of salt water, can actually catch fire. Even at temperatures of over 2000°F the destruction of the body doesn't reach the extent indicated in the Case of the Cinder Woman . . .' What, evidently, Dr Krogman means here is that bodies don't catch fire *spontaneously;* for that they do catch fire he knows well – having 'burned . . . dozens of corpses'.

His own experience apart, that of others may yield some surprises, too.

The case has troubled him through the years. He makes a point of stopping by fire stations to ask veteran firemen if they have ever heard of anything resembling this phenomenon. None have. He also asks if they have experienced a type of fire that could cause so complete a burning of a human body as was indicated in the St. Petersburg case. Except for one peculiar [fire] in which the family silverware was melted while inside an only slightly charred sideboard, he hasn't heard of such a fire.

The reader of this book will realize how many 'such fires' *might* have come to the knowledge of these veteran firemen.

But the most surprising comment of Dr Krogman is that the *only* other recorded instance of a case resembling Mrs Reeser's was the 'fictional' one in *Bleak House;* the American bibliography on Spontaneous Combustion is almost as extensive as the European; and one of the classic articles, J. Knott, 'Spontaneous Combustion', in *American Medicine,* 1905, ix, 653-660, was actually published in Philadelphia, in a journal which is almost certainly in Dr Krogman's own university's library.

The first paragraph of the *Today* article mentions that 'Krogman's most celebrated case . . . was never actually solved', by which, I take it, one is to understand that it has been 'half-solved'? Is that it? For 'Krogman's theory of the crime', as described by *Today,* calls for a more thorough suspension of disbelief than the most improbable case of spontaneous combustion could ever do.

'Krogman's theory of the crime', says *Today,'* is that the woman was taken from the room and burned elsewhere at a temperature much in extreme *[sic]* of 2000 degrees, and then returned by the killer, who ingeniously supplied the other touches . . .'

Such as the greasy soot which festooned walls above a height of four feet, and the entire ceiling? Such as the hot doorknob – so hot that Mrs Carpenter, touching it, cried out in pain? Such as the candles, melted all but the wicks. . .? Such as the blast of hot air through the door?

'Krogman', *Today* continues, 'was impressed by the almost uncanny resemblance to the *Bleak House* episode. His suspicion is that the murderer was someone who knew a lot about burning, and who read a lot of Dickens.'

This murderous someone could also have read any of the many descriptions of the strange death of the Countess di Bandi, in any account from that of the *Gentleman's Magazine* to Sir David Brewster's *Letters on Natural Magic*, for it is in the case of the Countess that the unconsumed candle wicks appear. (Dickens, though he mentions the case, does not mention the candle wicks.)

Obviously, as so many reformers have pointed out, there may be grave dangers in the indiscriminate reading of books . . . I cannot do better here than to quote Gaddis:

> It's not easy to destroy totally a human body by fire. In crematories that do not have up-to-date retorts, the operators have to crush or grind the bones to fine grit or ash after the flesh has been consumed.
>
> Allan W. Eckert *(True,* May 1964) quotes a pathologist who tells of a fire in a Cleveland, Ohio, plant where materials for Thermite[32] welding were made. The fire was like a volcano – so hot that it melted concrete floors. Yet the bodies of the victims, although terribly charred, were still recognizable as humans.
>
> It takes more than a chair and fatty tissue almost to consume a body i.e. that of Mrs Reeser, leaving only a vertebra, a foot, and a shrunken skull.

---

[32] Thermite is a mixture of metallic oxides and aluminium, which, when ignited by magnesium, produces intense heat, the magnesium, a catalyst in this reaction, remaining unaffected.

Wrapping eight inches of human fat in a piece of cloth and watching it burn does not explain the intense heat which will reduce a human being to ashes in, sometimes, a matter of minutes.

Another expert opinion unexpectedly produced by the Reeser case was that of Julius H. Hagenguth, 'engineer-in-charge of the General Electric Company's man-made lightning experiments'. Mr Hagenguth comes into the story because of a suggestion that lightning may have been the agency by which Mrs Reeser met her death. Mr Hagenguth rejected this theory, and thus explained himself to the investigating committee at St Petersburg:

While the core of a lightning stroke attains very high temperatures, its diameter is very small, perhaps two to five inches at the most. It could have struck Mrs Reeser and paralyzed or killed her and also set her clothing afire. The stroke should not, however, have lasted long enough to completely consume her and the chair, leaving only the springs, a shrunken skull and a backbone. That is fantastic.

If a lightning stroke of such terrific force had entered the room through a window, there should have been some marks . . . While lightning can strike a house without causing the electric light to fail, a stroke of such unusual power certainly would have caused fuse blowing, which did not occur. . . Lightning could have been the cause, but if it was, it would be outside of any experience that we know about. It's like a first-class Oppenheimer [sic] mystery.[33]

In other words, it wasn't lightning.

Well might Baron Justus von Liebig deplore the absence of witnesses to the majority of such cases. Of course, there

---

[33] Reprinted in *The Woman*, July 1952, from the Atlanta, Georgia, *Journal and Constitution*; quoted by Vincent H. Gaddis, op. cit.

are witnesses: some who, like the Lincolnshire farmer and the New Hampshire doctor, see the flames beginning to sprout from between the shoulder blades of kneeling women. But in deploring the absence of witnesses, the scientists really mean 'expert witnesses', and few of the rare observers of the incidence of spontaneous combustion are ever that. The ideal witness is, naturally, the victim; but he or she is almost always unable to say what happened; not, I feel, because the victim does not know, or could not describe at least the circumstances in which the 'attack' took place, as because some type of Fire-induced amnesia prevents the victim's recalling 'exactly what happened'. Usually, though, the victim, when found, is beyond all speech.

Such evidence of this phenomenon as exists seems clearly to indicate that, like other catastrophes in the experience of man, it is possible to take avoiding action – not all those threatened by the Fire have perished. Mr Hamilton put out his own flames, the Binbrook farmer and the New England doctor beat out those spurting from the women's backs, and I think that Mr Richard Vogt, driving home to Eagle Band, Minnesota, from Osakis, on the night of 10 May 1961, also avoided the death which overtook ex-actress Mrs Olga Worth Stephens, of Dallas, Texas, as she sat in her parked car.

It was October 1964 when suddenly passers-by in East Grand Avenue saw Mrs Stephens become a 'human torch', burning up both Mrs Stephens (who was seventy-five) *and* her clothing. The car was not burned, and firemen could find nothing in it which might have caused the fire in which its owner died.

Three years earlier, as Mr Vogt drove home, something happened at a little before midnight which has not yet been explained, but which, all things considered, must be regarded as Mr Vogt's lucky 'near miss'.

He testified afterwards that as he drove along the main highway he saw 'a ball of fog, about three feet in diameter,

174

and slightly elongated, descending towards his car at about a 45-degree angle'. The 'ball of fog' approached far too fast for the driver to avoid it, and it hit the car at the upper part of the hood. Mr Vogt said that the noise of the impact was what one might have expected from contact with a 'shovel full of fine gravel', hitting the car at a high speed. Immediately after the impact of the 'ball of fog', the interior of the car began to heat up so quickly that the scared Mr Vogt braked and jumped out. He saw that the windscreen had been cracked and that the body of the car not only was pitted from contact with the 'fog', but that it was now too hot to touch for more than a second. The frightened man wondered if a 'disintegrating rocket cone or similar weapon' had showered red-hot particles down on his car.

Scientists studying this odd occurrence under Professor W. J. Layten at the University of Minnesota were unable to explain, though like scientists elsewhere, they were ready with a 'probable explanation' – in this case 'either a collection of small meteorite fragments surrounded by some gas, or . . . something like ball lightning'. As in the case of the helmsman of SS *Ulrich,* the sky was perfectly clear at the time of the occurrence.

Robert Burch, an electronics mechanic, looked into the mirror just in time to avoid 'an orange-red ball of fire' coming at him through the open window of his room in the Bremerton, Washington, YMCA. Burch had hardly thrown himself aside when the ball of fire was in the room, bursting with a blinding flash and a deafening noise.

There was nothing subjective about this experience: the noise brought Burch's room-mate in on the run – he had heard the noise in the bathroom, three doors away.

Apart from having burned Burch's right arm badly, the ball of fire had set fire to the contents of a wastepaper basket, the men's baggage and two radios. And, as both were shaking with reaction, a witness entered the room: a policeman, he had seen the ball of fire enter the room and had heard the bang. He sent for an ambulance, and as Burch worked at the Puget Sound Navy Yard, the injured man was taken off to Bremerton Naval Hospital.

Is this 'ball lightning', a common enough phenomenon, something which, 'if unattended to', becomes, grows into, the Fire which consumes everything? In the case of Robert Burch there was the common enough loud bang, but there are many cases in which this electrical phenomenon comes to wreak its mischief in complete noiselessness. Were the kneeling women whose backs were aflame caught by a noiseless fire ball? From the position of her few remains, the Countess di Bandi had been kneeling at some stage of her final experience, and though it was the terrified scream of the kneeling and burning woman which brought the New England doctor to her rescue, a servant girl who died in the late eighteenth-century was scrubbing the floor on her knees, unaware that her back was on fire.

I was once trimming my nails by a closed window, in the light of a moon so brilliant that I did not have to switch on the electric light. Concentrating on the scissors, I had not seen a small ball of blue radiance approach – the first that I knew of it was when it ran along the scissors, *shocking* them out of my hand, and giving me a sharp twinge, no more. I do not recall that there was any other noise than my startled cry. Was this the Fire in embryo? – a baby fire, trying out its powers?

I think that, often, we see the beginning of a series of happenings which, carried through to their 'natural' conclusion, would result in authentic Fire. For some reason – as inexplicable still as the Fire itself – the sequence does not develop; we see the initial phenomenon or phenomena, and then the sequence stops, and the malignant influences depart.

176

What are these phenomena, which hint at – which seem obliquely to belong to – the nature of fire? Are they adumbrations of more serious assaults on the human mind and body? Are they, in respect of the Fire from Heaven, what the *aura* of an attack is to the epileptic? Or are these *hints* of fire no more than the 'threatening' weather which, in actuality, threatens nothing? One senses, as one studies the history of the Fire, that in this, as in other cosmic activities, there are unsuccessful trial sketches, essays, attempts, just as there are the successful completions. Are all the 'near escapes' no more than 'serious attempts' which did not quite succeed? Are they different from the total combustion of a Countess di Bandi, a Mrs Rooney, a Mrs Reeser, only in the fact that they were unsuccessful efforts?

One of the greatest – if not the greatest – triumphs of the human mind over the last century is the ever wider recognition of the ancient knowledge that the partition of human living between 'mental' and'physical' is a foolish misconception completely unjustified by even observed facts. The concept implicit in the neologism 'psychosomatic' – 'that which appertains equally to the mind and the body', but generally meaning 'bodily irregularities generated by some malfunctioning of the mind' – is completely unjustified by human behaviour. The distinction between those illnesses which are 'organic', and those which are 'psychosomatic' is an unreal distinction: in human life there is no division of human activities between those which are 'controlled by the body' and those which are 'controlled by the mind'. Mind and body are one, their functions complementary and indivisible; and the totality of their meshed activities constitutes what we call 'life'.

Soon, very soon, one hopes, the obscuring, confusing, misleading terms by which too many have been forbidden their rightful view of the obvious and important truths will be swept away. Such terms as 'psychic', 'occult', 'supernatural', 'paranormal', and so on, will either be dropped altogether from our terminology or will regain their proper meanings.

For far too many people to-day, telekinesis – the power to exert force at a distance without *apparent* contact between the person moving and the object moved – is 'weird', 'spooky', 'mystic'. In more 'scientific' phrasing, telekinesis is 'para-normal', 'paraphysical'.

Such people – both the 'simple-minded' and the 'educated' – will tell you without hesitation that telekinesis is a 'function of the mind', presumably because when Mrs Nelya Mikhailova causes a match box or a compass needle to move, she doesn't push either with her finger.

But what of the telekinetic abilities of the prisoners in Clinton Prison, Dannemora, New York, which so astonished Dr Julius Ransom, Chief Medical Officer, who described those abilities, and their astonishingly 'irrational' cause, in the *Electrical Experimenter* for June 1920? The thirty-four convicts admitted to the prison hospital had been stricken with botulism – infection by *B. botulinus,* a highly toxic organism usually found in undercooked food. The men attributed their serious illness to their having been given canned salmon.

During the course of these cases, it was discovered by accident that peculiar static electric power had developed in the patients. One of the patients who was convalescing crumpled up a piece of paper and attempted to throw it in a wastepaper basket; it absolutely refused to leave his hand. The matter was reported to me, and I found that every case of *botulinus* poisoning developed this strange power.

All sorts of experiments have been tried, and it was found to be a constant condition. The compass needle of a surveyor's instrument could be rotated with any piece of paper electrified by these patients. *A steel tape suspended would feel the*

178

magnetic field in a remarkable manner, and sway from side to side.[34]

The ability to electrify was proportional to the severity of the disease; as the patient convalesced he gradually lost his power, and when quite well lost it altogether.

Was this telekinetic ability 'physical', 'paraphysical' or 'psychic'? If telekinesis be a 'function of the parapsychic' (whatever that could possibly mean!), then what is the relation between infected red salmon and the strengthening of the so-called 'mental powers'? That there *is* a relation, as Dr Ransom argued, seems to me to be beyond dispute; but there is nothing more 'weird' in the fact that *B. botulinus* steps up the power of the human magnetic field than that a dose of mescalin (or even a stiff dose of alcohol) can endow the observer with some unusual powers of perception.

The close and causal relation between the stomach (including the food that it ingests and digests) and the mind was known and recognized as a matter of ordinary fact by all the Ancient World.

All religious activities in the Ancient World were related to some specialized ritual food, which in variety ran upwards from yoghurt to human brains. The ritual food of the Aztec priests was the living human heart; that of the priestesses of Korè the Maiden, 'little cakes'. The initiates of Mithraism drank the blood of bulls; the votaries of the Lares – the Family Divinities – worshipped them with salted wheat. Cybele, the Mother Goddess in her demon aspect, was worshipped, paradoxically enough, in the eating of

---

[34] My italics. Note particularly the relation between Mrs Mikhailova's telekinetic abilities and the "prostration" from which she suffers after any prolonged experimentation, usually conducted by Dr G. Sergeyev, of the A. A. Uktomskii (Military) Physiological Institute, Leningrad.

curds-and-whey (thus, perhaps, our word for a feast: 'junket'). In these ritual foods – and we must here not overlook the ritual bread and wine of Christianity – the devout worshipper found a releasing translation to a higher plane of consciousness: no worshipper of *any* religion of the Ancient World would have found anything incredible in the fact that the eating of poisoned salmon would have bestowed on the eater the 'gift' of causing objects to move by the very act of will. Indeed, had one told any of these ancient worshippers that Caroline Clare, of London, Ontario, would, in 1877, fall into spastic and catatonic states, and thereafter attract to her body metal objects, so that they could be pulled away from her only by force, the ancient worshipper would have had only two questions to ask: 'Which God does she worship?' and 'What is her ritual food?' – questions which, perhaps, might with advantage have been asked in some modern investigations.

Even less astonished would our hypothetical ancient worshipper be to hear of the case, reported by Hereward Carrington from his own observation, of a child whose over-eating of chestnuts caused his death from acute indigestion. It is a curious case which links this gastric-psychic type of phenomena with both telekinetic ('PK') abilities and vulnerability to the Fire.

Preparing the child's body for burial, the neighbours were startled to see that the corpse was already enshrouded, as it were, in a 'bluish glow'; a glow which, moreover, was associated with a considerable degree of heat. It is said that 'efforts were made to extinguish this glow' – but one cannot imagine what those efforts could have been. Perhaps the wish that the glow would vanish had its effect on the odd phenomenon, for it did vanish, and the body was prepared for burial.

In this case, we have that 'mirror image' of happening on which I commented earlier in this book: the child's body bore no burns, but the sheet on which it lay had been scorched. With the incidence of the Fire proper, it is usually the other way around.

Indeed, the association of illness and disease (that is, abnormality of bodily function) with the so-called 'psychic' phenomena is so well attested that there should be no doubt of its happening. A truly scientific approach to the study of the 'luminous sick' has been made less easy by the reluctance of even trained observers to study the phenomena objectively; preconceived views and ineradicable prejudices have tended to make the observer see rather what he wished to see and not what was there to be seen. Thus, though the French researcher, Dr Charles Féré, records two cases of 'luminous illness', both in women of hysterical character, he includes the case in a work called *Annales des Sciences Psychiques.* In Féré's reported cases, luminous halos of an *orange* colour, lasting some two hours, appeared about the heads and hands of the two patients.

But the truly secular medical press is full of such accounts; the records showing the manifestation of luminescence in almost every part of the human body, and in almost all its products.

In their *Anomalies and Curiosities of Medicine* (in which title the loaded and misleading word 'Anomalies' is to be deplored), Dr George M. Gould and Dr Walter L. Pyle cite the scientifically observed occurrence of luminosity in perspiration, urine, ulcers; while others have recorded luminous saliva and blood. Gould and Pyle note two cases of luminous halos about the heads of tubercular patients; and one case of a complete bodily aura which enveloped a sufferer from psoriasis.

As Gaddis points out, much has been learned in recent years of the chemical and mechanical facts governing the phenomenon of luminescence in living creatures, all of them of non-mammalian phyla: a range of sea-creatures, from the

181

'basic' plankton to the highly organized squid, and, in the lower depths of the oceans, scores of fish whose coloured lights attract their prey; in the non-mammalian terrestrial creation, chick-beetles, glowworms and fireflies; in the plant world certain fungi, and in the sub-microscopic world, below (or removed from) these convenient classifications, the bacteria.

The bio-luminescence of the firefly is a sexual manifestation – the male literally 'lights up' to attract the female. Present in the firefly's tail are two chemicals, luciferin and luciferase, an enzyme, both of which will luminesce when brought into contact with adenosine triphosphate (ATP), a chemical found in all living organisms, mammalian and non-mammalian alike. Modern scientific opinion considers adenosine triphosphate to be 'the key source of energy in biological systems'. In the case of the amorous firefly, a nerve impulse brings the luciferin and luciferase into contact with the adenosine triphosphate, whose characteristic it is to convert chemical into mechanical energy, which makes it the initiator and controller of muscular action. So far as the firefly is concerned, adenosine triphosphate converts chemical energy into radiant energy – that is, light.

Perhaps 'illness' is not the correct word when it comes to our observing the link between persons suffering from some ailment and their developing bio-luminescence. Would it not be more precise to describe 'illness', not so much as a *malfunctioning* of the human economy, as a change of state, perhaps even a change of function?

Gould and Pyle tell of a woman whose cancerous breast showed such powerful bio-luminescence that the glow could be seen from several feet away, the light being so strong that the time could be told from a watch held some inches away.

This bio-luminescence seems to occur most frequently in the region of the chest – but surely that is only another way of saying 'that part of the body around the heart'? When Signora Anna Monaro was an asthma patient in the general hospital at Pirano, Italy, it was noticed that while she slept at night, 'a flickering bluish glow emanated from her breasts, remaining visible for several seconds'. This bio-luminescence persisted over a period of several weeks, and was witnessed not only by many responsible medical men but also by Italian government officials. The bio-lumines-cence was accompanied by an accelerated pulse-rate and by profuse sweating, which *shews* that, in this case again, the phenomenon of luminosity was associated with *heat,* though not to a dangerous degree.

Closely allied with the phenomenon of bioluminescence – especially when one considers the class of persons affected – seems to be that of hyperthermia or 'super-heating': an abnormal condition which was first 'officially' reported only as recently as 2 February 1875, when Mr J. W. Teale, a respected medical practitioner of Scarborough, England, read a report to the Clinical Society of London. Mr Teale announced that a lady patient had, after a fall from a horse, maintained, *for seven consecutive weeks,* a tempera-ture which had never fallen below 108°F (42.2°C), and which, on four separate occasions, had risen to the 'fatal' level of 122°F (50°C). Despite this, the doctor reported, the patient had recovered, to enjoy excellent health.

The Teale Report was the signal for the established medical profession to assail him with all the weapons that science always has to hand: ridicule not the least of those (quite often thoroughly effective) arms. Commenting on Mr Teale's history of the hyperthermic patient, the *British Medical Journal* (1875, I, p. 347) asked ironically whether or not Mr Teale had ever seen a case resembling that of St Denis, who walked about with his head 'tucked underneath his arm'?

But the Teale records had been scrupulously kept, and in *The Lancet* – then, and still, the not-less-respected rival of the *British Medical Journal* – the facts, both of the case and of Mr Teale's precise recordings, were given. No fewer than seven thermometers were used for the observations of the hyperthermic temperatures; three had been made specially to record the temperatures in question; four others were found to be accurate to within the tenth of a degree. Aware that he had come in contact with a phenomenon of 'intrinsic incredibility', Mr Teale contrived that each thermometer used had been inspected by trustworthy witnesses before and after each taking of the patient's temperature.

More, the routine oral temperature-taking was supplemented by observations from other parts of the body – sometimes the severally located observations being made at the same time.

And finally, these most elaborate observations were continued *daily* for nearly ten weeks, in the last three weeks of which the patient's temperature dropped gradually back to a normal 97° or 98°F (36.5° or 37°C).

It was impossible to question the accuracy of Mr Teale's records; it was impossible any longer to accuse the Scarborough medical man of faulty observation or of fraudulent imposture: there remained only the disagreeable choice of accepting a 'fact against nature' or rejecting Mr Teale and his records altogether.

That was a century ago. Now comes another and even more striking case of hyperthermia: that of an Italian priest, Father Forgione, chaplain of a convent at Foggia. This priest, whose undoubted sanctity has already earned him 'unofficial' popular canonization under his respected nickname of 'Father Pio', has been tested perhaps even more rigorously than was Mr Teale's hyperthermic patient of a century ago.

The hyperthermia of 'Father Pio' – discovered when he literally blew the mercury up in a standard hospital thermometer – is not an isolated phenomenon connected with his sanctity: his hands and feet display the by no means uncommon stigmata of the crucified Christ; so that one may assume that 'Father Pio's' body is more than normally subject to the impulses of his mind.

The priest was first tested in a scientific manner at the well-known Trinity Hospital in Naples, where, after having broken the regular thermometers, the Father's body recorded, on a bath thermometer, the astonishing figure of 118.4°F (48°C). A decided sceptic – at least, in regard to the reports of Father Forgione's hyperthermic temperatures – was the writer on medical and other scientific subjects, Dr Georgio Festa.

Taking with him an instrument of great precision, Dr Festa called on the Father, obtained his permission to record the priest's body temperatures, and – found what the hospital authorities at Naples had found: that the priest's morning and evening temperatures were slightly below normal, but that, during a hyperthermic crisis – which could last continuously or up to two days at a time – temperatures of between 118.4° and 119.3°F (48° and 48.5°C) were recorded.

The reported phenomenon of excessive skin heat – during one 'exaltation' onlookers observed that 'Father Pio' seemed to glow, and that his skin became too hot to touch – goes back, of course, far beyond Mr Teale's patient; but only within the last century has it been possible to make precisely controlled observation of the phenomenon of *non-lethal* hyperthermia – and then only with two subjects. In the case of the modern priest, he does not lose consciousness – he does not even feel unwell.

That the heat-regulating mechanism of these two hyperthermics is abnormal goes without saying; but in what does the abnormality consist? George Zorab, on whose account I have mainly relied, asks: 'Did they by chance *possess* proteins not coagulating at these high temperatures, or, perhaps, body cells provided with some kind of air-conditioning, enabling their organisms to withstand temperatures which could be fatal to others?'

The relevance of this proven hyperthermia is its apparent relevance to the 'harmless heat' to which I referred on page 45: such for instance, as that which caused the walls of Mrs Mable Metcalf's house to become 'almost red hot', but where no fire followed. The hyperthermia of Mr Teale's patient and of 'Father Pio' seems analogous, in that the body temperature rises to 'lethal' heights, but without progressing into total and truly lethal combustion. It would seem here that the abnormal heat-regulating mechanism of these hyperthermics acts rather to put a brake on the sudden rise of temperature than to cause normal body temperature to rise. Like Mr Hamilton, they actually fight – successfully, too! – the Fire from Heaven.

From a scientifically recorded hyperthermia which may – and, as we have seen, often does – raise the body temperature of a human being above what, normally, would be a lethal heat; from this non-flaming heat to the heat which is seen as actual flames, there would appear to be no great step. And, indeed, the non-lethal flame in a living person is as well-attested as the presence of the lethal.

The phenomenon was well-known in the past; we noted, on page 44, the fact that Theodoric the Great's body, when rubbed, gave out flames – that is, non-lethal flames; for the King of the Ostrogoths and of Italy lived to what, for the fifth and sixth centuries of our era, was a ripe old age: seventy-one. There are many other instances from history; all dismissed – *because* history records them as 'legends', 'fables', 'myths'. To-day, the scientific investigation of body-produced non-lethal flame is going on all over the world;

and nowhere more thoroughly than in Russia, where Dr Genady Sergeyev, of the A. A. Uktomskii (Military) Physiological Institute of Leningrad, the investigator of Mrs Nelya Mikhailova's telekinetic talents, is recording the flame-producing abilities of another Russian telekinetic: Nina Kulagina.

An interview with Dr Sergeyev appeared in the London *Sunday People* for 14 March 1976, in the course of which the famous Russian parapsychologist described how Miss Kulagina 'can draw energy somehow from all around her'. He described how, 'on several occasions the force rushing into her body left burn-marks up to four inches long on her arms and hands'.

'I was with her once', said Dr Sergeyev, 'when her clothing caught fire from this energy flow – it literally flamed up. I helped put out the flames, and saved some of the burnt clothing as an exhibit.'

Here the Fire, though not lethal, is not *quite* harmless: '. . . the force rushing into her body left burn-marks up to four inches long . . .' In the case of Lily White, the young woman from Antigua, BWI, whose clothing was burned (see page 260) without Miss White's being even scorched.

The Fire, as I have said or implied elsewhere, covers, not only the widest range of victims, but the widest range of heat, too. It seems to manifest itself at every marking on the thermometer's scale, from heat that we do not notice as unusual, through heat which is merely uncomfortable to heat which is flameless but beyond the limits of fever heat; through the heat of non-lethal flame to killing, all-consuming heat which must operate at temperatures around 3000°F to effect what, in fact, it does.

Let us note that there is a 'mirror image' of bio-luminescence – we might call it 'necro-luminescence', the glow of thoroughly *dead* things.

This glow, commonly most noticeable on stale fish, and less commonly on 'high' meat and 'turned' vegetables, is attributable to bacteria which, like the firefly, the glowworm and the chick-beetle, secrete luciferin and luciferase. Since here it is not the dead fish, meat or vegetables which are glowing, but only the bacteria which thrive in what only custom impels us to call 'corruption', the highly mannered 'explanation' by psychiatrist Dr Carlos Saiz of Signora Anna Monaro's pectoral luminescence may have been based on an insufficiency of facts. The bluish luminescence observable over Signora Monaro's breasts was caused, said Dr Saiz, by 'electrical and magnetic organisms in the woman's body, developed in eminent degree'.

The more one observes the behaviour of this abnormal heat – here making a Signora Monaro merely sweat, there burning up a Mrs Reeser to a few pounds of ash; here 'concentrating' so closely upon the *individual* that even (as in the case of Billy Thomas Peterson) his underclothes escaped the burning; there so scattering the fiery attack that in October 1871, not only the city of Chicago, but towns and villages throughout six great states – Michigan, Missouri, Illinois, North Dakota, South Dakota and Wisconsin – together with *vast* tracts of forest, were destroyed. The authors of *The History of the Great Conflagration*, James Sheahan and George Upson, both associate editors of the *Chicago Daily Tribune*, comment wonderingly on the fact that fire seemed to strike simultaneously places many miles apart. Their contemporary testimony makes it clear that it was not a question of a central fire's spreading to take in outlying villages and towns, but rather scattered focuses of flame gradually (and not by any means slowly) coalescing into one vast blaze. Reporters told of buildings, far beyond the line of fire, that burst into flames simultaneously from the interior 'as if a regiment of incendiaries were at work. What latent power enkindled the inside of these advanced buildings while externally they were untouched?' And there were references to a 'food for fire in the air, something mysterious as yet and unexplainable. Whether it is atmospheric or electric is yet to be determined.'

It is sure that, to the *contemporary* observer, there was nothing either 'accidental' or even 'natural' about the Fire of 1871.

And then one meets the attack in which the blindly impersonal and the individually concentrated seem to be equally apparent. In a burst of spontaneous fire the cotton dress of Mrs Charles H. Williamson suddenly flared up. It was on a January morning in 1932, in Bladenboro, North Carolina; but though it was a cold day, Mrs Williamson had not been standing near any type of fire, open or closed. Her dress had never been in contact with cleaning fluid or other volatile, highly combustible liquid. Her dress simply caught fire. But now follows a curious fact which induces us to believe that, quite apart from its 'causeless' outbreak, it was no ordinary fire.

Mrs Williamson's husband and daughter tore the blazing dress off with their bare hands – the dress now no more than a charred tatter of cloth. Yet not one of the three was burned in the slightest degree.

Was this first attack directed at Mrs Williamson *personally?* It is hard to think so; or, perhaps the 'individual' pattern of attack was changed to a more 'general', less 'individual' one.

For now the objects of the attack changed: a pair of pants of Mr Williamson's hung up in a closet burst into flames; a bed caught fire; curtains in an unoccupied room blazed up. Flames as from a gas-jet consumed various articles throughout the house without touching adjacent objects. The flames could not be put out, but vanished of their own accord after having burned up the object of their

189

attention. There was no smoke and no smell, even from the burning articles.

For three days, with many neighbours to witness these odd happenings, the Williamsons stuck out the attack; on the fourth day they moved. All relevant 'experts' – gas, electricity, arson, police – were called in, and came away without having found the reason for, or even the nature of, the Fire. Said an Associated press report: 'The fires started, burned and vanished as mysteriously as if guided by invisible hands. There has been no logical explanation.' On the fifth day the fires vanished.

The Williamsons moved back into their house – the attack was over . . . for good.

12

POKER-DICE AND POLTERGEISTS

It is known that some people win 'against the odds', and some never win, even 'with the odds'. The adventurer-financier, John Law, gained the capital needed to start his private bank by studying the calculus of probability in dice-throwing and card-playing; even he, as he admitted, could not 'rationalize' the element of 'luck'. Do the dice fall according to the calculus of probability? Or do they fall according to some energy pattern whose nature may have been long suspected, but which is only now beginning to be examined? Yes, the hard-headed owners of Las Vegas gaming saloons recognize, in their practical way, that 'lucky' throws may be not so much 'lucky' as induced; that some of their customers must have a telekinetic power to control the fall of the dice, the sequence of the cards. Suppose, say, that some – or even all – of those salmon-poisoned prisoners from Dannemora had been taken to Las Vegas, and instead of controlling the needle of a compass, the swing of a hanging steel rule, their botulism-induced telekinesis had let them control the play of the cards, the fall of the dice, the spin of the roulette wheel.

And this brings me to another important question: at which point, seeing that there appears to be both unconscious and conscious control by telekinesis, do the *unintentional* – control of the compass-needle by the poisoned prisoners of Dannemora – and the *intentional* – control of the compass-needle by 'officially investigated' TK mediums, Mrs Nelya Mikhailova, or Alla Vinogradova – meet?

191

It is a question which accompanies us into the strange world of the poltergeists. It is a question which asks: How much of this apparently aberrant activity is 'unintentional', how much under the willed control of mind?

The question of the poltergeists' activities arises here because so much of 'officially classified' poltergeist activity seems to border on phenomena which would 'normally' be classified under the heading of 'spontaneous combustion'. I am here led to ask, and it is asked by no means for the first time: Is spontaneous combustion a poltergeist phenomenon, differing from the more common poltergeist phenomena only in that the combustion appears to be unaccompanied by those activities generally associated with poltergeist phenomena?

The word *Poltergeist,* a German word, is usually explained as 'noisy spirit'; but this seems to fail to convey the exact meaning. It is true that the verb *poltern* means 'to make a rumbling noise', but *Polterabend,* 'polter-eve', means the night before the wedding, hours in which – especially with the peasantry – the boozy junketing is accompanied by the harmless licentious grossness, the rude and rustic practical jokes, with which bride and groom are prepared for the end of their celibacy.

Polter, then, would seem to mean, not so much 'noisy', as 'boisterous, rambunctious, frolicking', nor is this careful search for the correct translation of *polter* idle hair-splitting. It is essential that we see and recognize the mental image that most people have formed of the poltergeist – not as that of a noisy, so much as of an erratic, irresponsible, childish – and often maliciously childish – entity.

We have already seen the case of the Williamson family, in which Mrs Williamson's dress burst into flames and was utterly consumed, and in which neither Mrs Williamson nor her husband and daughter was harmed. This aberrant manifestation of fire is strictly in the tradition of spontaneous combustion.

On the other hand, as I remarked, what followed was rather in the tradition of the poltergeist: the selective fires appearing all over the house; this selective type of fire burning up small objects without communicating itself to the rest of the room or even to adjacent small objects. And the fact that, after the first alarming day, at least three competent witnesses – Mr J. A. Bridger, the Mayor; Dr S. S. Hutchinson, the family doctor, and Mr J. B. Edwards, from the Wilmington Department of Health – were present at most of the manifestations argues for poltergeist activity, since 'the boisterous spirit' is notoriously extrovert.

At which point do telekinetic manifestations cease to belong to the classification 'poltergeist', and move into the classification 'spontaneous combustion'? This question, of course, inevitably raises another: is spontaneous combustion merely a more forceful manifestation, a 'logical extension', as it were, of the poltergeist activity which rocks tables, hurls objects with more or less violence across rooms, and sometimes contents itself with a few harmless (though frightening) raps on the wall?

The events at Binbrook Farm, to which I shall now return, would seem to suggest that the answer to that latter question is yes.

Lincolnshire, England, is flat, featureless, fertile country whose broad, seemingly endless plains clearly betray its origin as land recovered from the sea. It has a look of Holland, and indeed, it was the Dutch who, centuries ago, recovered much of its now rich soil from the North Sea.

Both physically and psychically, Lincolnshire is an odd place: one of the three known districts on the earth's surface in which the standard gravitational acceleration – slightly over 32 feet per second per second – is *not* the rule. Things fall oddly in Lincolnshire, not at all as fast as 'the rule' lays it down that they should. It is here, also, that both poltergeist and spontaneous combustion activity are seen at what may well be called their most typical.

It was at Louth, in Lincolnshire, that Ashton Clodd, it will be recalled, died of burns in mysterious circumstances; a death of which a witness at the inquest remarked: 'If there was a fire in the fireplace, it was very little.'

And near Louth, too, at the time when Ashton Clodd was dying of burns from a fire in a cold grate, something literally unnatural was happening in the Lincolnshire village of Binbrook, about fifteen miles from Market Rasen on the road which leads to New Waltham and Grimsby.

The facts were collected by the Reverend A. C. Custance, of Binbrook Rectory, and collated in detail by Colonel Taylor, for the records of the Society for Psychical Research. Knowledge of 'odd happenings' in Lincolnshire was already reported in the *Liverpool Echo* and through that esteemed newspaper the facts got wide publicity throughout the England of 1904-5 – that strange period in which Margaret Dewar found her sister dying of burns in an unburned bed.

The manifestations of some unusual paraphysical force made themselves first noticed, according to Colonel Taylor, on 1 December 1904. At first the manifestations, though sufficiently alarming, as such manifestations always must be, were of the 'low tempo' kind: objects began to hurl themselves about the rectory, and three times, near a 'not very good, or big, fire', things burst into flames.

On 25 January 1905, almost two months after the outbreak of poltergeist activity in the rectory, the *Liverpool Echo* printed a letter from a Binbrook schoolteacher, describing how she had found a blanket on fire in a room which had no fireplace.

Three days later the *Louth and North Lincolnshire News* reported that the poltergeist (it didn't call it that) had reached the Binbrook farmhouse, and told of the unaccountable falling of objects from shelves and mantels, and of the mysterious transportation of objects.

Interviewed by journalists, Farmer White told of the inexplicable and terrifying pressure of some unusual force both inside and outside his farmhouse. Here are his words:

> Our servant girl, whom we had taken from the workhouse, and who had neither kin nor friend in the world that she knows of, was sweeping the kitchen. There was a very small fire in the grate; there was a guard there, so that no one can *[sic]* come within two feet or more of the fire, and she was at the other end of the room, and had not been near [i.e. the fire]. I suddenly came into the kitchen, and there she was sweeping away while the back of her dress was on fire. She looked around, as I shouted, and seeing the flames, rushed through the door. She tripped, and I smothered the fire out with sacks. But she was terribly burned, and she is at the Louth Hospital now, in terrible pain.

The newspaper was graciously pleased to confirm at least the verifiable part of Farmer White's account: 'This last sentence is very true. Yesterday our reporter called at the hospital and was informed that the girl was burned extensively on the back, and lies in a critical condition. She adheres to the belief that she was in the middle of the room, when her clothes ignited.'

There was something else loose in that cold Lincolnshire January even less easily explained than the 'spontaneous' igniting of the servant girl's dress. *Something* that both Farmer White and the editor of the *Louth and North Lincolnshire News* thought unconnected with the poltergeist manifestations in the rectory, house and farmhouse; yet that Charles Fort believed to be a part of a totality of aberration: the torture-killing of Farmer White's chickens.

The newspaper reported this as though, for all that it was happening to Farmer White, employer of the burned girl and neighbour of the poltergeist-tormented rector and schoolteacher, it was something outside the general pattern of disturbance: 'Out of 250 chickens, Mr White says that he has only 24 left. They had all been killed in the same weird way. The skin around the neck, from the head to the breast, had been pulled off, and the windpipe drawn from its place and snapped. The chicken-coop had been watched night and day, but whenever examined, four or five chickens had been found dead.' It is necessary here to note that whatever animals, birds and reptiles share with humans, it does not generally[35] include spontaneous combustion.

For Charles Fort, as has been pointed out, all these separate incidents were part of one cosmos-wide pattern of oddity: 'In London, a woman sat asleep, near a grate, and something, as if taking advantage of this means of commonplace explanation, burned her, behind her, but I had no data on which to speculate. . .' Neither, for that matter, had the coroner, as was reported in *Lloyd's Weekly News*, of 5 February 1905.

Charles Fort continues:

But if we accept that, at Binbrook Farm, something was savagely killing chickens, we accept that whatever we mean by a *being* was there. It seems that, in the little time taken by the farmer to put out the fire of the burning girl, she could not have been badly scorched. Then the suggestion is that, unknown to her, something behind her was burning her, and that she was unconscious of her scorching flesh. *All the stories are notable for the absence of outcry or seeming unconsciousness of victims that something was consuming them.*[36]

---

[35] For a rare possible example, see page 218.

[36] My italics. Not quite all − Fort exaggerates here. It was the victim's screams which brought Dr H. B. Hartwell of Ayer, Mass., to the assistance of the woman burning in the wood.

To make the subject more up-to-date, I quote two stories from newspapers of December 1973. One story concerns some very mysterious cattle-maiming; the other a not less mysterious case of spontaneous combustion.

Unlike the Binbrook combustions of human beings and bedding, with the strangely savage mutilation-killing of the hens, the oddities of December 1973 do not seem to be connected in *place:* the combustion taking place in Hoquiam, Oregon; the maiming of cattle around Concordia, Kansas. But there *is* a startling linkage in *time:* 'Mortuary Fire Baffles Police' *(The Oregonian,* Thursday, 20 December 1973); 'Deaths puzzle Farmers' *(Kansas City Times,* Saturday, 22 December 1973):

When a 500-pound heifer owned by state Sen. Ross Doyen of Concordia was found Thursday morning two miles east of Concordia . . . part of its left ear was missing and a six-inch hole had been gouged in its belly. At first, investigators believed the ear and hole were cut with a knife and they were ready to add Doyen's Angus to the mystery. But an autopsy performed at the veterinarian diagnostic laboratory at Kansas State University indicated the heifer died of acute bloating of the stomach. The hole and ear marks apparently were made by coyotes, officials said.

What the Diagnostic Laboratory had failed 'scientifically' or even 'apparently' to explain is the absence of the minutest trace of blood at the site of these maimings – all of which involved cutting with a sharp instrument:

Concordia, Kan. – A dead heifer's ear had been sliced or chewed to the skull. A bull was found with a pound of meat removed from a front quarter. Another had no tongue or nose and again was missing an ear . . . almost all the deaths have been black cows, mostly Angus . . . many bore knife marks on the carcasses, including the apparent butchering of the sex organs from both bulls and heifers . . .

No blood, and no footprints. Not being a skilled technician of the Diagnostic Laboratory, Under-Sheriff C. P. McGuire, of Could County, offered no explanation:

'We worked on this thing trying to come up with some kind of pattern but just aren't coming up with a thing.

We had one that was basically in a mudhole, maybe twenty feet by seventy-five or 100 feet . . . When they called and told us it was in a mudhole, we were gung ho [sic], thought sure we'd have foot-prints.'

He shook his head. 'You can understand why we're up against a stump.'

The Sheriff of Harvey County, Galen Morford, did, however, have a theory, though not one likely to have been approved by the experts of the Diagnostic Laboratory:

I'm really not going to be surprised if this isn't some cult type of thing. When they let witches practice over at the state industrial reformatory at Hutchinson there's no telling what will happen.

One may well sympathize with Sheriff Morford's theory – even if one does not accept it.

McGuire said more recent kills . . . had only their sex organs and parts near the head and neck removed.

'They take the eyeballs, the tongue, snouts or maybe a swish of the tail', Deputy Sam Budreau said, 'but 27 had their sex organs removed, predominantly the heifers. Some had their external organs taken, and some had their complete reproductive areas removed.

There was no blood loss in any of them [my italics – MH], and some were still warm enough . . .

198

'Another thing, they do such a clean job', Budreau added. They clean the bones, no bleeding, and take the ear at the base of the skull.' Pointing at snapshots of some victims, Budreau said: 'When they cut the eye out they've taken the membranes and eyelids and all.'

Another aspect puzzling investigators has been *the absence of a death mark on the cattle* [my italics – MH]. No fatal stab or gunshot wounds have turned up on the cows, McGuire said, nor had there been a blow to the head.

Altogether, some forty cattle were thus mutilated; and in the previous year six similar cases were reported from Sweden. There may be a 'psychic' link here between Emory Eklund, a Minneapolis farmer who lost a cow, and Sweden from which his family originally came.) Charles Fort would have been interested in this cattle-maiming; he would not have been astonished. What would most have interested him would have been the 'classic' pattern of the maimings: the odd (and to us still inexplicable) motivation, the specific oddness of the absence of blood from the killings, the 'scientific' cover-up, and, to complete the pattern, the precisely contemporary oddness of a spontaneous combustion with features unusual even within that oddest of all phenomena.

The death of Mrs Sam Satlow, fifty, of Hoquiam, Oregon, links her, in the tables of mortality, with Billy Thomas Peterson, twenty-seven, of Pontiac, Michigan, who, it will be recalled, managed to commit suicide in his car by attaching a flexible pipe to the exhaust. There is another link in that both these deaths took place in December: Mrs Satlow's on 7 December, Billy Peterson's on 13 December. They were also linked in so far that they were subjects ('victims' seems the wrong word here) of posthumous spontaneous combustion, for the autopsy revealed that Billy was dead of carbon-monoxide poisoning before the Fire hit him; and Mrs Satlow had been dead a full three days before the Fire hit *her*.

This appears to have been one of the cases in which there was a smell of smoke; at any rate, 'a resident of an upstairs apartment' gave the alarm which brought the Hoquiam fire department to the Chapel of Rest in Coleman's Mortuary early in the morning of 10 December 1973.

Due to be buried on the following day, Mrs Satlow lay at what should have been her final rest in her coffin; *the lid on, and screwed firmly down;* the family and friends had paid their last respects on the previous day.

Hoquiam's Police Chief Richard Barnes said, understandably: 'The burning of a woman's body in a coffin inside a locked funeral home remains a mystery!'

For that is exactly what the firemen found at Coleman's: 'She was completely consumed to the hips', said Chief Barnes. 'We have no proof that a crime has been committed, and', he added, with an honesty unusual in an official, 'no evidence of it. It's all conjecture. We have no evidence, either, which would point to arson; investigators can't determine the cause.'

As in the case of Mrs Reeser, the charred coffin with what was left of Mrs Satlow's corpse was sent to the Treasury Department's (FBI'S) laboratories in Washington, D.C. The report which came back to Chief Barnes told him no more than he knew already: that the cause of the fire was 'inexplicable'.

'We really need a logical explanation', Mr Barnes is reported to have told the *Oregonian,* 'to put an end to so many wild, baseless rumors that are going around the community.'

But the oddity of Mrs Satlow's posthumous burning and the many oddities of the 'cattle-rustling' which produced neither footprints nor the least sign of blood were not all the oddities which troubled the more rural areas of North America in 1973.

Commenting on the cattle-maiming in the privately circulated journal *Anomaly*,[37] the editor had this comment to make:

> Fortunately, there have not been any verifiable reports of mutilations in UFO ('Unidentified Flying Objects') flap areas, areas in which the real or supposed sightings of UFOS have caused a 'flap', but there have been several rather mysterious deaths. Some were apparently caused by lightning, but others resulted from *concussion,* distinguishable by bleeding from the nose, mouth and ears. In 1973 there was a sharp increase in which UFO witnesses received mysterious red marks on their necks, on the major nerve just below the ear. Persons suffering such marks usually have absolutely no memory of the period when they acquired it. *They simply see a strange light or object approaching their cars, then – ZAP – the next thing they know they are home in their own bed wondering if it was all just a dream* [my italics – MH].

To pursue the connection between those phenomena generally described as 'UFO sightings' and the phenomena of the Fire would take me far beyond the scope of this book. That all the phenomena of the odd are, as Fort maintained, linked in origin, may hardly be denied; it is no more than saying that all energy shares a common basic origin. But here we are concerned only with those phenomena which seem to be associated with radiant energy: with, primarily, heat above the temperature of combustion; fire; and then, in a less important degree, the aberrations of light and of non-fiery heat.

I have now reviewed the evidence for that phenomenon which the Darmstadt Assize Court declared to be 'absolutely

---

[37] Published irregularly by Specialized Research, Box 351, Murray Hill Station, New York, N.Y. 10016.

contrary to the law of nature',[38] but which yet, in its fiery vagaries, seems to have burned every type of organic substance, from papers in a locked safe to the cotton stuffing of an easy chair; from a hay-filled barn to a human being. Only, as I said earlier, do animals seem generally to have been excepted.

Is there a theory to account for this burning? I think that there is. Let us see now what that theory offers in explanation of the Fire from Heaven.

---

[38] Dr Krogman, a century later, expressed himself in precisely similar words: "It is absolutely contrary to natural law." See p 167.

13

FEEDBACK FROM A MIRROR WORLD

William Bolitho, the brilliant South African essayist who died far too young, once commented wonderingly on the fact that human beings will insist upon believing things which they know are untrue. He could have added that this impulse to believe what is known to be untrue is of considerable use to us human beings in 'accounting for' – and so accepting – many of the most fundamental phenomena characterizing the material world.

For instance, children are being taught to-day, as they have been taught for the past three centuries, that the centrifugal force 'does not apply' to objects (including Man) on the surface of our rapidly turning world because of a 'counter-force', commonly called 'gravitational attraction', which keeps loose objects attached to the world's surface – the loose objects including the molecules of its air-envelope, of course.

Now, the ability to calculate the centrifugal force – that force which causes, say, waterdrops to fly *away* from the tyre of a rapidly revolving bicycle wheel – has long been with us; the formula for the simple calculation may be found in any mathematics primer. And this formula tells us what force would be needed to counteract the centrifugal force generated by the world's spin, and thus keep any loose object on the world's surface. By the calculations – and by the calculations alone – this counteracting force would appear to be a very powerful one. Even at the equator, the centrifugal force is quite small compared with the gravitational force, and the net effect – the force which keeps us and the air and the mountains and the seas all firmly moored to the earth's surface – is just that of the gravitational force *minus* the much smaller centrifugal force. Even so, the gravitational force seems to have its conveniently overlooked anomalies, since, for all the powerful 'attraction' of the earth, human beings and animals do manage to lift their feet, walk, jump – actions hardly possible if gravitation were so very much more powerful than the centrifugal force that it cancels out. Ah yes, 'explain' those to whom the anomaly is presented: but gravitational force exactly matches centrifugal force in the particular case.

But by the time that one has seen the fallacies inherent in the taught 'facts' of centrifugal force and its counteracting force, 'gravitational attraction', one has also reached the stage at which one has learnt that, in default of a correct explanation of phenomena, *any* explanation will be given.

Yet there are so many facts obviously waiting to be discovered in the one fact that objects – conscious and otherwise – do remain on the earth's surface, being neither ejected violently into space nor crushed into the soil. Why, for instance, may a fall of twenty feet kill, while a fall from *six thousand feet* leave the faller alive and unhurt (save for some shock)?

Ah yes! – but the fall was into snow on a mountainside.

True, but if the acceleration formula is correct – acceleration at a rate of thirty-two feet per second per second, reduced by air resistance to a constant of about 120 mph, then the snow would hardly have presented a soft surface to anything – or anyone – hitting it at 120 mph.

But did the faller from 6,000 feet hit it at 120 mph? In Lincolnshire the 'gravitational constant' doesn't seem to apply; it was the harmless fall of a First World War aviator from five hundred feet on to Lincolnshire turf which first called attention to the gravitational anomalies of that strange part of England.

And then . . . what is gravitation? Perhaps the act of a young woman who toured the vaudeville theatres before the Second World War may help us on the way to answering that question? This young woman could, apparently, control her own weight – that is, she could control the so-called 'gravitational force' which was holding her down to the stage. A young woman of slim build, probably weighing no more than 125 pounds, she would cause herself to be lifted by some volunteers from the audience, and then, *by an act of will*, would make herself so heavy that even the strongest man present could not lift her an inch from the ground. This power to change one's bodily weight was one of the genuine powers of the often fraudulent medium, Eusapia Palladino; and it is faculty by no means uncommon in what used to be called 'psychic' activities.

We may ask, then, what happens when a young woman of slim build challenges a strong man to carry her – and the man finds it impossible to lift her? Who was changed? – the young woman (in growing suddenly heavier)? – or the strong man (in growing suddenly weaker)?

These are by no means the same questions: the added 'weight' of the young woman involves considerations of gravitational attraction; the diminished muscular power of the man involves a number of other considerations, all of them of a physical nature. But, above all, this phenomenon of varying weight, apparently controlled by the human will, must bring the whole problem of weight – that is to say, of gravitational attraction – into question. If, 'by taking thought', the young woman could add a good many pounds to her weight – her *apparent* weight – may it be that *all* weight is eventually reducible to a mental, rather than a physical factor? That the so-called 'gravitational force' is an attribute of the consciousness, and not of the plenum? That it is not an inherent quality of matter (or, more precisely, of mass), but bestowed on mass by the deeply subliminal consciousness of the entity which, for its own needs, wishes to be 'attracted'? In other words, we stay on the earth because we *need* to stay on the earth; that we are able to defy the enormous centrifugal force of the spinning earth, not by any 'gravitational force' of the earth, which could keep us from flying off earth's surface only at the cost of squashing us flat against its soil, but by an effort of the subconscious will.

It is when this will becomes a conscious faculty, when we learn to control it, that levitation becomes possible – as in the well-reported and more than adequately witnessed cases of Apollonius of Tyana, St John of Copertino, Daniel Dunglass Home, and so many others.

Children have a game which enables them to demonstrate how it is possible to control the weight of the body – or to moderate 'gravitational force'; whichever expression is preferred.

Some years ago, when Professor Joad was conducting an 'Answers' column for the now defunct *Weekly Dispatch*, a reader wrote to ask him how it was that five small children could lift – and with the tips of their little fingers, too! – even a heavy adult, provided that actions were synchronized, not only with each other, but with a breathing controlled (as by a musical conductor) by the boy fugleman of this 'inexplicable' exercise in coordinated effort. The reader described what happened.

The person to be lifted sits in a hard chair, back straight, chin up, hands on knees, legs together, feet flat on the ground. He must remain unmoving.

Using only the tips of their fingers – one fingertip to a child – the children touch the sitter beneath each elbow, under each knee, while the fifth child (the 'fugleman', the 'conductor') places a fingertip beneath the chin of the sitter's head.

As soon as all five fingertips are in position, the 'conductor', beating time, as it were, with his free hand, gives the breathing orders: 'Bre-e-a-athe *i-i-i-i-n;* bre-e-a-athe *ou-u-u-t;* breathe *iiiiin;* breathe *ou-u-u-t . . .*' Now comes the third order to 'breathe in', but this time the order to 'breathe out' comes with a difference. The conductor, as he says 'Breathe OUT!', raises his free hand in an upward-sweeping gesture – and all the fingertips go up too, carrying the heavy adult with them. To those who see the sitter sailing aloft at the end of their fingertips it seems as though the sitter weighs nothing. As high as the small arms can reach, the sitter rises – and then, after he has been held, in apparent weightlessness, for a moment or two, the conductor gives the order: 'Now . . . ge-e-ently . . . down.' Five small children, with their fingertips, have lifted a human being weighing, say, 150 pounds, as much as three feet.

'How is it done?' the reader asked Joad.

Professor Joad could not explain why five small boys can lift a *seated* grown man, and nor, for that matter, can I. But it should be noted that we *could* do it – and we did not, so far as I remember, invoke the 'highly practical' explanation of the 'division of weight.' Perhaps, young as we were, we could spot the fallacy inherent in that 'theory' at once. The 150 pound weight of a seated man, divided among five boys, works out at 30 pounds a boy – and which of us could lift 30 pounds with the tip of a little finger?

We were all country boys; we knew – had known from our earliest years – what a two-stone bag of potatoes weighed. *That* wasn't the sort of weight to lift with a fingertip.

And then there's Nijinsky – the great Nijinsky – whom I saw in London when my father and uncle took me to see the Russian dancer, for, as my uncle said, 'a very special reason'.

My uncle was most mysterious over our pre-theatre dinner.

'Never mind about the others', said Uncle Percy, authoritatively; 'there are hundreds just as good as they are. – they're just dancers, doing their bit. But', said Uncle, fixing me with a blue eye which had learnt its business quelling natives, 'just you concentrate on this chap Nijinsky. I shall take care to ask you afterwards', said Uncle, menacingly, 'so just you keep your eyes open and see what George and I are taking you to see'.

'But what am I to look for, Uncle?' I asked.

Uncle Percy decided to explain a little more.

'It's not exactly the *leap* I want you to watch carefully – what I want you to watch is not how he goes up, *but how he comes down.* You'll see. . .'

'Well', said Uncle afterwards, 'I see that you spotted what I meant. It's extraordinary, isn't it? The first time I saw it, I thought my eyes had been deceiving me; but I've seen it too often now to know that I wasn't mistaken that first time. But I'm glad that other people have seen it, too . . .'

'Dozens of others', said Father.

And I *had* seen it. Of course, the urgings to keep my eyes peeled, to watch out for something unusual, not to miss 'something quite extraordinary', had obviously sharpened my youthful attention. For it was not as Nijinsky leapt up that one saw the oddity – he *was so* obviously a strong man that 'superhuman' leaps hardly astonished. It *was as he came down* – 'like a gull landing', said Uncle. – that one saw the strangeness: only in dreams could one have realized the possibility of controlling one's *fall.* Up the Russian had sprung – up and high across; and then the slowing-down, to fall as lightly as a leaf or thistledown.

The tale had gone around – and the two believers had gone to see the miracle. I don't know now whether or not I had gone to see Nijinsky in a spirit of uncritical accept-

208

ance. I do know that I saw him dance, but in a fashion possible only to one who could levitate. Nijinsky, the 'madman', had learnt how to control 'gravitational attraction'.

All the biographies and biographical articles which have been written about Nijinsky or Diaghileff or, indeed, about anyone concerned with the Russian Ballet in the days of its greatest splendour, have mentioned this *apparent* ability of Nijinsky's to do what I have since learned is called 'the slow vault'. I know that I saw him *float down* – control and retard the speed of descent. But, like most other people with memories which stretch back into earliest childhood, I have sometimes doubted what I thought that I remembered that I saw. Did I really see, as both my father and my uncle said that *they saw,* Nijinsky – Uncle's words here – 'go up like a rocket; come down like thistle-fluff'?

When I came to write this book, and remembered Nijinsky, I began to make enquiries about this ability to 'control gravity'. I present my findings here.

Before the last war, a French acrobat used to tour the fairs and circuses of England. I am still awaiting his name, but several of my friends saw him perform the 'slow vault' – and another, much earlier, practitioner of this unusual art was that 'slow vaulter' who was performing at side-shows in England as far back as 1776, and who is mentioned in *The Romance of Magic,* by 'Old Man o' the Mow' – a book which has long been out of print.

But that Nijinsky's 'trick' is not unique, we may now state with confidence. 'Slow vaulting' is one of the secret arts of the peasant; part of that 'underground' corpus of knowledge which is the heritage of the countryman, and no longer that of the city-dweller. Belonging to that corpus of knowledge was the fact known to everyone who lived in the country (as it was to me) that even the most severe haemorrhage may be staunched by the application of the 'cloth' spider's-web.

It was this fact, known, as I say, to every peasant, but unknown to the physicians of the Tsar's court, which enabled the peasant Rasputin to staunch the haemorrhages of the Tsar's haemophiliac son and heir, and thus to gain ascendancy over the Imperial family. Using another bit of peasant lore, Nijinsky contributed 'something unique' to the ballet . . .

In the vast spectrum of phenomena, in which every manifestation of light and heat has been seen and recorded, one senses the action of what one may compare with a rheostat – a mechanism which enables Force X (as we may call it for the moment) to operate from its mildest, least harmful aspect, to the very totality of hurt.

If we scan the manifestations, the operations – if you prefer – of Force X, we find a pattern of this kind:

HEAT

Harmless

Called to the home of Mrs Mable Metcalf, of Alstead, New Hampshire, on 23 July 1961, firemen found that the walls were 'almost red hot'. There had been a violent electrical storm. In the Metcalf house there was no fire, smoke or short-circuiting. Simply *the non-fiery* heat of the 'red hot' walls.

Harmless to Humans

'Inferno-like blast' hit several Portuguese towns in the early morning of 6 July 1949. Lasting only about two minutes, the temperature was raised, during the 'heat blast', from a normal 100°F to 158°F. No persons hurt, but thousands of chickens and ducks died, while the drying up of the Mondego River in the intense heat killed millions of fish, as they gasped their life away in the mud.

LIGHT

Harmless   Lights of changing colour, white to amber to
                          pink to yellow, in belfry of St Joseph's R.C.
                          Church, Jersey City, New Jersey, in the spring
                          of 1954, returning after a similar manifestation
                          exactly thirty years earlier.

Harmless to Humans   Flammarion's report of a fireball at Marseilles,
                          1898. Ball entered room, approached young
                          girl seated at table, circled around her, broke
                          through paper pasted over hole in ceiling (site
                          of a former stove-pipe) and exploded violently
                          on reaching outer air. 'In like a lamb, out
                          like a lion', commented Flammarion.

HEAT

Harmful   The 'fire cyclone' of Sunday, 8 October 1871,
                          which hit Peshtigo, Wisconsin, killing over half
                          of the town's 2,000 inhabitants and destroying
                          all its buildings – about 400.

LIGHT

Harmful   Tucumcari, New Mexico, 13 December 1951:
                          'fireball' hit a 750,000-gallon water tank,
                          collapsing tank, and destroying twenty build-
                          ings and killing four persons.

Harmless	St Bernadette (of Lourdes) could hold her hands in flames for several minutes without harm to them. See also many other cases of 'human salamanders' quoted in this book.
Harmful – moderately	Mr 'H.' (James Hamilton) of Nashville University. (See page 78.)
Harmful – to person through clothing	Miss Phyllis Newcombe's dress caught fire at dance at Chelmsford; she, twenty-two, was burned to death. (See Page 103.)
Harmful to person but not to clothing	Billy Thomas Peterson, twenty-seven, found badly burned in his car at Pontiac, Michigan, 13 December 1959, after he had committed suicide with CO. (See page 84.)
Harmful to person *and* clothing	Mrs Mary Reeser, 1 July 1951, at St Petersburg, Florida. (See page 136.)
Fatal – with total destruction	Perhaps all or most of the cases of 'disappearance'.

In each of the classifications listed above there are degrees of 'mildness', degrees of 'intensity'. The death of the Countess von Görlitz involved some burning of adjacent furniture. The death of Mrs Mary Reeser consumed all the furniture in close proximity to the body, save only the metal parts. In the case of Mrs Rooney, where consumption of the body was as total as in the case of Mrs Reeser, the corpse burned its way through the floorboards. In the case of the

212

'slim widow of sixty-nine', reported by Dr Gavin Thurston, furniture was not even scorched.

We may further subdivide the classification. For instance, we might classify by the presence or absence of smoke, by the presence or absence of odour, by the presence or absence of normal or abnormal sound (noting that rarely has a cry been heard). In the case of the Countess di Bandi there was thick smoke with a foul smell; in the case of Mrs Reeser thick smoke without any detectable odour. In neither case was any outcry heard by domestics or neighbours.

When Justus von Liebig deplored the fact that no 'previous' evidence was available, he merely stated what researchers have been echoing for more than a century. Even the most careful enquiries fail to note what is – what *must* be – contributory evidence of an essential kind: a poltergeist (to give it a name) fires the papers within a locked drawer, a locked safe.

Some have opinions, some have not: we have the opinions and non-opinions (in detail) on record. But what we never have – and Father Herbert Thurston, SJ, tells of a classic case which happened in Bombay – is a *description* of the papers within the locked drawers, the locked safes.

What were these papers? Were they dangerous to the possessor? – illicit love-letters, stolen documents, writs, blackmailing demands? One feels that the fact that they had been locked away reveals them as no ordinary papers. Did their existence haunt the mind of their possessor, so that it was an anxiety-generated energy, manifesting itself as incinerating heat or flame, and not some incarnate poltergeist, which destroyed the hated papers?

There is a short passage in Colin Wilson's *The Occult: A History*, which, though not concerned with the phenomenon of poltergeist burning of hidden-away papers, contains a sentence so relevant to my theme that I should like to quote the passage here. I have italicized the most significant sentence.

> Reich's comments about sexual excitement raise a point of vital importance . . . Sexual excitement occurs in two parts: a mental part, where the imagination is important; and a physical part, where the body takes over and explodes into physical climax. We take this for granted; but it is almost unique in the realm of human experience. If I am moved by a piece of music, or by the smells of a spring morning, my 'imaginative' excitement increases, then it recedes, without any physical counterpart. This imaginative part is 'intentional': that is, a sudden noise can break my concentration and ruin the whole thing. The teenager who experiences an orgasm for the first time recognizes the astonishing nature of the occurrence. It is almost as strange as if he sprouted wings and flew. *What had before been largely an 'intentional' mental excitation has burst into the realms of the physical*. And this itself seems amazing; for after all, the body catches colds, gets hungry, feels fatigue, without asking my mind's permission.

How many other things does the body also do, without asking the human mind's permission? – rapping on walls, throwing furniture and small objects about, pinching and nipping people (and in this vitally important aspect of the poltergeist phenomenon, even the painstaking Harry Price never told us *what kind of people they seemed in relation to the presumed adolescent focus of the phenomena)*, setting dogs howling? And if within the table of poltergeist phenomena we may include such ardent expressions of its power as the burning of Mrs Williamson's dress, the burning of Mr Williamson's pants, and then the 'individual' burning of various small objects about the house, may we not include those obviously intentional (even though only subconsciously intentional) burnings of hated or feared papers in a locked drawer?

One recalls the story carried in January 1952 on the wires of the Associated press and United press, about some very odd happenings in Louisville, Kentucky, at the home of Mr Henry Thacker and his family.

Objects were defying gravity by flying and floating about in the air. Crowds milled around the house. Scientists from the University of Louisville and the University of Kentucky joined the curious onlookers.

Mrs. Thacker was quoted: 'It's just unbelievable to us. Sometimes just a few small objects move, but at other times it's like a shower of rain with things flying over your head.'

Two county officers swore they saw a pin, bottle caps, and Christmas cards mysteriously move from one room to another. Patrolmen Jack Fischer and Russell McDaniels reported they watched floating objects, including cans and knives.

In this case, as in so many others of similar type, there was a small girl – Joyce, aged eleven – and again, as in so many other cases of poltergeist phenomena supposedly triggered by the presence of an adolescent child (usually female), Joyce was an unhappy foster child, placed in the Thacker home, with her two sisters, by the Jefferson County Children's Home, of which they had been made wards. 'Her mother was dying of cancer. She was in a strange home during the holiday season.'[39]

In my opinion this case is unusual, and so proportionately important in that both the child and the unnamed 'investigating officers' were 'sensitives'. One of these investigating officers connected the presence of the eleven-year-old girl with the phenomena. Even more unusual was not so much the confession extracted from the child – these 'confessions' regularly appear in the record – as the nature

---

[39] Vincent H. Gaddis, op. cit., from whom this account is taken.

of the 'confession'. Under pressure the (usually adolescent) child, accused of having 'thrown things', 'set fire to things', and so on, 'confesses.' The value of the 'confession', which ignores the impossibility of the culprit's having been able to do the things charged, is that it enables (as Fort noticed long ago) the file to be closed, and the police to proceed to other matters.

It may be asked: But aren't police and other investigators on the right track, at any rate, when they fix the blame on an adolescent child? (It's wrong of them to *blame* the child – but aren't they on the right track in assuming some relation between child and poltergeist phenomena?)

However, in this case, Joyce's 'confession' ventured interestingly outside the 'traditional'.

It was, in the nature of things, required of little Joyce that she give a 'logical, rational' explanation of the events at the Thacker house, so that this 'explanation' could qualify as the truth through the simple fact of its being written down, by an official, in the official record.

Very well. Joyce did 'confess' – that she had thrown things about . . . the 'investigators' ignoring the fact that those 'things' had been 'thrown about' in such a manner that crowds, including members of the two neighbouring universities, had come to see them floating in the air above the house. They got their 'confession', but not, one feels, in the form in which they would have preferred it.

It wasn't exactly that Joyce, having reached the decision to give her questioners what they asked, denied the harsh impeachment of 'complicity'; it was that she refused the plenary admission of guilt. For Joyce hedged – and her half-confession sets her apart from those victims of adult pressure who 'confess' in full.

For what she said was this. 'I didn't throw *all* those things', and then, perhaps as bewildered by the odd phenomena as the witnessing scientists from the universities of Louisville and Kentucky had been, Joyce ventured her own 'explanation': 'people just imagined some of them . . .'

There is – there must be – some semantic connection, even though deep within the human consciousness, between the concept of 'liberty' and the concept of 'fire'. The old phrase, beloved of the more romantic novelists, 'she burned to be free' is expressed in words *literally* interpreting the human perception of its own basic values.

Gaddis is right when he says that 'poltergeist fires are so clearly related to the agents that it is not necessary to actually – figuratively – slap little girls into confessions'. But he might have noticed that such 'obvious' agents seem always to belong to one type – which, of course, is why they are agents and obvious agents at that. They are all 'lost' – temporarily or permanently. They are lost in the emotional horror of encountering the physical and psychic changes of adolescence without the reassurance of a compassionate warning against, and explanation of, those changes. Odd and terrifying things happen at puberty to the bodies of boys and girls, and though in recent generations it has not been the custom to explain these changes – the custom being to let the children sweat out their terror in nightmares and furtive concealments – yet the alarming signs of puberty were the more easily borne in a home in which, though not helpfully explanatory, parents were at least familiar – and usually kind.

Fourteen-year-old Jennie Bramwell was an orphan of the peculiarly 'lost' type: ill as well as adolescent, and with a painful illness whose more memorable effects act upon the consciousness. Jennie contracted meningitis after Mr and Mrs Robert Dawson, of Thorah Island, Beaverton, Ontario, had taken her from the Belleville Orphanage.

Meningitis affects the brain directly and indirectly – and its disturbing sequels include a drowsy condition resembling trance. In one of these trance-like states Jennie suddenly pointed up at the ceiling over her bed and shouted: 'Look at that!' The ceiling was on fire.

Doused with water from a bucket fetched by Mrs Dawson, this first fire was followed up by *several hundred* others. The roof flamed, the walls flamed. 'While one blaze was burning at one end of the structure, a picture on the wall at the opposite end flared up and was consumed before the eyes of witnesses.'

Almost nothing in the house escaped; fire sprang out of wallpaper, towels, logs, woodwork, furniture. At one time, fifty fires, big and small, occurred in one day. And, unlike the fires that Mr and Mrs Williamson's daughter 'caused', the fires that Jennie Bramwell started were real enough to harm human beings: Mrs Dawson, attempting to put a fire out, was severely burned.[40]

Not only were the human beings in the Dawson household hurt, but the pet cat as well. As Mrs Dawson's brother was sitting in a chair, with the cat on the floor before him, the animal suddenly started burning, and yelling as only cats know how, bolted for the open – once outside, however, it was free of flames.[41] It was noticed that blazing objects, taken outside, immediately stopped burning. What could have happened to the cat had it remained indoors, obviously no one can say, but by dashing out of the house it apparently saved its life – only its fur was singed.

---

[40] A detailed account of the extraordinary happenings in the Dawson household in 1891 is to be found in Exploring the Super-natural, by R. S. Lambert; Toronto: McClelland & Stewart Ltd, 1955.

[41] The burning cat in the Dawson household does not contradict my statement (see page 196) that I have no record of any animal's becoming a victim of spontaneous combustion. At the moment, as I distinguish between ignition which is spontaneous and that which is induced, the Dawson cat falls into the latter category.

No two cases of poltergeist activity are exactly alike. In the case of Orphan Jennie, one of the most striking (and disturbing) features was the intense *heat* noticed – as distinct from the all-prevalent fire. The fires seemed to the wretched Dawsons to be hotter than fires usually are; if a wood-panelled wall caught fire, the wood would be instantiy charred to the depth of half an inch, and the other side of the wall would be too hot to touch.

Of course it was Jennie. When they sent her back to the orphanage, the Dawson household suffered no more.

Girls, rather than boys, are the 'prime movers' in poltergeist manifestations; but boys, whose puberty is also accompanied by distressing physical changes, can upset, in their terror, the cosmic equipoise. Willie Brough, twelve, of Turlock, California, had the basilisk-glance: he could set objects on fire by merely looking at them. Accusing him of being possessed of the devil, his parents threw him out and a farmer, pitying the lad, took him in, gave him a home, and sent him to school. Willie obviously didn't like school. 'On the first day', the *San Francisco Bulletin* reported, on 14 October 1886, 'there were five fires in the school: one in the center of the ceiling, one in the teacher's desk, one in her closet, and two on the wall. *The boy discovered all,* and cried from fright. The trustees met and expelled him that same night.'

Though it is now the common belief, among students of the paranormal, that a 'poltergeist' is not a separate entity – an independent, free-acting 'rambunctious spirit' – but, as Dr Fodor so neatly expressed it, 'a bundle of . . . repressions', projected from the (usually adolescent) repressed, the pinning-down of the 'culprit' has always been rendered harder by the presence, too often, of so many candidates for 'blame'. For it is in families with several children that the liveliest (and not rarely the most malicious) poltergeist

219

activities are seen. This is especially the case where the poltergeist activities involve heat or fire.

Who, for instance, is the focus of poltergeist activity in one of the most recent poltergeist manifestations: that of the van Reenan family, with Mr and Mrs van Reenan and their *eight* children? The case, reported in *The National Enquirer* (New York) of 4 November 1975, defies the pinning-down of 'blame' on any one person.

As reported in *The National Enquirer,* the van Reenans have had to move from their home in Plettenberg Bay, South Africa, because of 'fiery persecution' which involved no fewer than one hundred fires in some three months after the first outbreak on 5 May 1975. There was hardly an object of domestic use – carpets, toys, curtains, chairs, beds – which would not suddenly burst into flame, 'putting us', said Mrs van Reenan, understandably, 'in continual terror'.

'Our two family bibles began showing scorch-marks. They got worse day by day; until one day both bibles caught fire at the same time.'

It was this 'attack' on the bibles – and not, apparently, the hundred or so other 'attacks' on more secular objects – which convinced the van Reenans that they and their house were under siege by 'something evil' – an opinion shared, if not perhaps originated, by the Reverend Jacobus van Zyl, of the African Methodist Church, witness himself to at least a dozen fires spontaneously bursting forth in the van Reenan home. The *predikant* was not the only stranger to witness the fires. 'Apparently local housing officials and policemen have also seen things suddenly smoulder and blaze, and [my italics] *a forensic examination of various items concludes that no chemicals were causing the phenomena.'*

It would be absurd to protest that a 'forensic examination' *never* reveals the cause of such 'poltergeist-fires'; however ill-directed such 'technical', such 'scientific' tests,

220

it is right and proper that they should be made, as often and as thoroughly as possible, if only to convince the doubting Thomases that 'no chemicals are causing the phenomena', and to lead them to a conclusion already reached by the Russian investigators of such phenomena: that the electroencephalograph and not the test-tube will give the better chance of finding the truth.

It is certainly no argument against large families that, as I said above, the presence of several people in a household makes the pinpointing of the 'poltergeist-focus' more difficult. Investigators had no chance of doing much about such pinpointing at Paris, Kentucky, where Charles Johnson's home became an object of 'poltergeist-attack' – by fire. In that striken house lived no fewer than *thirteen* people – is there any significance in the number? We may think that there well might be, when we read that, in three days in December 1958, the number of fires (all minor, but full of the threat of worse) which broke out 'causelessly' in the Johnson house were exactly *thirteen*. No more; no fewer. Just one apiece for each member of the family . . .

In the case of the Johnsons, there is an unusual feature in that the older persons set up a round-the-clock watch – but without, obviously, determining the cause of the fires, which concerned themselves mostly with bedding (a favourite target, as we have already seen) and the children's clothing.

There were fewer persons in the home of Mr and Mrs George Byrnes, who lived with their *fourteen-year-old* daughter, Evelyn. One senses the easy explanation in the fact that Mr and Mrs Byrnes were awakened, early one morning in February 1959, by Evelyn's screams. She had gone to sleep in the living-room, and awoke to find her bedding ablaze. It would seem that, 'cast out' into the livingroom, Evelyn's resentment was subconsciously 'energized' into fire-poltergeist activity. An interesting remark in the report is that Evelyn helped her parents to 'drag the smouldering bedding into the front yard'. Evidently here the force was not great enough to make the bedding 'blaze'. Note the place: *Miami, Florida* – and see page 112.

Recalling the connection that Charles Fort established between 'anxiety states' and the onset of the Fire, one may well be justified in seeing a connection between the Fire and the fact that the buildings that it attacks are often either under-insured or not insured at all. In the week beginning Sunday, 9 September 1945, 'about thirty' fires broke out in the house and adjacent buildings belonging to Mrs Annie Bryan, of Midland, Arkansas. The first of these approximately thirty fires – (but we would say *exactly* thirty: the number of days in September) – began in a table drawer. Curtains, clothing, wall-paper, furniture: all blazed – on the Wednesday of that disastrous week, Mrs Bryan's barn burned down. On the afternoon of the following day, nine objects 'burst into flame, apparently without cause; and again there seems to be something *numerically* significant here. Thursday, when *nine* objects burst into flames, out of what would be a total of *thirty* fires, was 13 September. But there are thirty days in September, and the first fire (in the drawer) occurred on 9 September. It is as though *something* was trying to call Mrs Bryan's attention to an important fact. Indeed, that was just what that something *was* trying to do. On 13 September – unlucky day – *nine* fires. September, the *ninth* month. Thirty days hath September. Thirty fires. To what was that *something* trying to call Mrs Bryan's attention? that she was not insured. And the nature of that *something*? Mrs Bryan's subconscious, acting out its rôle of poltergeist . . .

The 'precaution' of disconnecting the electricity supply after the outbreak of an 'inexplicable' fire serves no purpose; the fire will break out just as easily in a house which is without an electricity supply – in a house in which, as in the multiple-fire case of the Hackler farm at Odon, Indiana, in 1941, not even a domestic fire was burning.

The first fire broke out at 8 a.m., and was extinguished by the local fire department, which had no sooner returned to its station than it was hastily called back to the Hackler farm to put out another blaze – this time, not in a mattress, but in the paper put between the mattress and the bed-springs.

Even allowing for the acceptedly erratic nature of the fire – whether poltergeist-manifested or otherwise – its behaviour at the Hackler farm was distinctly unusual. As a variant on the burning of a human body within its unburnt clothing, the Hackler fire ignited the contents of a book without burning the covers. (And the book was quietly burning inside a closed drawer.)

'A calendar on a wall went up in a quick puff of smoke', ran the report of The Travelers Insurance Company of 19 April 1941. 'Another fire started in a pair of overalls on a door. A bedspread was reduced to ashes while neighbors, standing in the room, stared in amazement.'

The reaction of the Hacklers to this 'attack' was as unusual as some of the fires' tricks: after twenty-eight fires had been dealt with by the fire department, the Hacklers moved their beds out under the trees, and then, in the following week, pulled down the house and built a new one with the salvaged timber. Perhaps that was what someone in the Hackler home had been wanting to do for a long time . . .

Mrs Charles King, of Glendive, Montana, walked into her living-room at 8 a.m. on 10 January 1958, and saw a curtain burst into flame. She disconnected the electricity – and a mere half-hour later another fire broke out. The local fire department smothered the blaze, which had not done much damage. At 4:30 p.m., a workman visiting the house saw, through a window, that a wastepaper basket was burning.

Entering the house, he threw a bucket of water over the fire.

Two teenage girls were watching television in the living-room – Mrs King had reconnected the electricity supply – when they smelled smoke; a curtain was burning in a bedroom. During the next week, despite the fact that though George Smith, head of the Glendive Fire Department, had ordered the removal of 'all materials in which spontaneous combustion might possibly occur', and had ordered the disconnection of the electricity supply, five more fires broke out. Once more we have the family's sitting up at night – a useless precaution against the fire-poltergeist, as we have seen, and as the Kings found out.

In the King case, the objects of the attack were exclusively articles of cloth – and the fire showed that it could reach them wherever they were.

One of two fires in the bedroom of a granddaughter destroyed all the clothing in a portable wardrobe; the other, the contents of a closet. Another fire burned a tablecloth; another started inside a drawer.

There was nothing 'imaginary' about the fires at the King house; Mrs King's married daughter was badly burned about the hands, and her husband was overcome by smoke. No reason known to the members of the state Fire Marshal's department could be adduced to account for the outbreak – and, as suddenly and as inexplicably as they had started, the fires ceased.

Once again we have a 'high concentration of women' – at least five, of which at least two were of adolescent years. Cutting off the electricity and sitting up all night evidently have no effect on the repression-bred intentions which manifest themselves in poltergeist activity.

The presence of adopted children is almost commonplace in sudden and multiple attacks by a 'fire-poltergeist' – certainly it was so when Mr and Mrs Robert Dawson adopted Jennie Bramwell (see page 217) and it was so when Mr and Mrs Douglas MacDonald – he was a retired Salvation Army officer – still had living with them three of the many children, boys and girls, whom they, having no children of their own, had spent a lifetime adopting and raising. But note that the remaining three adopted children – Sheila and Marie, both twenty-five, and Betty, twenty-one – were all girls; and, unusually in such cases, were all 'officially' above the age of puberty.

The pattern of the fire-attack on the MacDonald house in Glace Bay, Nova Scotia, which began in an upstairs bedroom on the afternoon of 16 April 1963, followed that which has now become 'classic' – even to the fire's beginning with curtains, and including the fact that the electric current – because the fire might have been caused by a short-circuit – was cut off. The damage done was extensive, but not enough, apparently, to satisfy the ambitions of the 'poltergeist' – the second fire occurred as Mrs MacDonald was in the house talking to the adjuster from the insurance company. Fire succeeded fire – all showing the pattern of such visitations: paper igniting in boxes and drawers and closets; clothes and curtains catching fire wherever they were. The fires broke out as neighbours, drawn by curiosity, were in the house. No one could say why the fires had arrived in the first place – any more than it was ever explained why the fires as suddenly ceased. It may be of significance that the MacDonalds' house was seriously under-insured – had this fact ever been discussed in the family, with the expressed or implied explanation for the under-insuring, that the MacDonalds' need to provide for so many had made it impossible for them to afford full insurance coverage? And, if so, was this remark or implication seen as a rebuke to one or all of the three adopted daughters – and resented accordingly?

A woman figures, too – and an ill woman, at that – in one of the most extraordinary cases of Fire-*poltergeistismus* on record; the place: the new Dominion Golf and Country Club, outside Windsor, Ontario; the time: one o'clock in the morning, when a guest came shouting out of the men's washroom: 'Hey! – a piece of paper in there just caught fire for no reason at all!'

That near-hysterical cry was to mark the beginning of what, to Mr Nicholas White, who both owned and managed the club, was a fiery reign of terror. Once again – especially when the female element seemed to be dominant – the Fire concentrated its attack on cloth; but this time with most distinctive differences. As Mr White hurried off to the washroom, a waiter's cry of alarm called attention to the fact that a tablecloth had burst into flames; within a minute or two, all the table-cloths were – well, not exactly burning (though that would have been alarming enough) but covered with 'tiny dancing blue flames', like the St. Elmo's Fire. Jugs of water, strangely, doused the flames on the tablecloths – water usually has quite an opposite effect when cast on to flames of this abnormal type. But now the 'Fire-poltergeist' was busy in the kitchen: all the towels on the rack blazed up. Mr White ran into his office, to telephone the fire department. He opened a drawer to take out the directory, but, as he opened it, flames erupted. The operator got the number for the distracted club-owner.

Suddenly, Mrs White, ill as she was – she had been lying in bed – was standing, screaming, at the top of the stairs; the blue 'dancing' flames had reached the curtains in her bedroom – and were playing over the curtains and other things in seven out of the ten bedrooms. By the time that the Fire Department turned up, Mr White and his staff had extinguished no fewer than *forty-three* fires. On the following morning, the Fire Chief arrived with an insurance investigator and James S. Pooler, a reporter from the *Detroit*

226

Free Press (a paper which was later to carry the even more astonishing story of Billy Thomas Peterson, 'charred to a crisp' within his unburnt clothing). The club staff were clearing up, and one of the cleaners leaned his broom against a table some feet from where the disbelieving Fire Chief and the insurance man were hearing the unlikely account of the 'fire plague'.

'Do you mean to tell me', the investigator said incredulously to Mr White, 'that various things just burst into flames? For example: like that broom over there?' Pooler, the reporter, is a witness of what happened next. The insurance man leapt from his chair, shouting, 'put out that broom! It's on fire!' – and so, obligingly enough, the broom was.

In all such fire attacks, there is always at least one detail to distinguish it from all other attacks of a similar type. The attack on the Whites is unique in that a stranger – and an unbelieving stranger at that – had, apparently, some control himself over the 'dancing blue flames'. The focus of the poltergeist activity was almost certainly Mrs White, who was ill (and therefore, if only temporarily, unhappy). But had the insurance man – the chance witness whose unthinkingly facetious remark actually generated yet another fire, this time in the broom – some repression of his own to work off? Had he become *personally* involved in the lively poltergeist activity simply by finding himself in an active poltergeist environment?

This accidental introduction of another element into the existing pattern brings to mind a mysterious death in Walker, a suburb of Newcastle-on-Tyne, England, on 23 August 1974, and reported in the London *Daily Mirror* on the following day. Thomas Watt died in a fire at his home; but it was not the fire which had killed him. The fire had attacked him, as it were, *obliquely* – just as, we might say, the poltergeist activity generated by Mrs White's illness and

227

consequent depression had been *diverted* to take in the emotions of the insurance adjuster.

For Mr Watt was killed by the explosion of two aerosol cans, which burst from the heat of a slow fire – and, in bursting, caused a far more extensive and damaging blaze. There was no mystery about Mr Watt's death – the explosion of the aerosol cans had caused that; what was mysterious was the heat which had exploded the cans; there was no 'logical' (which, in the jargon of the 'investigators', usually means 'acceptable to the unthinking public') explanation. Here it would seem as though the Fire had struck in two stages: killing Mr Watt, not directly by heat, but by an explosion caused by heat – and then 'finishing him off' by the type of Fire usual in such cases.

There is a fact within the phenomena of poltergeist activity which ought to be noticed. It may have no significance; its connection with 'aberrant' flame may be coincidental, fortuitous. Nevertheless, I feel its presence in the record should be noted – its significance if any, may be apparent later. I refer to the incidence of cancer in several cases involving the various aspects of light/heat, from harmless luminosity to actively destructive fire.

Cancer is not a disease in itself, but is the sudden withdrawal of control of cell-growth. Of course, cancer is the cause of disease; but simply because there is not room in the fully developed human organism to accommodate the surplus growth. Between the development and growth of a human embryo and those of a cancer, there are striking analogies; the fundamental difference between the two growths – both, by every definition of the word, parasitical within the host-body – is that the embryonic growth is reproductive of the genus; the cancer reproductive only of itself, and thus sterile and, so far as is now known, useless. Yet the analogies are plainly to be seen on the physical plane; on the paraphysical, analogies may be even more marked and even more numerous.

The female cancer patient reported in *Anomalies and Curiosities of Medicine* (see page 183) was so luminous that a watch could be read by her radiant light. Joyce Thacker's mother was dying of cancer as Joyce's misery found its paraphysical expression in modifying 'gravitational force'. Billy Thomas Peterson (see page 84) committed suicide because he believed that his serious kidney trouble was cancerous – as it almost certainly was, despite his relative youth.

The oddest story involving the connection of cancer with heat/fire is that of Mr Thomas Young, a farmer, of Duke-dom, Tennessee. The story was told in *Fate* magazine, issue of February 1955, by Mr H. M. Cantrell, a Nashville, Tennessee, businessman.

Mr Cantrell called at Mr Young's farm in October 1932. The visitor noticed that the farmer had suffered severe disfigurations: 'had a badly scarred face, and part of his lower jaw was gone'. Despite these injuries, Mr Young seemed cheerful – 'utterly unaware that he looked unusual'. Mr Cantrell asked Mr Young what had caused the disfigurements.

'Well, sir, last June I was almost dead from cancer. I was so weak that I did nothing but lie in bed or on a hammock out under the trees. One day I was on the hammock when a storm came all of a sudden, and then lightning struck one of the trees. The bolt came down the hammock-wires, and I was almost killed. The shock stunned me, and even ripped the soles from my shoes. A few days later I felt a lot better. Then I noticed the cancer sores looked different. They began to heal, and, sir, I got well. It was certainly the Lord's work.'

Mr Cantrell was so impressed with this strange tale that he called on Dr J. E. Taylor, the physician who had attended the farmer. Asked by Mr Cantrell if the story were true, the physician replied:

'Without a doubt it was cancer. The old fellow was getting weaker all the time, but now he is apparently cured. I've never been able to cure a patient in such advanced stages as he had reached, so I guess we'll have to believe the lightning did it.'

There is one other connection between cancer and (if not exactly fire, then) a combustible product. In some cases of carcinoma of the stomach and bowels, methane is generated internally. Methane (CH_4), first hydrocarbon of the paraffin series, is an odourless, invisible, highly inflammable gas which, mixed with air, forms an explosive vapour.

Methane, known colloquially as fire-damp or marsh-gas, and usually the produce of decaying or fossil (e.g. coal) organic matter, has been known to become ignited when produced in the human body. Writing in *The British Medical Journal*, Dr Stephen Power, of the Royal Homoeopathic Hospital, cites such a case, though here the methane was generated in a patient suffering from a duodenal ulcer, and not from carcinoma.

The patient, a clergyman, was blowing out the altar candles after a church service when 'his breath caught fire'. Alarmed, but otherwise unhurt, he lost no time in asking medical advice, when the curing of the ulcer ended the generation of methane.

What the connection – if any – may be between cancer and the phenomena of fire and heat I cannot say, but that all possible connections with these phenomena should be noted goes, I suggest, without saying.

Our remote ancestors firmly believed that there was some intimate connection between lightning and human health; and from the primitive belief, it was not a difficult step to the derived theory that lightning was intimately connected with human morality (that is, human mental health). These beliefs were especially strong among the Greeks, the Etruscans and the Romans.

In those fragments of *Leges Regiae* which have come down to us from the days of Numa Pompilius, second King of Rome (died 672 BC), there are two laws[42] respecting deaths by lightning:

1. *Si hominem fulmen Iovis occisit, ne supra genua tollito.* ('If the Fire from Heaven kill any man, you shall not lift him above the knees.')
2. *Homo si fulmine occisus est, ei iusta nulla fieri oportet.* ('If any man be killed by lightning, it is not fitting that the customary burial rites be carried out.')

These curious laws regarding the victims of lightning caused me to renew my acquaintance with Professor O. W. Dilke, of Leeds University, who kindly referred me to some relevant passages in Sir John Sandys' *Companion to Latin Studies*, of which the following seems to me to be the most apposite:

The other part of the *disciplina (Etrusca)* was the expiation of lightning. Here again the practice was common to Italians, as indeed to Greeks, but was specially elaborated by the Etruscans. The Romans, for example, regarded all places struck by lightning as sacred, and enclosed them with a fence which, from its resemblance to a well, took the name of *puteal* or 'well-cover' (also *bidental,* from the sacrifice of a two-year-old victim offered there). But the Etruscans developed this practice by making the spot itself into a *templum;* and among other regulations of theirs may be mentioned the singular one that, if a man were struck

---

[42] Quoted here from L. R. Palmer, *The Latin Language* (Faber & Faber, London 1954). Festus (*De Verborum Significatione*) quoted No. 1 as *si hominem fulminibus occisit*: 'If any man be killed by lightning' etc. – but Scaliger, the sixteenth-century Italian philologist, suggested that the text should be amended to the more likely version given above.

by lightning, his body was disposed of by inhumation instead of being burnt.[43]

But, as Professor Dilke pointed out to me, there are two contrary indications to this:

(a)   A Persius scholiast says, *'quia fulminati supra terram positi non mandatur sepulturae'* – '. . . shall not be consigned to burial' – and

(b)   Johannes Lydus, *De Mensibus,* p. 182. Winsch, following Greek sources, says something similar. But the *nulla is* regarded as genuine, presumably meaning that such a body had to be moved without being lifted right up, and could not be given regular burial. A lightning-tomb was found at Vulci in Etruria, with a Latin inscription, and a *puteal* near the Baths of Diocletian in Rome. So evidently the correct procedure was to build a special tomb or *puteal* on the spot.

To which I should add my own observation that the very king who promulgated these laws concerning deaths by lightning stroke, Numa Pompilius (whose name shows him to have been an Etruscan), gave orders that after his death he was not to be burnt, as was the Roman custom, but buried – a form of disposal then reserved to those struck by lightning.

Still unsatisfied that the exact meaning of the prohibition 'You shall not lift him above the knees', had by no means been ascertained – the *words* were clear enough; the *significance,* hardly so – I wrote to Professor Dilke suggesting that, as the same basic sounds linked the Latin words for *femina,* 'woman', and *femur* (Old Latin, *femen),* 'thigh' – so that the word, *feminalia,* means 'coverings for the

---

[43]   Sir John Sandys: *Companion to Latin Studies,* p 168.

femina', that is, 'the thighs' – and the words for both 'knee' and 'to beget', these homophonies might, in primitive thinking, have established a semantic connection between 'thigh' and 'woman'; between 'knee' and 'procreation'?

I was delighted to receive, by return mail, a most inspiring letter from Professor Dilke, who, in the meantime, had been in touch with another leading contemporary Latinist, Professor M. J. Boyd, of the Queen's University, Belfast. I quote the relevant parts of Professor Dilke's letter to me:

> Thank you for your letter of the 25th, which has quite an intriguing story in its first paragraph. I had a brief word with Professor Boyd, who will help you as far as he can. On the question of the significance of knees, he directed me to R. B. Onians, *The Origin of European Thought* (Cambridge, 1951), Chapter 4 (pages 174-86), which is entirely devoted to knees. On page 181, note 6, Onians quotes your Passage and wonders whether the association between a *genius* (spirit within a Roman male which perished at his death) and life may explain this old taboo attributed to Numa. He quotes Apuleius, *De deo Socratis* in *De philosophia*, ed. P. Thomas (Teubner), 151-2: '. . . those Prayers by which men entreat the *genius* and the knees *(genium* or *genua)* seem to me to bear witness to the union and bond in our nature, since they comprehend under two names body and soul, of which we are a communion and a linking.'

Or, in more modern terms, we are a 'communion and a linking' of two corporate bodies, the 'physical' and the 'para-physical'; the 'earthy' and the 'etheric'.

My own ponderings on a possible semantic link between the words for 'woman' and 'thigh'; between the words for 'knee' and (in the biblical sense) 'knowing' – ponderings confirmed in Professor Dilke's and Professor Boyd's having kindly referred me to R. B. Onians – dredged up from the depths of my memory a striking passage in the publishers' advertisement for a most unusual book, that I had read some years ago: *The Psycho-analysis of Fire,* by Gaston Bachelard.[44]

> Is fire a symbol of the generative seed, and flame a sexual metaphor? Does the hearth[45] connote a human drive to intellectuality, and is heat a fundamental image of the womb?
>
> . . . Bachelard's analysis is a brilliant statement of the mind's petal-like coördination between fact and myth. Metaphors, he said, summon one another, and through poetic imagination the most diverse images may be fused. The fusion is, of course, often at the expense of scientific knowledge. But our reveries create us.

In the aspect of the Fire, perhaps our reveries also destroy us. Were the victims of 'Jove's thunderbolt' denied the customary burial rites in Greece, Etruria and Rome – and certainly in some other places – because of a primitive human belief, more 'sensed' than consciously acknowledged, that, in some inexplicable fashion, men can, and do, 'call down Fire from Heaven'? Was the inborn belief that men do somehow cause themselves to be struck by lightning – that they attract it, summon it – which made the lightning-struck, animate and inanimate, men and places, taboo?

How ancient this belief is, and how strong a hold it retained, and still retains, upon the deeper sentiments of mankind, I may illustrate by a story out of my own experience.

In the country, some two miles outside the cathedral city near which I lived as a boy, there was an artificial hill, several hundred feet high: one of those tumuli which are scattered over southern England, and which were old when

---

[44] London: Routledge & Kegan Paul, 1964. (Translated from the French, *La Psycho-analyse du Feu,* by Alan C. M. Ross.)

[45] Latin: *focus.*

the first wave of Celts arrived. It was a 'tump' – an almost regular cone, upon whose flat and broad top a ring of tall and ancient elms enclosed a grassy sward from which one could look across thirty miles of the surrounding country in any direction. It was to give that advantage, perhaps, that the hill had originally been raised maybe as much as four thousand years ago.

Around the trees, the local council had erected wooden benches; but even without the benches, the hill would have had an irresistible attraction for lovers.

One sunny August day a girl in her teens – the 'respectable', pretty daughter of a well-to-do storekeeper of the city – climbed to the top of the hill with what must have seemed to her romantic eyes the very *beau idéal* of manhood: a young Belgian officer. 'The War was on' as we used to say – and it was accounted almost a duty on the part of everyone to be rather more than ordinarily kind to the Belgians, whose 'small but gallant' country had been the first victim of the German attack.

The couple climbed the hill and sat down on one of the wooden benches under a tall elm, and, as the officer smoked three Turmac cigarettes (they counted the stubs), they gazed out over the grey, muddy, twisting river, over the ruined keep of the castle, and the pointed spire of the cathedral. They must have been talking as the clouds gathered for a summer storm, and lightning struck the elm under which they were sitting.

After the storm had passed, others climbed up to the top of the hill and found the two bodies. The Belgian officer had been killed outright; the girl was alive, but in deep shock. When they got her to the hospital they found that she had been partially paralyzed, the paralysis being more noticeable in her face.

She was no longer a pretty girl . . .

No-one would speak, save in hushed and – so it seemed to me – shocked and disapproving tones, of what had happened to the girl whom we had all known and liked, though our cook now remembered that she had called her 'flighty', and had said that 'she would come to no good'. The girl, released from hospital, crawled about the city like a leper. But if everyone was reluctant to discuss her case, no one would talk at all of what she had been doing when God struck her and the foreigner (he had dropped so far in the social esteem that he had become that by now).

Even the servants couldn't be persuaded to gossip – and from all this silence I could only assume the worst: that the girl and her foreigner had not only been struck down, but had been struck down in their wickedness.

Some years later, though not quite grown-up, but no longer a boy, I climbed with my father to the top of the hill. Greatly daring in my imminent manhood, I mentioned the girl and the Belgian officer, or, rather, I mentioned their having been struck by lightning, and I hinted that 'I knew' more of the story than had come out at the inquest.

My father was indignant at this slander on a young woman who still lived in our city, and whose twisted face reminded many of what they (as well as she) would rather have forgotten.

'Why', he said, 'what stories have you been hearing?' – and he told me that it was evident that they had been doing no more than sit under the elm, and gaze out over the city and river. 'Why, he was smoking – they counted the ends!'

I know now that it wasn't for any sexual irregularity, real or supposed, that the girl and her companion had been censured by all the city, educated and uneducated alike; it was because she and her friend had been struck by lightning. It was *that* offence which had condemned the dead

236

soldier to obloquy and the living girl to social oblivion. The year was 1916.

Dr Nandor Fodor, emphasizing the purely subjective nature of poltergeist phenomena, wrote in *The Haunted Mind:* 'The poltergeist is not a ghost. It is a bundle of projected repressions.' (Here precision has been sacrificed to epigrammatic brevity. More precisely put, his concept would have been expressed as: 'The poltergeist . . . is a bundle of perceptible phenomena *set in action* by the released energy of an over-repressed psyche.') Colin Wilson seems to me to put the thought better in his already-quoted passage: 'What had before been largely an 'intentional' mental excitation *has burst into the realm of the physical.'*

It is curious how often investigation − investigation of anything, of everything − seems to be halted at self-set limits. The perception that made the investigators of poltergeist phenomena realize long ago that such phenomena were most likely to be encountered, and so examined, in 'puberty-ridden' households did not take them the essential step further − to examine the 'repressed' emotions, and thus the *expressed* intentions of the poltergeist-creator (usually − though not always − an adolescent girl).

The events at Wild Plum School, Richardton, North Dakota, were fully and accurately reported in *Time,* issue of 24 April 1944 − a report which would have attracted even wider notice had it been published in peacetime.

A 'classic' of poltergeist phenomena, the Wild Plum School incident is yet another 'psychic' case in which the help of the FBI was enlisted − with no better results than in the case of Mrs Reeser.

The odd happenings, described by State Fire Marshal Charles Schwartz as 'simply beyond belief', began with a restless stirring of the coal in a bucket, which, a few seconds later, began to bombard the walls of the classroom, rebounding to frighten Mrs Pauline Rebel, the teacher, and her eight pupils – one of whom, Jack Steiner, was hit on the head. The coal bucket then overturned, and its contents started to flame. To the accompaniment of the children's screams, nine window-blinds began to smoulder, a dictionary to move across its stand, a bookcase to blaze up. 'It looked as if it had been set on fire with a blowtorch', said one of the investigating officials who came quickly in answer to Mrs Rebel's panic telephone call. They arrived to find the coal 'still acting up', and the chemists and the FBI moved in as the scared children and their teacher left.

The coal was 'analyzed'. Nothing was found out of the ordinary – of course. The coal bucket and the dictionary were taken away by the FBI. To give themselves something to do, the 'experts' gave Mrs Rebel and her eight pupils a 'lie-detector test'. This grotesque item from the mumbo-jumbo branch of modern technology gave the scared teacher and her pupils the all-clear. They were, declared this 'scientific' instrument, 'telling the truth'. A really scientific instrument, such as an ouija-board, would have given much more positive results.

In the case of Wild Plum School, we have not the name of the 'culprit' – possibly because all the children were of the same age, and thus, not only of similar physical development, but also – one assumes – similar in their dislike of school. Perhaps we have here a concerted 'projection of repressions', for it is clear that it was school, and not Mrs Rebel, which was the prime target for the telekinetic attack.

For observe: the 'attack' begins on the school building itself – the walls are bombarded, the window curtains set afire. Then the essentials of the disliked act of teaching: the dictionary, the books in their case. Especially the books, without which Mrs Rebel cannot teach; she must let the children escape.

The intention clearly exposed by the poltergeist manifestation is even more obvious in the already-mentioned case in which Willie Brough was the generator of the paraphysical phenomena.

Kicked out of his own home – at twelve – Willie excited the compassion of a farmer, who seemed to be providing the boy with what his harsh parents had taken away: a friendly home. Then the farmer shocks Willie by condemning him to what to the boy must have seemed little better than the unloving and unloved house out of which he had been driven: a school.

In Willie's case he seems to have divided his animosity pretty evenly between the school and the teacher who ran it.

Of the five fires which broke out on Willie's first day as a pupil, three – one in the ceiling, two on walls – were directed towards the destruction of the school itself; while the other two – one in the teacher's desk, one in her closet – struck first at the teacher's ability to teach at all, and second at her ability to walk about at all. For a 'subconscious' attack on school and teacher, Willie's subconscious seems to have planned the attack pretty well. Destroy the school building, destroy the books, and destroy the teacher's clothing. Had all this happened as planned, Willie would have been in no further danger of instruction.

The newspaper report of 1886 says, as we have seen, that 'the boy discovered all, and cried from fright. The trustees met and expelled him that same night'.

But wasn't that exactly the result for which Willie, albeit 'subconsciously', had been aiming? It is hard to resist, in considering some of these cases, the conclusion that intention is much more 'conscious' than is realized by the investigators or admitted by the 'culprit'. What the culprit *doesn't* know is *how* he or she achieves the spectacular and disturbing poltergeist effects. But that the powers which bring about these effects are as conscious and controllable

239

as the movements of a hand is a conclusion to which all honest students of the phenomena must eventually come.

Dislike of the surroundings will, it seems, generate enough force in certain people – not necessarily children, though to them the dislike-generated force appears to be more easily accessible – to enable them to 'poltergeist' a solution to their immediate problem, which is how to get out of their unsympathetic surroundings. Certainly this was the case with the pupils of Wild Plum School, with Jennie Bramwell, with Willie Brough. . .

Was it the case also with the British TV actor, Derek Boote, whose strange and alarming experience while 'going on the set' was told in the (London) *Daily Express* for 14 October 1974?

The actor was ready to begin in a Welsh-language 'space comedy' to be shot at the British Broadcasting Corporation's Cardiff studio: *Maldwyn Aldwyn*. He had put on his space-monster costume, and was awaiting the call when something caused him to cry out; his screams bringing fellow-actors and studio staff to his dressing-room. They found Mr Boote in flames – *and quite unable to explain how he had come to be on fire*.

Taken to hospital, the doctors there pronounced him 'critically ill', though, unlike many another victim of the Fire, he did survive.

And what of Mrs Booley, so 'fire-prone' that, when questioned by police about the *seven* fires which had broken out in her vicinity, she said indignantly, 'Fires seem to follow me around. But I swear on my child's head that I didn't start them.'

Mrs Booley is a cook, and, as is mentioned elsewhere in this book, 'admits to a temper'. What is far more important, I think, as an admission, is her stating to the police (who seem to have attached a different importance to the statement) that 'she had had rows with the management twenty-four hours before a blaze-up, but swears she had no hand in the fires'.

The seven fires which 'followed her around' were:

1. Berkeley Vale Hotel, Stone, Gloucestershire, August, 1971. Mrs Booley worked there as a cook. She had been given notice; the fire occurred on the night before she left.

2. St Hilda's School, Bridgewater, Somerset, November, 1971. Two pupils smelled smoke and raised the alarm. There was a fire in one of the dormitories.

3. Bath High School for Girls, Bath, Somerset, Easter, 1973. Said Mrs Booley: 'Because I'd had a few words with a housemistress the previous day, police tried to pin the fire on me.'

4. Swan Hotel, Tewkesbury, Gloucestershire, August, 1973. A car caught fire in the hotel parking lot. The police accused Mrs Booley.

5. The same, two days later. A fire broke out in a furniture storeroom; the police again questioned Mrs Booley.

6. The same, a week later. Another fire in a storeroom. Though Mrs Booley had left the Swan Hotel by this time, the police again questioned her.

7. Torbay Hotel, Sidmouth, Devon, early October 1975. On the day following her dismissal by the management, a quantity of bedding, left on a staircase, caught fire. Mrs Booley, who was 'serving out her notice', helped to put out the blaze. 'One hell of a coincidence!' the outspoken lady commented, adding that she wished that the police had charged her, so that, in court, she might have been able to establish her innocence of blame for all the fires.

One does not wish that Mrs Booley had been charged; but one does wish that she could have had the opportunity of, not demonstrating her innocence (for I do not think that she would be able to do that), but having her innocence demonstrated for her. But when coroners set their faces resolutely against admitting the phenomenon of SHC, *who* would speak up for a 'fire-prone' Mrs Booley?

One of the oddities of this odd case – and a point on which I have commented elsewhere in this book – is that Mrs Booley's unintentional fire-raising, described in the London *News of the World* for 19 October 1975, is that her circuit of dismissals included the city of Bath, and that, at Bath, *exactly at the time when Mrs Booley was being fired from the Sidmouth hotel,* a boy was being charged before the Bath Juvenile Court with the very offence with which the police had refrained from charging Mrs Booley: 'setting fire to things'.

The evidence against the boy – unnamed, because of his youth, in the *Bath & West Evening Chronicle* of 3 October 1975 – must have read somewhat strangely to the court though it must have a ring familiar enough to the reader.

According to the police, the boy entered an empty house and there 'lit a fire', which 'went out of control', so that the boy, to kill it, thrust 'it' down a hole in the floor, in the hope that it would then stop burning.

The police 'suggested that the boy panicked and called the fire department' – did he? or did he not? – and that, when the firemen arrived on the scene, found 'another fire going not far away'. As is common in such cases (of most of the cases involving children in this book), the boy 'admitted' causing both fires (to the police), but his counsel, in court, protested that this admission had been gained only 'under pressure', and the Court reprimanded the police for having begun their interrogation of the boy before the arrival of either his parents or his legal representative.

The Court found the boy not guilty, a decision which – as *The Fortean Times* cynically remarked when reviewing the case – 'leaves two unexplained fires'.

A case which bears – despite the accused's 'pleading guilty. . . to arson' – many of the by now familiar signs of spontaneous combustion and poltergeist-agency is that of David Webb, aged twenty, who was arrested on the night of 25 March 1976, for being drunk in a street in Paddington, West London.

Taken to the police station on Paddington Green, Webb was put into a cell, *after having been searched*. He was, he said later, sitting quietly in his cell about half-an-hour after he had been locked in, when flames began to rise from the mattress on which he was 'quietly' sitting. Alarmed by the inexplicable happening, he jumped out, tried to put the flames out with his coat, collapsed because of the smoke, and was dragged out of the cell by the guards. When he had recovered from the smoke, he was charged with having set fire to a mattress, the property of Her Majesty the Queen, in the lawful custody of the Right Honourable the Secretary of State for the Home Department for the time being, and by him placed in the keeping of the Commissioner of police for the Metropolis. According to *The Paddington Mercury*, issue of 26 March 1976, young Mr Webb pleaded guilty. The evidence, which is not uncommonly confused (and confusing) in such cases, was even more so when Detective-Sergeant Hawkins gave his evidence in Marylebone Police Court. The Magistrate heard that the defendant 'had a drinking problem', and was 'frequently in suicidal depressions. . . committing acts he could not later recall'. I see no reason to challenge the accuracy of this testimony, which is familiar from many other cases in which objects and people have been set on fire by spontaneous combustion. If Mr Webb could not recall what had happened when his mattress caught fire and the guards had dragged him, nearly asphyxiated, from the smoke-filled cell, his plea of guilty could well have been expected in the circumstances. ('I tell you, Sergeant, I can't *remember* . . . *Yes,* well, if you say no one else could have done it, I suppose I must have done it . . . though I tell you, I don't remember a thing . . .') In Court, the defendant, while acknowledging his 'logically probable' guilt, insisted that he could not remember having set fire to the mattress – nor did the learned Magistrate ask how, if all fire-lighting objects and combustible materials (as well as more obviously 'dangerous' objects as knives, knuckle-dusters, bicycle chains, bottles, cordage, etc.) are removed as a matter of course when the prisoner is taken into custody, with what did Mr Webb ignite his mattress? Perhaps, as must often be the reflection in such cases, the judge decided that some questions are better left unasked . . .

No charge was brought by the police against Terry Nelson, 33, of Digby Street, Scunthorpe, Lincolnshire (a notoriously Fireprone county), when he was taken to the hospital to have the serious burns on his leg treated. Mr Nelson had been asleep when *his* mattress (the property of Terry Nelson) caught fire. Apparently, it is only when mattresses blaze up 'inexplicably' in prison cells that the temporary occupant is charged with arson. I say 'inexplicably', because, after Mr Nelson had narrowly escaped death by burning on the night of 18 October 1974, the *Scunthorpe Evening Telegraph* of the following day reported that the firemen could assign not even the most improbable cause to the fire . . .

Nor, indeed, was any charge of arson made against Mr Roland Davies, of Corby, Northamptonshire, whose bed, as reported in the London *Daily Express* of 27 August 1974, caught fire 'from an unknown cause' as he was lying in it asleep. Perhaps because, as the *Daily Express* mentioned, Mr Davies was feeling 'rather poorly' in the hospital – he has since recovered – the police decided that it would be unprofitable to pursue what by now ought to be recognized as the unpursuable.

We must now ask two important questions relative to all the phenomena assembled in this book: Are the fires of the poltergeist manifestations and that of spontaneous combustion identical in nature? And, whether or not, of what type is the energy responsible for each class of phenomenon?

14

TO WISH AND TO WILL

There is a passage in the writings of the seventeenth-century philosopher Joseph Glanvil that Edgar Allan Poe rescued from undeserved oblivion and made immortal by quoting it at the head of his tale, *Ligeia:* 'And the Will therein lieth, which dieth not. Who knoweth the Mysteries of the Will, with its Vigour? For GOD is but a great Will, pervading all things by nature of its Intentness. Man doth not yield himself to the Angels, nor unto Death utterly, save only through the weakness of his feeble Will.' This book has told of many who 'yielded themselves to Death utterly', but also of many – many more, in fact – who evaded the totality of destruction, and suffered only a little, or, in some cases not at all. And so we ask ourselves: How much of intention, conscious or subconscious, was involved in these takings and in these escapes? – or, in the phrase of an older philosophy: How much of *will?*

In a recent *Sunday Times* article concerning Mr Nixon's health, the author brings forward, as though it were a theory of startling originality, the proposition that human beings may live or die as they wish; that they may will themselves to survive or will themselves to give up that struggle which, even with the healthiest, the most fortunate, of us, is still an unequal battle.

All but the 'scientifically trained' *know* that all bodily health, all mental stability, all happiness, all optimism, are matters for human choice – that is, they are controllable by, and most ordinary people think *only* by, the human will.

246

What is it, then, that this powerful human will is controlling? It is will which keeps us alive: more specifically, it is will which provides and maintains those 'optimum' conditions in which, alone, we may hope to survive. We live in a world which, though it permits us to live, does *not* provide ideal living conditions. It is often said that man has been able to survive only by having been willing to adapt himself – it is realized only by a few that this 'adaptation' is not a matter of 'ancient history', of palaeontology; of some 'adaptation', millions of years ago, by which man 'evolved' from something or other, and became 'what he is to-day'. If man is still slowly evolving, he is still rapidly adapting; for the fact is that, if he did not adapt *every second* of his earthly existence, he would soon be dead.

Man's body, to survive, must be able to operate within a relatively narrow temperature range, and this ordinary earth conditions do *not generally* provide, even in the so-called 'temperate zones'. It is man himself who must alter his ambient temperature *all the time, so* that he may maintain, in his own body, that temperature which is essential to his existence, and outside of which he will die.

We are born into a world in which we are threatened with dangerous, indeed fatal, extremes of heat and cold; to these extremes, it is said, 'our internal temperature adjusts automatically'. This is a convenient way of putting the facts, but it is rather a loose way, for all that. We do not adjust 'automatically', though we do adjust unconsciously; yet there are times when the extremes of either heat or cold are such indeed, that our temperature-controlling mechanism leaves the unconscious or subconscious, and begins to involve our conscious. These are the times when we flap our arms, rub our cold limbs, or, if heat is troubling us, retire to the shade or divest ourselves of excess clothing.

Threatened with cold, the body is protected by a number of 'adjustments' over which a (generally) subconscious

247

mental control takes charge. Heat is required to counter the cold, so that temperature-control in the brain orders the body to shiver so as to generate heat. Cold makes us hungry, because food generates heat, and when we encounter cold, the control steps up the output of the hormones which stimulate the heat-producing metabolism so that we get the utmost from our eating. Next comes the order to conserve the body's own heat, and this is helped by the closing of the pores and the contraction of the surface blood vessels, slowing down the loss of heat to the colder atmosphere. And in cases of extreme cold, the muscles are ordered to cut bodily activity down to its minimum by locking the body into the foetal position.

Another part of the brain takes care of the problems set by excessive heat. The body begins to sweat, so that evaporation of the sweat will reduce the surface temperature of the skin; the surface blood vessels dilate to increase the surface through which body heat may be lost.

Our hunger goes, so that we shall not generate unneeded heat in the process of digestion, and a self-protective lethargy inhibits bodily activity; metabolism is slowed down through a reduction of those hormones which control the thyroid gland.

Now this instantly acting, and seemingly quite automatic, control of the body's temperature is governed by a will planted so deep in the human organism that it may hold fast to its intentions, never relax its constant watch over bodily temperature, and give its orders, even through the body's falling into sleep, unconsciousness, catatonia and even imbecility and the fearful 'vegetable state'.

But sometimes, it would appear, this will, as does the human being whose mechanical activity it controls, sleeps too.

Except in special, and relatively rare, circumstances, we do not see human energy: only its results. Persons gifted

248

with a 'paraphysical' range of perception may see, not only human activities not perceptible to 'normal' senses, but they may see, too, the electrical and chemical sources of the energy which makes those activities possible.

Over the past century, science has provided us with substitute, and thus necessarily inferior, perceptors, with which we may measure and even photograph the magnetic field of a human body, may measure the electrical potential of that energy that we see revealed in the now-photo-graphable *aura*. These prosthetic instruments, enabling us to detect only a fraction of that range of paraphysical phenomena accessible to a trained 'sensitive' or an unspoilt savage, have had the effect of demonstrating to the obstin-ately materialistic that there is 'something' beyond normal perception — and to such materialists 'something' is accept-able, believable, so long as it may be measured with non-mystical instruments, as I remarked in Chapter 11.

What, then — in terms of 'measurable' force — is the energy involved in all those phenomena that have been considered in this book?

Despite the claims of the Russian public relations industry, the first serious and successful attempt to invest-igate the laws governing 'dowsing' was made in 1962 by Professor Y. Rocard, Professor of Physics at the Sorbonne in Paris. Dowsing — that is, the ability to detect, by the telekinetic twitching of a hazel twig or other simple appliance, the underground presence of water, minerals, etc. — is a faculty not controlled by the *conscious* will of the dowser.

Assuming that the dowser 'knew' (even though subcon-sciously) of the presence of, say, water, when his forked wand bent downwards 'of its own accord', Professor Rocard studied the relevant phenomena, and discovered two facts which are already recognized to be of prime significance: (1) The presence of water in the soil produces changes —

though admittedly very small – in the terrestrial magnetism; (2) The change in terrestrial magnetism, slight though it be, seems strong enough to relax the dowser's muscles, thus causing the rod or wand to dip.

One of the most interesting aspects of Rocard's objective investigation of the phenomena of dowsing was his examination of the 'biophysical effectiveness' (the Russians' jargon) of subjects who were not professional dowsers. The professor discovered what the makers of commercially produced 'pipe-locators' could have told him years before: that nine out of ten ordinary people can operate the dowsing rod successfully, or, in Rocard's more scientific phrasing, 'that the capacity for detecting weak magnetic gradients is not rare at all'. Rocard, by careful measurement, demonstrated that an average subject – dowser or non-dowser – discriminates between magnetic changes in the range 0.3 to 0.5 mOe/m, 'which would seem much too small to be detected, except that they are of the same order of magnitude found among animals by biologists'.

A more direct investigation, not so much of telekinesis (TK), as of the electrical energies involved in TK, was made in the United States by Dr Mayne R. Coe, Jr., who had already begun the study of 'paraphysical' phenomena in connection with his research into that partial or total immunity to fire described in Chapter 5.

The importance of Dr Coe's study of telekinesis is that, remembering the established connection between the botulism of the Dannemora convicts and their temporary acquisition of telekinetic powers, Coe adopted, as his working hypothesis, the theory that telekinesis might be a physical, rather than a 'psychic', phenomenon.

Dr Coe was fortunate in that, like so many of the Russian investigators of the 'biophysical effect' (dowsing, telekinesis, 'blind-sight', etc.), he was able to produce the phenomena that he wished to study. When an investigator is himself or herself aware of the reality of the phenomena through personal experience, that investigator is free of the lingering suspicion − always hampering the research worker who has to accept the evidence of phenomena on hearsay − that 'it's all fraud'. As not only Dr Coe, but most members of his family also, could move small strips of aluminium foil, pivoted on the points of needles, by passing their hands over them, he knew that a telekinetic force existed − and might be demonstrated.

From these promising beginnings, Dr Coe moved on to more ambitious stages of experiment, looking much further afield for examples of telekinetic ability, and looking for both evidence of, and explanations of, telekinesis in the deep study of unorthodox science. Dr Coe was especially attracted to, and impressed by, the kundalini, the 'secret bodily force' of the yogis. Just as Dr Coe had discovered in himself a latent but untrained power to perform simple acts of telekinesis, so now he embarked earnestly on those exercises of mind and body − yoga − which fitted the Eastern adepts for so many paraphysical abilities, and which would, Dr Coe hoped, enable him to develop his own bio-electricity.

He succeeded. He describes how, sitting one evening in an easy chair, he felt a powerful current passing downwards from his head through his entire body. 'It was unmistakably an electric current', he said afterward, 'bio-electricity generated in my muscles'. It was a current of high voltage, though of low amperage.

Now that he could generate and control this electrical force, he found that he could move a large − 7 ft 6" long by 7" broad by 5" deep − cardboard box, suspended from the ceiling by a single cord, in every required direction; sometimes, when the air in the room was dry, from as far as eight feet.

Having proved that he could project this electrical energy (generated in the muscles) – changing the electrostatic pattern by what he found to be quite instinctive movements of his hands – Dr Coe then sought, in two most important experiments, to identify this bio-electrical force.

Coe, for his first experiment, charged his body with 35,000V DC and then moved the hanging box, demonstrating the positive proof that the induced charge that his body was radiating was of the same type of electrical energy as that produced in his body by 'paraphysical' means.

For his second experiment, Dr Coe, again charging himself with 35,000V DC, took an aeroplane to find dry air at some 21,000 feet. He found that, whenever he took off his blanket or touched metal seat-handles, 'blue-white sparks flashed'. He explained that to him this was the reason for the more striking quality of telekinetic and other paraphysical phenomena in Tibet, whose mean altitude is not lower than 12, 000 feet.

This scientific demonstration of how bio-electricity may be generated in the body, and controlled by the will, seemed to Dr Coe to provide a theory of telekinetic and personal levitation. If the electrostatic force of the human body could charge objects negatively, then the negatively charged earth would repel them, and they would rise. (Similar signs repel; opposite signs attract.) The charged human body must attract objects with no charge – as in the famous case of Caroline Clare, of London, Ontario (1877), to whose body metal objects would cling – but, by induction or contact, the body may charge them with its own sign, and thus repel them. In the case of Caroline Clare, her body acted as a magnet in which it was impossible, or Caroline did not wish, to reverse the magnetic field. Objects attracted by her body stayed attracted; if she held a knife for more than a few seconds, considerable force was needed to pull the knife from her hands; she could give a powerful electrical shock to as many as twenty people, if they linked hands, and one of the twenty touched her; the steel ribs of her corsets became heavily charged by mere contact with her body. This (perhaps not so much excess as) erratically controlled electrostatic force came to her when she was seventeen; still within the age of puberty, and, one imagines, at a time which brought with it distressing 'personality changes'. She became moping and listless, a prey to melancholy; and from these morbid mental states she progressed to spastic and cataleptic conditions.

After the lapse of a year and a half the electrical charge, which had been gradually diminishing for some months, left her altogether, and with regained normality she recovered both her health and her mental balance. A report on her case was read to the Ontario Medical Association in 1879. Ten years later medical science became interested in a case which, in its general outline, recalled what may be more than a myth: Antaeus, the Libyan giant, son of Terra and Neptune, who acquired fresh strength from his mother, Terra (the Earth), every time that he touched her. Hercules overcame this giant by lifting him off the ground, and squeezing him to death in his arms.

The dowser, Frank McKinstry, of Joplin, Missouri, was a latter-day Antaeus in that both were in abnormal magnetic relationship with Mother Earth. The difference is that, whereas Antaeus received strength from that contact, McKinstry was weakened. In the case of McKinstry, Earth's magnetic pull was so powerful that, unless he kept on the move, he would be, in the old phrase, 'rooted to the spot'. He would ask a friend to lift one of his legs, at which McKinstry would be able to lift the other, and so for a few minutes he could break the magnetic lock. As the terrestrial current was broken, observers always saw a momentary flash between the earth and McKinstry's feet.

Dr Coe always maintained that he had by no means reached the limits of the electrostatic force with which specific muscular movements could charge the human body. Although he had, in his opinion, doubled or even trebled the original latent force, he gave it as his opinion that a continuation of his yoga exercises could have increased the force even more.

To what limits? Dr Coe cited other 'magnetized' persons, obviously deploying far greater electrical force; and he called attention to the peculiar abilities of 'electrical marine life', in which the ability to produce shocks, offensively or defensively, is shared by many marine genera, most of them of unrelated species. He instanced the electrical abilities of the electric eel, which, though producing shocks of relatively low voltage, 600V, lasting only 0.002 seconds, can deliver more than four hundred of these shocks a second.

Dissection of the electric eel makes it clear that it is a specialized electrical machine; half of the creature's body consisting of three sets of electricity-generating organs, as similar in design as in function to the cells of a storage battery. These organs are modifications of the lateral muscles but they are larger than normal muscle cells and contain more saline solution. This highly specialized electrical equipment enables the electric eel to give up to 500,000 maximum-intensity shocks over a period of some twenty minutes, after which a five-minute rest is sufficient to restore the eel to full shocking-power. Direct contact is not necessary for the eel when shocking its enemies or prey: the electrical field generated by the eel can shock at some distance from its body.

It was in the study of the relationship between the eel's specialized musculature and its power to shock that Dr Coe theorized that the muscles of the human body might be – or be brought to be – in relationship with an electrical force: a discovery already made, perhaps thousands of years ago, by Eastern adepts.

In the Coe theory of human electrostatic force he asks us to imagine that each muscle cell is a battery consisting of potassium chloride and sodium chloride in a saline solution, with poles of protein as acid or base. By this theory, one cubic inch of such 'cell-batteries' could generate 400,000 volts, provided that the amperage – whose heating effect is destructive of human tissue – be kept harmlessly low, the body, says Dr Coe, may take charges of up to 1,000,000V – energy sufficient to light electric lamps, as Charles Bockett, of Port Talbot, and Brian Williams, of Cardiff, did for the *Daily Mirror,* on 16 September 1952 (in the 1930s Count John Berenyi, of Budapest, Hungary, supplied the current to light neon tubes): 'explode lead discs and melt metal rods.'

In the case of the convicts' botulinus-induced telekinetic abilities, already quoted, Dr Coe believes that the convicts' muscle cells, affected by the food poisoning, generated a powerful force, electrical in nature. Dr Coe mentions that in other cases of botulinus poisoning, patients have been known to develop bioluminescence, so that they glow in the dark.

Much higher voltages are mentioned in the speculations of other scientists. As against Dr Coe's speculation that, if each cell generated 0.01V, a cubic inch of cells could generate 400,000V, Dr Andrija Puharich[46] has calculated that, 'under certain conditions', the intensity of the electrical field surrounding even one potassium ion (an *ion* is an electrically charged atom or group of atoms) can reach approximately 3.6 *million* volts per cubic centimeter.

---

[46] *Beyond Telepathy*. (Doubleday & Co, New York, 1962), chapter 11. Quoted by Gaddis, op. cit.

Observations of this potential have revealed not so much a differing *rate* of discharge as a differing *method* of discharge – a mode of discharge which varies between the 'continuous flow' (as of water flowing through a pipe and out of a tap) and the ejection of energy in 'bursts' or 'quanta'.

'Safety' in the matter of bodily concentrations of electrical energy is a simple matter of keeping the amperage at a considerably lower level than the voltage – to which, theoretically, there seems to be no limit. If, for instance, there is discharged upon an object a release of electrical energy of even very high voltage, but of low amperage, the object will not burn; that is, the radiant energy per square centimeter will not reach 70-100 calories but will travel as an ordinary brush discharge from an electrified substance. But as soon as the amperage increases, this brush discharge becomes flame – and the object catches fire. Gaddis makes the point that the objects burned 'are not free from some form of mental control . . . a woman's dress may be burned, but she herself escapes injury. This, as Dr Fodor once said, suggests a brain activity comparable to that of an electronic computing machine.'

Electrical energy at the level of 3.6 million volts per cubic centimeter would be more than sufficient to raise the temperature of the 'assailed object' – the body of Mrs Reeser, for instance – to the 3000°F stipulated by Dr Krogman as the minimum degree of heat required to convert the body to ash.

No scientist of past or present could have been more taken with the case of Frank McKinstry than would Leonardo da Vinci, in whose scientific thinking the earth was only the greater analogue of man; the analogy established and maintained by the presence, in both the greater and the smaller, of the vital heat: the 'fire in the body of the earth' and 'the hot heart in the body of man'.

It is strange that there exist no theorizings of Leonardo on the phenomenon of combustion-by-no-detectable-agent, either of the spontaneous or of the poltergeist (usually non-lethal) type. It is one of those phenomena which should have caught and held his attention; one on which he would have theorized in the full liberty of his illimitably imaginative speculation. But if he wrote of the Fire from Heaven, no surviving MSS contain the references.

But on heat as the vital principle, Leonardo has much to say. If Glanvil, two centuries after Leonardo, was to find, in God, the Great Will, Leonardo had earlier found, in the 'fire-hearted' earth, the macrocosmic analogue of the 'fire-hearted man'. Life – that is to say, the constantly active, progressive, constantly self-renewing energy which informs and motivates all living things (including, for Leonardo, the earth itself) was, for this unique genius, immanent in, and manifested only in, the vital principle of heat – so that, long before the eighteenth- and nineteenth- century physicists had, with the kinetic theory of heat, equated it with movement, Leonardo had sensed their equivalence: heat was motion, and motion was heat.

'The heat', he writes, 'which is poured into animate bodies moves the humours, the basic constituents of organic matter, which nourish them. The movement made by the humour is the conservation of itself and the vivification of the body which contains it.

'One and the same cause moves the water, one of the four humours, through its spreading veins and moves the blood in the human species.

'The heat of the fire generated within the body of the earth warms the waters which are pent up within it, in the great caverns and other hollow places; and this heat causes the waters to boil and pass into vapour, and raise themselves up . . .'

This last observation is not astonishing in one who lived in a country of intermittent volcanic activity; but of what nature were the observations and proving experiments which inspired the following note? (Leonardo is discussing the heat-resistance of the left ventricular wall of the heart.) 'And it is of such a density *that the fire can hardly burn it* . . . And this great resistance to heat nature has made in order that it should be able to resist *the great heat which is produced* in the left side of the heart by means of the arterial blood which refines itself in this ventricle.'[47]

Was this observation on a 'density so great that the fire can hardly burn it' based on earlier observations of fires, such as that in which Mrs Reeser was to perish, which *had* the power utterly to consume even the abnormally 'dense' left ventricular wall? Had Leonardo, who seems to have encountered everything, as well as to have *seen* everything, encountered and theorized upon the phenomenon of spontaneous combustion, whose most striking characteristic is not that it should have found a victim (the theory of 'Fire from Heaven' would have satisfied almost anyone but Leonardo in the fifteenth century), but that it should have consumed him so completely?

The main function of the heart, in Leonardo's opinion, was the generation of heat. It followed, then, that if the pulse rate were speeded up, the heat generated would be proportionately increased. It is in this way that Leonardo explains fever. 'Heat is generated by the movement of the heart, and this shows itself because the more rapidly the heart moves, the more the heat increases, as the pulse of the feverish patient tells us, moved by the beating of the heart.'

---

[47] My italics. All quotations from K. D. Keele, MD, FRCS, Leonardo da Vinci – *Movement of the Heart & Blood* (Harvey & Blythe Ltd, London, 1952).

Heat, thinks Leonardo, and 'the vital spirit' are one. He observed that the heart 'is essentially the central heater of the body',[48] that the butter-churn-like mechanism of the heat imparted not only movement to the blood but heat to the whole body: 'Observe how milk, when revolved in the churn during butter-making, becomes heated.'

Leonardo's observations, and the thinking based on those observations, led him inevitably, not only to the theory that heat and the 'vital spirit' were one – '. . . this heat gives life to all things, as you see that the heat of the hen gives life and birth to the chickens, and the returning sun causes all fruits to blossom . . .' – but that an excess of this heat was as dangerous as a lack.

If Leonardo did not understand everything, the gaps in his comprehension are so small that we may only stand and wonder at the mind which opened up so much which had previously been barred to, or hidden from, human knowledge. His vision of life as heat – that is, his perception that heat was motion – causes him to present his ideas on physical life in the images of flame and smoke. In the following passage[49] Leonardo sums up as it were his whole thinking on the heart in its relation to human life. It is a passage which seems to bring Leonardo's vision close indeed to the subject of this book.

> If you do not supply nourishment equal to the nourishment which has been consumed, then life fails in its vigour; and if you deprive it of that nourishment, life is totally destroyed. But if you supply as much as is destroyed daily, then life is renewed

---

[48] Keele, op. cit.

[49] Quoted from *Leonardo da Vinci on the Human Body;* C. O'Malley and I. B. de C. M. Saunders; New York: Henry Schuman, 1952.

by as much as is consumed: just as the flame of a candle is –
a light which is also continually restored with the speediest of
assistance from below by as much as is consumed above in
dying, and the brilliant light, on dying, is converted into murky
smoke.

Such a death is continuous as long as the smoke continues:
and the continuance of the smoke is equal to the nourishment
i.e. of the flame by the fuelling beeswax, and in the same instant
all the flame is dead and all regenerated simultaneously with the
motion of its nourishment. Its life also receives from it its flux
and reflux, as is shown by the flickering of its tip. The same
thing happens in the body of animals by means of the beating
of the heart . . .

Diastole, systole; dilation, contraction; flux and reflux;
enlargement and diminishment – Leonardo saw and noted
it all. What he saw too, was that the heat which is motion,
even as the motion which is heat, are forces so finely
balanced that there must be no slightest imbalance to affect
that ideal equipoise of matter and movement on which the
healthy functioning of the human body depends. In spontaneous combustion that equipoise has given place to
imbalance; heat has slipped its control; heat has, somehow,
been converted to motion which is runaway, totally destructive.

How has this imbalance occurred? Why has the controlled
heat of the human body suddenly slipped its leash?

Lily White was the name of a young woman living in
Antigua, BWI, whose odd story was told in the *New York
Times* of 25 August 1929. At home or as she was walking in
the street the clothing of this young woman was often
destroyed by fire, Miss White being unharmed at all times.
Kindly neighbours made good the deficiencies of her
mysteriously depleted wardrobe, and sometimes even of her
bedding, since the sheets would scorch beneath and above
her – though, again, without doing her injury.

260

Miss White was obviously the victim of a poltergeist attack – but who was generating the force which was burning her clothing or bedding? Herself or another person?

Whoever it was bore Miss White a specifically patterned enmity, since – whether the poltergeist manifestations emanated from Miss White or from another – the intention behind those manifestations did not include a desire to harm Miss White. Was it simply Miss White's clothing that the poltergeist disliked? In all the cases of poltergeist phenomena that we have been considering the force has been projected outward from one person to cause the discomfort of another, or of others. What if, in the case of Miss White, we have a powerful electrostatic force acting upon the subject herself? What if, in the case of Miss White, we have a link between the 'harmless' poltergeist phenomenon and the destructive (and usually fatal) spontaneous combustion phenomenon?

So that if we concede the operation of human intention in the first phenomenon – of human will – may we not equally concede human intention, human will, whether conscious or subconscious, to the second of these phenomena – the phenomenon of spontaneous combustion?

'I could have wished', people have said since speech was invented, 'I could have wished that the earth would have opened and swallowed me up' – traditional expression of a common wish for *instant and total* release from a dangerous (or merely acutely embarrassing) situation. Those who have made this remark know how free from taint of exaggeration it is: it is a *literal* expression of a wish involving the deepest of human emotions. It is what many people have wished for, and will continue to wish for: total extinction, with total oblivion – in a second of time.

Perhaps that is what those who perish in the total combustion of the Fire of Heaven have wished for. Perhaps that is what they secured for themselves.

It looks, then, as though we may, on the evidence, regard both poltergeist activity and spontaneous combustion as linked phenomena, differentiated by the object of the attack: the object, within the first set of phenomena, being external to the force-generator; within the second set, the object being the force-generator himself or herself. In both cases we may also subdivide phenomena into the intentionally and unintentionally caused.

The obstacle to our arriving at any definite conclusion in these dark matters is, as Justus von Liebig complained a century and a quarter ago, the almost total absence of *detailed* background knowledge. Father Herbert Thurston, writing learnedly on poltergeist activity, records the case of papers having burned within a locked drawer in Bombay. Of what nature were these papers? Who saw their contents, their existence, as threats to his or her peace?

In two recent cases we may tentatively put forward the theory that spontaneous combustion, self-willed, is plain suicide: Glen B. Denney, the forty-five-year-old Gretna foundry-owner (1952) and Billy Thomas Peterson, the twenty-seven-year-old General Motors welder, of Pontiac, Michigan. Both had embarked on suicide – Denney by cutting his arteries in five places; Peterson by inhaling carbon monoxide from the exhaust of the engine as he sat in his closed car.

Both succeeded in committing suicide by, respectively, knife and lethal gas; both were dead, according to the coroner's report, before the Fire overtook them; but who is to say that the mental agony which had impelled them to suicide was not capable of releasing an electrical force able to burn them up?

In other cases, where the suicidal impulse has been concealed from others' notice, testimony will be given that the deceased 'showed no evidence of depression; never mentioned a suicidal impulse' – and where the circumstances of the death appear, or are contrived to appear, accidental, no suspicion of suicide attaches to the dead. Just after the Second World War, I met, in a London bar, a naval officer whom I had not seen since before the war. I greeted him, made a few perfunctory enquiries about his health and career, asked him to have a drink, and then, because he was no intimate of mine, I joined some other friends, while he went over to speak to some people I did not know. I looked over at him once or twice, and saw that, though quiet (as was usual with him), he joined in the conversation, and 'stood his round' as bar custom ordained. He went straight from the bar to a block of flats half a mile away, took the lift to the ninth floor, and threw himself out of the window.

Commander C. hadn't looked depressed; he had looked as I had always remembered him: neat, quiet, reserved . . . Had the 'suicidal impulse' overtaken him, not *before* he had entered the bar, but *after* he had left it? It was accepted by the coroner that the dead man had decided to commit suicide before he had entered the bar for 'one last drink', and that, having said goodbye to his friends, he had gone quietly off to 'keep his appointment with death'.

All this I found an indefensible assumption. At which point of his life did Commander C. decide that life wasn't worth living, and that he had the wish, the will and the *means* to end it? Enquiries into death (as Justus von Liebig would have been the first to complain) are always full of so many irrelevancies that it is only by a miracle of accidental relevancy that the truth ever emerges. The impulse to 'end it all' may 'come in a flash' – in the case of spontaneous combustion, that colloquial phrase must be the literal expression of fact.

In spontaneous combustion, as it generally occurs, we seem to have the mirror image of the phenomenon by which Miss Lily White found herself walking naked and unharmed (but by no means unashamed) through the streets of Liberta, Antigua. In spontaneous combustion it is the *wearer* of the clothes who is burned up – the clothes generally escape harm.

By noting the 'victim' in each instance, we may distinguish between the objects of each emission of destructive force – and so between the intentions of the force-generator, in each case.

In the case of Miss Lily White the designated 'victim' was Miss White's clothing; in the case of Billy Peterson it was Billy (and not even his underpants); in the case of Mrs Rooney and Mrs Reeser both clothes and their wearers were marked down for a shocking totality of destruction.

What force destroyed them – and from where did it come?

The human body does not reach lethal temperatures because of the brain's imposition of a complex and marvellously effective system of temperature control. We saw how this control operates even from a brain so damaged that it can operate none of the conscious human activities; that, through a catatonia lasting perhaps many years (the result, usually, of a severe accident), the body is maintained at normal temperature by a brain which yet cannot make that body see, hear, smell, feel or even think.

It was observed that this constant watch over the body's temperature was maintained, though deep in the subconscious, by an act of will – and it was suggested that this will, like any other human faculty, could fail. Now we ask: Could it also fail, not by any mechanical defect, but by the command of the mind subconsciously operating that control? Unless we assume that the sympathetic nervous system, by which all the subconscious operations of our body are carried through, is a mechanical system not subject to our mental control, which makes us a sort of zombie or, better, robot, we must be able to influence the operations of that system.

It is never disputed that 'savages' – persons living in a simple economic environment – have a tight *conscious* control over their sympathetic nervous system; it is agreed that they may 'will' themselves to die, as indeed may animals.

And to Eastern adepts – particularly the Tibetans of the days before the Chinese Communist 'liberation' – is also conceded the ability to control the sympathetic nervous system. Only 'we' have lost, or never possessed, this ability. So the legend goes. And one may well ask: why have 'we' – the smugly self-satisfied, cockily complacent 'lords of creation' – been denied the gift that Tibetans and others enjoy?

The fact is that 'we' don't lack this gift – but it is a fact that we have trained ourselves to fear it to the extent that we rarely use it. Lord Adare reported to the Dialectical Society that he had been the witness of Daniel Dunglass Home's ability to manifest his control over his own sympathetic nervous system (which, of course, includes the generating of electrostatic force) in a marvellous way. Not only could this greatest paraphysical demonstrator of the nineteenth century make any part of his body luminous at will; like gas jets he could spurt tongues of fire, up to nine inches long, from his body, for all the world to see.

A fire consumes a human body, leaving ashes, soot and a few scraps of charred animal matter. To achieve this combustion outside the special circumstances in which the body was utterly consumed, we should have to use heat in the range of some 3000°F – and then we should have the problem of burning the body without touching the clothes.

There are two possibilities to consider, and I think only two, when the question of the fire's 'triggering' comes up: burning by personal intention (even though, perhaps in the majority of cases, subconscious intention) and burning through a mechanical defect in the system of temperature control. It is clear that, in the cases of Denney and Peterson, the fire followed their actual suicide – one may say that the fire *assisted* them to make that suicide certain. It is not clear in other cases that the suicidal impulse was clearly recognized by its victim: the servant girl scrubbing the floor, unaware of the fire burning between her shoulder blades, the woman crouching in a glade at Ayer, Massachusetts, whose screams of terror brought Dr T. H. Hartwell to her aid, were obviously either suicides unconscious of the fact, or unfortunate subjects of the human organism's mechanical failure. It would not be hard to suggest reasons why a late eighteenth-century 'slavey' should dream, not so much of suicide as of Nirvana – to such an extent that the Fire came 'because it was called'.

And what might be happening when control breaks down? What energies are then released? We have seen their effects in a totality of combustion – and we have guessed at both their nature and their force. From where do they come?

As was remarked in Chapter 5, man has two bodies, the physical and the paraphysical (or 'etheric' – the label hardly matters; the identification does). But it would be foolish to consider that these two bodies, the physical and the etheric, lead distinct existences. They do not. They are different – perhaps 'differently organized' is a better way of expressing the fact – but complementary. How they are complementary it will be one of the triumphs of twenty-first-century parapsychology and paraphysiology to discover.

What seems to be apparent, from the very limited amount of evidence now available to us, is that these two human bodies, these composite organisms linked by a natural paraphysical twinning, exist on two different energy levels, which seems inevitably to imply different rates in the dimension of time.

Let us suppose that, normally, the control of the human physical body – let us call this Body I – is so far beyond the meddling of even the human subconscious because this control has both Body I and Body II (the 'paraphysical' body) in its care. We have seen, in Chapter 5, when the researches of the Kirlians were examined, that the organization of Body II appears to involve chemical and electrical energy on very high levels.

Now let us seek a simple analogy in the boiler of a steam engine fired with, say, coal. Suppose that the fireman, sticking strictly to his duty, continues to shovel coal into the firebox, but suppose, also, that the steam in the boiler, raised by heat to a dangerous pressure, cannot escape because the engineer has permitted the steam-valve to become inoperative.

Somehow the energy within the boiler, the *surplus* energy, that is to say, must find its release. It does find it. If not through the stopped-up steam-valve, then through the walls of the boiler tubes. But escape it does.

Is it like this? Is one of the functions, perhaps even the principal function, of the physical body to feed energy to the paraphysical body, there to be converted into energy of a different type (because intended for a different set of purposes), possibly in different time? Is Body I merely the 'firebox' for energizing the 'boiler' of Body II?

There is man-made energy and there is, and always has been, 'accidental' energy; and the time has now come when man-made energy seems about to approach, in both type and force, even the most powerful of 'accidental' energy releases and transformations.

At 7:17 on the morning of 30 June 1908 a 'fireball' was seen to pass over the Siberian steppes, in a south-north direction, to strike in a forest in the Tunguska, some 550 miles north-east of Irkutsk. Passengers on the Trans-Siberian railway who were looking from the windows clearly saw the 'fireball', and all on the train felt the appalling concussion as it hit the forest. The noise of the explosion, heard within a radius of over 600 miles, caused the needle of the seismograph at Irkutsk to quiver for more than an hour. Trees were stripped to a distance of nearly forty miles from the fireball's impact. The explosion was registered on the paper of the majority of the world's seismographs as a tremor of magnitude. Most seismologists interpreted the recordings of their instruments as the indication that an earthquake of violent type had taken place. The Russian Government told the world that an unusually large meteorite had hit the Siberian Tunguska, and to the world the fireball remained a 'meteorite' for decades to come. But several scientific expeditions, each equipped with progressively more refined and sensitive apparatus, have conclusively proved that, whatever the fireball was, it was not a meteorite.

No one yet knows what it was. There are theories, of course. Some say that exiled Russian scientists constructed an atom bomb, sent it aloft by balloon, and caused it to detonate over the Tunguska, in which case, their 'primitive' bomb was of an incredibly high order of magnitude. Others say that a 'fragment' of anti-matter reached earth, and, on encountering matter, 'naturally' exploded. Whatever was the nature of the fireball, its radiant energy was such that it set fire to trees eleven miles from the explosion's focus, and had a flash so bright that secondary shadows were cast at a distance of 124 miles.

Calculations of the energy involved in the explosion indicate a force of 2.8×10^{23} ergs – equivalent to the energy released by nearly thirty 10-megaton atom bombs.

This was explosion on the 'nuclear' scale – and with all the discernible effects of high-level radiation on dead and surviving humans, animals and plants. One may say that the energy responsible for spontaneous combustion isn't of a 'nuclear' type – but how may one say that, when the first person to have his remains examined by a Geiger-Müller counter was Billy Peterson, because of the 'nuclear' way in which his unburnt hair was poking through his charred-to-a-crisp skin?

What would the charred bodies of Countess di Bandi or Mrs Rooney have shown had the Geiger-Müller counter been switched on in *their* presence?

We don't know *what* the 'fireball' of 1908 was, save that it was of unprecedented force and power.

And why do I call it a 'fireball'? – linking it, in type, if not in power, with that which was described by Camille Flammarion (which went up a stovepipe and exploded outside the house) or that which destroyed the barn of retired Boston banker Robert Bowen, at Sudbury, Massachusetts, on 28 April 1965? Well, we have seen that, compared with other manifestations of radiant energy – lightning, poltergeist activity, spontaneous combustion, and so on – the 'fireball' is relatively harmless to human beings. Or perhaps it would be more precise to say that the 'fireball' is rarely lethal.

And how much damage, that is to say, compared with its terrifying potential, did the so-called meteorite, the actual 'fireball', of the Tunguska do? It had enough energy to have flattened fifty Dresdens or Hiroshimas; yet it fell (must we say 'by chance'?) on what was then one of the least populated parts of the world – 'undeveloped' land, over which a relatively few nomads grazed their herds of reindeer and ponies. And while there were some deaths – a handful of nomads, but whole herds of reindeer – the deaths were nothing compared with the power which caused them. So remote, so 'private', was this release of titanic energies that for decades the world did not even know what had hit it.

Indeed, when we come to consider its energy, and relate it, *proportionally,* to the world itself, was it so powerful? Was it, *in proportion to the world,* any more powerful than was the force which consumed Mrs Reeser, proportionally to her 175 lb?

Leonardo would have seen at once that this external heat, striking the macrocosm, earth, was small, compared with the heat which so often struck the microcosm, Man.

Is it like this? When the control breaks down, a control which must superintend and ensure the perfect functioning of the two linked and interdependent bodies – not merely of one – is the sudden excess energy of Body II blown off through Body I, in a sudden, titanic burst of force which leaves Body I nothing more than 'a rag, a bone and a hank of hair' . . . and often not even that?

15

FACTS AND THEORIES . . .
A SUMMING UP

We are now reaching the end of that wide detailed survey of the mysterious Fire which behaves – for fire – in so seemingly capricious a manner: burning people, but not their clothes; burning clothes, but leaving the wearers unharmed. We have seen pretty much everything of how the Fire acts – and on what it acts. We have seen enough to know why our ancestors called it The Fire from Heaven – when they did not call it (perhaps with more reason) The Fire from Hell. But, at the end of this close look at the Fire, may we say that we are any nearer to understanding its nature; any nearer to the ability to state, not only what it does, *but what it is?*

Cautiously – very cautiously indeed – I would venture to suggest that we have by now accumulated a sufficient quantity of fact on which to base at least one plausible theory, and, in my opinion, more than one, even though a single master theory is all that truth requires or, in fact, is able to handle.

Let us see where the *facts, as we have surveyed them*, leave us.

Fact No. 1 – the master fact – is that the phenomenon of SHC is as undeniable as the testimony of responsible witnesses can make it. But no more. And we must not forget that the testimony of responsible witnesses is not always enough to earn for any reported occurrence the acceptance, by the world, of that occurrence as 'fact'. If the testimony of responsible witnesses were always accepted, then such phenomena as 'flying saucers', levitation, telekinesis, teleportation and some other 'fantasies' would be accepted by the mass of mankind with no more argument than it accepts the 'fact' that the sun rises in the East and sets in the West – though Velikovsky is not the only one to have collected impressive evidence that, even in historical times, there was a period when the sun reversed its direction *and rose in the West.*

Fact No. 2 – and a fact almost as important as Fact No. 1 – is that poltergeist activity and the Fire are connected; or, to express this most important fact in a more precise way, poltergeist activity may – and, as we have seen, quite often does – include fire-making among those actions that it can control and use. To refresh the reader's memory: poltergeist activity is the expression, in physical action, of subconscious, normally suppressed, wishes whose 'containing' has proved too much for the wisher – a time comes when they have, as it were, to burst out, making themselves apparent in all those activities which are normally associated with the non-existent being that ancient belief called 'the poltergeist', the 'restless spirit'. We know now that the force which activates the 'poltergeist' originates in, and is supplied by, a human being – the so-called 'focus' of poltergeist activity, and that, thus, this human being (usually, though not exclusively, a young person – more often female than male) can levitate and teleport objects, though *how* we cannot as yet say. One of the most fortunate facts in the history of research into the poltergeist was the emergence of a 'poltergeist-focus' – a boy – intelligent and educated enough to be able to study his own powers. In *The Link*,[50] the world, for the first time, had the advantage of reading an account of the most vigorous poltergeist activity from the subjective point-of-view

---

[50] Now available as a Corgi Books paperback, published 1975.

– from the point-of-view of the intelligent, completely self-aware 'focus'.

The author of *The Link*, Mr Matthew Manning, is still, at the time of writing, under forty; his poltergeist-life, to coin a phrase, began when he was between eleven and twelve, and involves not only the transfer of 'apports' – books, vases of flowers, candlesticks, and so on – from one room to another, *through solid walls*, but, if we may accept the impressive evidence of automatic writing and drawing, communications from those people whom it is the custom to call 'dead': Dürer, Blake, Goya, Beardsley and many others.

The poltergeist manifestations originating in Mr Manning were as frequent at his school as at home; and though he may describe, in calm and detailed prose, his actions and reactions throughout the time from which he first began to be the focus of a poltergeist, he cannot account for the power that he subconsciously deploys to transport a candlestick or book from one room to another. One might ask then: What has Mr Manning, even though writing from the standpoint of the 'focus', to tell us that we did not know before? – that is to say, if he cannot tell us how he manages these unusual happenings?

It is in the revelation of Mr Manning's character that his book has much to tell us; for in comparing his character with his poltergeist actions, we see why – and how – other characters, less pleasant, less balanced and less placid than that of Mr Manning, might well be associated with poltergeist phenomena of a different and far more sinister order.

Willie Brough, as we have seen, may be said to have 'burned himself out' of the school that he hated; and at Wild Plum School the whole class seems to have been involved in using poltergeist-fire to rid themselves of lessons (or a teacher) repugnant to the children.

But, although his headmaster asked for his removal on no fewer than three occasions, Mr Manning disliked neither the school nor its headmaster. He is not an only child; he gets on well with his parents; though no extrovert, he is not a solitary. He was not bullied at school – a fact that I find almost incredible, seeing that he was different from the other boys in a marked degree, and only the most minor differences, in the usual way, are made the excuse for bullying. Mr Manning escaped all this – and so it is (or so it seems to me) that his placid, happy nature is reflected in the fact that none of the poltergeist activities associated with him have that element of the malicious which appears to inform so much of poltergeist activity. But one wonders what would have happened had Mr Manning been born with a cruel streak – or had hated either school or headmaster. Would Oakham School have burned down? – or merely been rendered uninhabitable by fires of the type which broke out in Wild Plum School . . .?

Yet, when I said a little while back that the poltergeist activities associated with Mr Manning, and splendidly recorded in *The Link,* did not include any appearance of the Fire, or, indeed, anything of a malicious or harmful character, I was stating that the power – the so-called poltergeist power – generated and controlled by this young man (albeit subconsciously) was not harmful to others. It should be noted here that the element of the harmful-malicious, almost always present in poltergeist activities, is *not* missing from the Manning record, but here assumes a curiously reversed form, in which the subject is not only the principal, but indeed the only, victim of malicious intent. Mr Manning's subconscious is unwilling to hurt others; it is not unwilling to hurt Mr Manning, though never – so far – in any dangerous degree.

One evening as I picked up a cup of coffee I received a startling electric shock from the handle. I was taken so much by surprise that I knocked the cup over and spilled its contents. Perhaps I would have thought no more of it, but for the fact that the following day I had the same experience, on placing my hand on a door handle.

This phenomenon continued at odd and unexpected times for a period of nearly a year. It seemed that almost any object had the ability to give me a small electric shock, whether it was metal or another material. I remember receiving such electric shocks from books, windows and even while holding strawberries. On one occasion I put my hand in a large open refrigerator in a shop to lift out a can of soft drink. To the surprise of the watching shopkeeper I dropped it almost immediately I had picked it up, as it gave me such a shock.

I never found any obvious explanation for the electric shocks that I received from assorted objects.

It is a pity that this 'self-hurting' aspect of Mr Manning's *Poltergeistismus* was not investigated with the same care as that with which other aspects were carefully and scientifically examined, for the phenomenon of auto-shocking has been studied, particularly in Russia, and with such 'electric' shocks, the energy-levels may be measured. It is to be hoped that, should the phenomenon of auto-shocking recur in Mr Manning's experience, he will submit himself for examination to some eminent parapsychologist of, say, Professor Genady Sergeyev's status.

A far more curious example of this 'energizing' of nearby objects is the case of the 'whistling egg'.

I had on my desk an alabaster stone egg. The egg was five feet away from the tape recorder *(which, from a blank tape had sounded with the rumble of distant gunfire, the muttering of crowds and the music of Nazi marching songs)* and about eight feet from the microphone.

For no obvious reason this egg, which was on the desk, about eighteen inches from where I was sitting, began to emit a whistling sound which started off as a low 'buzzing' and mounted to a *noise comparable to an electronic feedback.* [My italics – MH] Still the tape recorder *was* switched on.

I put out my hand to pick up the egg, and as soon as I got within an inch of it, the noise intensified to a level that hurt our ears. One of my friends stretched out to touch the egg and the noise stopped. He picked the egg up, and, he said, it was quite warm; it should not have been warm as it was solid stone, and had not been handled before.

He handed the egg to another friend and it again began to whine. When I took it, the noise rose to its former level until I put it back on the desk, where it just continued emitting a low hum.

Whoever touched the egg caused it to produce a different noise which was sometimes a high-pitched whistling sound and sometimes a low humming. *The noise increased most when I touched it.* [My italics – MH]

This . . . continued for just over fifteen minutes. We had started the tape recorder when this whistling started and recorded everything while it went on. When we played it back the noises and our voices were clearly recorded.

That this phenomenon had an objective as well as a subjective character is proved by the fact that the noises emitted by the egg – an object, be it noted, which appears in abnormal form in several of H. G. Wells's fantasies – were recorded on the magnetic tape. Note also that, though the noise was *hurtful* when Mr Manning touched the egg, the noise either stopped or did not rise to 'hurtful' levels when touched by any of his friends. And note, too, that Mr

Manning's comparing the noise to that of 'an electronic feedback' seems to me but the literal statement of fact: he was hearing an 'electronic feed-back' – the source of the electrical energy being himself.

But the most significant thing that Mr Manning has to say in his important book is this:

Approaching me one evening . . . was another boy whom I did not know. I was shocked . . . by seeing to my surprise that the boy was encircled in a pear-shaped aura of colours that looked very much like coloured heatwaves . . .

I discovered that I could switch myself 'on' or 'off' like an electric light switch. If I switched myself 'on', as though I were going to write *(i.e. automatically)* but without actually doing so, I could see auras surrounding people. I cannot describe in words how I achieve this switching on and off.

Mr Manning then goes on to describe the different colours of the aura seen by him, and to explain how he has come to interpret this 'colour-coding': 'By finding out what colours surrounded people that I knew well, I found that each colour was representative of a particular facet of their character. I distinguished six basic colours . . . Around those who are ill or have a major ailment [the coloured aura] . . . is often weak, and I have noticed that a darker coloured shadow surrounds any area of the person's body that is diseased or affected by illness. If, for example, someone has a tumor, it will darken the aura around the area in which it is sited.'

Here, for the first time, we have a 'psychic' of unusually varied gifts, not only with the power to observe and record his own paranormal gifts and experiences, but who has been fortunate enough to have found himself in an environment where he has not been forced to conceal his abnormality. We may be grateful to Mr Manning's family and school that his gifts have been permitted to develop in what is clearly a genuinely sympathetic attitude.

Now what may we learn from this 'psychic' of such varied and impressive paranormal gifts? A great deal, I suggest.

One aspect of his power is, to my mind, the most significant of all his gifts: the something more than a mere beginning of the ability *to direct and control* his power; and, in reading his book, I had the impression that Mr Manning has a greater control over his powers than he yet appreciates.

On 25 June 1974, Professor Douglas Dean took several Kirlian photographs of Mr Manning's fingertips, and said afterwards: 'The results we have received are absolutely unique! I have never seen anything like this before.' What was unique in the taking of these photographs was that the pictures fall into three distinct groups, each group being 'selected' by the subject: the first group showing Mr Manning's normal radiation; the second (showing greatly increased radiation) after he had intentionally 'switched on'; the third when, after having 'switched on', he was asked to (and did) 'focus the energy to pinpoint'.

Mr Manning, remarking on the 'uncanny ability of the poltergeist to carry out almost anything that anyone happened to suggest, including the turning-on of lights and taps', seems to have avoided (or not perceived) the inevitable conclusion that he himself is 'poltergeistly conditioned' to carry out the suggestions by paranormal means. I find also that his remarking on the poltergeist's 'affinity for electrical appliances' is an observation of particular significance, though its full significance seems to have gone unnoticed by him. The fact is that poltergeist activity is nothing more (but, note, nothing less!) than the translation into visible, physical manifestation – here as always – of the paranormal energy of Mr Manning himself.

This is true, of course, of all poltergeist activities.

I have considered the case of Mr Manning at some length in this final, summing-up chapter because, as I said in a letter to the world's foremost student and historian of the Unexplained, my friend Jacques Bergier, Mr Manning is, as it were, a one-man laboratory of the paranormal, in which every aspect – or nearly every aspect – of the paranormal was available for study, *with the willing, close, self-observant and highly intelligent cooperation of the subject.* I should have added that this unique laboratory of the paranormal was an experimental one . . .

I said above that we had not encountered the Fire in the case of Mr Manning's poltergeist activities. This was said in a strictly literal way, for the heating of the alabaster egg makes it evident beyond doubt that Mr Manning's paranormal powers do command the raising of temperature in material objects. Had Mr Manning been malicious or unhappy, or even disliked his school or the house that his father had taken for his family, then we might well have had the Fire appearing in Mr Manning's paranormal record.

There is, in my opinion, a highly significant remark in Mr Manning's account of the whistling egg – a remark all the more significant in that Mr Manning does not seem to realize its significance.

One of my friends stretched out to touch the egg . . . He picked the egg up, and, he said, it was quite warm; it should not have been warm as it was solid stone, and had not been handled before . . .

That is to say: it had not been handled before *by Mr Manning.* It was *his* egg. A friend had 'stretched out to touch the egg . . .' That 'the friend' had 'stretched out' to touch the egg seems to imply that the friend had made an unusual effort to touch the egg; had leaned across the table; had (perhaps) pushed Mr Manning aside; had made some

279

inconvenient or even irritating movements . . . And Mr Manning's placid nature had warmed up (I use this expression now literally!) into a mild temper. For, after all, it was *Mr, Manning's* egg . . . and no one else had the right to touch it. The 'warming-up' was – if the friend (and Mr Manning?) had only realized it – no more, though no less, than the warning growl of the dog or cat: 'Take your hands off me! – or there's decidedly worse to come!'

So, not only from a study of Mr Manning's unusual gifts, but from a general survey of all that we have learned of poltergeists and SHC, we may, I think, come to the following conclusions, in the setting forth of which 1 shall make use of a new word, coined by me for future use in the context of SHC and associated phenomena: *ekenergy* – 'the energy which is outside of us, but which may be used when we know the right words.'

We may say with confidence that we have learnt this:

1. SHC, fatal or non-fatal, belongs to the extensive range of poltergeist phenomena.

2. Physical movement of every sort, ascribed to 'a poltergeist', is movement generated by the ekenergy controlled by the conscious or subconscious will of a human being.

3. This 'ekenergy' is that part of the cosmic force which is not normally used by us because it is 'hidden' by being in balance with those other aspects of the cosmic force which are apparent to us.

4. Cosmic force is balanced between the physical (corporeal) body and the 'parallel' body, known to the Ancients, and now 'authorized' by the proof implicit in the Kirlian photographs.

5. SHC and other forms of ekenergetic phenomena are 'powered' by the energy released when the balance between 'normal' and 'held in reserve' energy is disturbed by the *will* – conscious or

subconscious – of the 'poltergeist-master'. In this connection, it is of great interest to observe that Mr Manning's 'poltergeist activities' included the appearance of carefully arranged 'balancing acts' – on one occasion a broom was balanced so precisely across the horizontal handrail of the staircase that 'only a touch' was necessary to put it out of balance. Mr Manning was so impressed by the 'poltergeist tricks' involving balance and order (e.g. the precise laying-out of plates and cutlery on a table) that he gave this 'orderliness' a separate classification. Had he reasoned the matter further, he must have arrived at the conclusion that his subconscious was 'acting out' the basic cosmic truth of the Eternal Equipoise, that – though in only a trivial degree – the paranormal powers of such as Mr Manning are able to disturb.

6. SHC and poltergeist phenomena imply action and reaction between the 'force generator' and the 'victim' – the 'force' being the result of deliberate *intention,* even though the intention may not be consciously known to the human being generating the force – though here it should be noted that many children (especially girls) seem to have appreciated to the full the connection between their own emotions and the poltergeist phenomena that they have the power to initiate.

7. SHC can be both outward-acting and inward-acting: a Willie Brough or a Jennie Bramwell may generate and direct a fire-raising force to burn the school or foster-parents' home detestable to them; but Charles Fort was the first to note and record the fact that fires of strange origin, some fatal, some not, seemed frequently to happen to or in the proximity of 'no-hopers'. In the mysterious fire death of Mr William Seale, 65, of Brighton, on the night of 15/16 September 1976, a neighbour, Miss Christine Harmer, remarked: 'Mr Seale had chronic bronchitis and bad legs. He could not get around by himself. He used to stay in his room all day. I think he got fed up not being able to go out . . . He was a lonely man . . .' Mrs Ellen Steers, 79 (see Page 110), who died, again in the night, on 29 August 1974, had buried her husband the day before. She had 'a

281

history of hypochondria'. The victims of SHC are all – rich or poor – seen to be dropouts to a greater or a lesser degree; lonely, neglected – or thinking themselves so; suffering from a sense of injury, whether justified or not. But the victims of *self-induced* SHC – the U.S. term, 'auto-oxidation', has much to recommend it – need not be old to feel lonely and neglected; children feel the sense of deprivation in what to them is literally a frightening degree. Little Peter Seaton (see page 10) had been put to bed, by *himself,* in a room of which the door had been closed upon him. Who may say what terrors of loneliness did not come to agonize the child before he sought – and found – the final and irrevocable release in SHC?

8. That the force generated to initiate the Fire can come from either the non-sentient or the inanimate seems highly doubtful. All the evidence so far collected appears to point conclusively to the human origin of the Fire – though that does not necessarily mean that all the ekenergy is derived from either Body I or Body II of the 'force-generator', though it seems probable, at least to the writer, that the 'force-generator' provides both the initiation (by his or her will) and the directing of the force manifesting itself as the Fire.

9. Against the contention that the 'paranormal' *selectivity* of the Fire – burning this, and leaving that unscorched – indicates its origin in human intention will, perhaps, be advanced by the fact that explosions often exhibit a seeming selectivity – the removal, by bomb- or shell-burst, of a soldier's clothing or merely his boots (the boots being found afterwards with the laces still tied), without doing more to the victim than shocking him, is commonplace in warfare. How this happens we do not yet know. But is this selectivity in explosions comparable with the selectivity *shewn* in the incidence of the Fire? Obviously not. The Fire selects its victim – the human being inside clothing with which the Fire has no concern – while the bomb or shell selects, when it does select, the very objects with which the bomb-aimer or gun-layer is *not* concerned: the soldier's boots – while the intended victim of bomb or shell escapes with no

282

more than shock. How, as I say, the selectivity of explosive substances may be accounted for, we do not know; but it has nothing to do with that operation of the consciously or subconsciously exercised human will which is behind the selectivity of the Fire.

Shall we ever understand the true nature of the Fire from Heaven? Indeed, yes; the Fire is but one of the hundreds – even thousands – of mysteries that Man has encountered on his slow and often faltering climb upwards. Some of the most 'obvious' facts of physiology – the property now of children as a part of their basic general knowledge – were mysteries, less than a century ago, apparently no less insoluble than the mystery of the Fire is to us to-day.

And the Fire, I am convinced, will not remain among the mysteries of the Unexplained for very much longer – indeed, I feel that *all* the clues to the explanation of this ancient mystery have been set out by me above, for all that I am not equipped, by scientific training, to interpret those clues.

However, what seems to me apparent is that the nature *and purpose* of the Fire from Heaven will be discovered through what is already accepted as a fact, especially by those scientists working directly on the various problems of the paranormal: that the Fire is merely one manifestation of that wide range of physico-psychic activity that we classify under the general heading of 'the unexplained' or 'the paranormal'.

Already, through the scientific investigation, under strictly controlled laboratory conditions, of the parallel body, of dowsing, levitation, 'shape-changing', telekinesis, and all the rest of what used to be (rather contemptuously) designated 'old wives' tales' or 'the stock-in-trade of the occult', the pattern of the unexplained is beginning to emerge – and when that pattern is fully revealed, its laws understood and the control of its dynamics assured, then the Fire from

Heaven will join malaria, diabetes, syphilis and a hundred other ills which were once inexplicable, but which are mysterious no longer.

Summing-up and Epilogue

In the little more than a decade since the first edition of this, the pioneer *full* study of the phenomenon of SHC, a fundamental change in the attitude of Press and (as a corollary) Public to this still unexplained phenomenon is now clearly evident. It is a change for which I like to think that I am greatly, even if not wholly, responsible.

The total 'unacceptability' of any book which professed to list and examine the incidence of an 'impossible' phenomenon (to be grouped among the 'imaginary' phenomena of ghosts, fetches, dowsing, telepathy, and so on) – that is, some thirteen years ago; no more – is evident from the many years and the large number of publishers involved in my placing of the book. At that time, and for some years after, SHC, in the general opinion of the doctors, the pathologists, the medical-officers and – above all – the coroners, was a contemptible non-fact; credible only to the most credulous of cranks. Up to that time, only one coroner, to my knowledge had had the plain commonsense (not to say great courage) to attribute a death on which he was 'sitting' to an incidence of spontaneous human combustion. This was the Dublin City Coroner, Dr P. J. Bofin, examining the death of Mrs Margaret Hogan, an 89-year-old widow. That was in April, 1970, and though the strange facts of Mrs Hogan's death, whom 'an intensive, devastating fire' reduced to 'a mere pile of ashes' was widely reported in the Irish Press, as was the finding of the Coroner, no other coroner, Irish or British, had the honesty and realism to follow Dr Bofin's example, and record a verdict of 'death from spontaneous human combustion'. Sixteen years of

284

'scientific rejection of the evidence followed Dr Bofin's unique finding, until, in 1986, a British coroner, unwilling to listen longer to the denials of SHC's factuality, pronounced, though hesitantly, for a verdict of SHC.

What changed, almost overnight, the attitude of the Press (taking the Public's opinion with it) was the scandalous, blatant cover-up of 'the authorities' in connection with the death of Miss Jacqueline Fitzsimon, a seventeen-year-old cookery student, who burst into flames as she was walking away from the school's instructional kitchen. The evidence was clear enough: the girl had attended a morning cookery class at Halton College of Further Education, at Widnes, Cheshire, on 28th January, 1985. She was coming downstairs – well away from the kitchen – and talking to some fellow-students, when she suddenly became 'a human torch'. Her friends beat out the flames, and she was taken off to Whiston Hospital outside Liverpool, where she died in the early hours of 12th February, after fifteen days of 'intensive care'.

In the case of Jacqueline Fitzsimon, the almost inevitable rejection of SHC as a possible cause of the girl's death was, curiously enough, not *quite* total: Mr Bert Gilles, Cheshire's Chief Fire Prevention Officer, is quoted as having said: 'I have interviewed seven eye-witnesses. So far, there is no clear explanation of the fire. Spontaneous combustion is a theory most of us have treated highly sceptically [why . . .?], but it should be examined.' Well: 'it should be examined' – here, at least, is a grudged admission that 'there may be something in it'. Alas! Mr Gilles's rudimentary broad-mindedness was not to inspire the other 'authorities' to a similar investigative spirit, and – would you credit it! – the coroner even brought up our old mischievous friend, the lighted cigarette, but here, Mr Philip Jones, a chartered chemist at the Home Office, found this all-purpose scapegoat – beloved of coroners both sides the Atlantic – too much to accept;

285

Mr Jones sturdily said that, 'contrary to popular belief,' it is very difficult for a cigarette to cause this sort of fire – a fact that I proved for myself by experiment, as I describe on page 88.

The investigation into Jacqueline's death covered a period of several months, and as one now long experienced in marvelling at both the opinions and the opinion-givers in any enquiry of this type, even I was astonished at the 'evidence' – most of it mutually contradictory – which was paraded, as lengthily as solemnly, in a farce which would have been laughter-making, save that it concerned the tragic death of a young girl.

One witness testified that, so far from Jacqueline's having spent fifteen days in the hospital's 'intensive care' unit, she had, when visited by some friends within a few days of the 'accident', sat up in bed and laughed with them. This, seems to have been 'confirmed' by the pathologist, Dr Cradwell, in his evidence of a bare two minutes that the burns on Jacqueline's buttocks and back were 'superficial', and that she had died of 'shock-lung'. Why, then, if Jacqueline had been – according to certain witnesses who had visited her in hospital – so well only a few days after her admission, how was it that the presumably minor burns had caused her death?

But how 'minor' were these 'minor' burns? A witness, John Foy, and his friend, Neil Gargan, were walking upstairs as the three girls passed them on their way down. Both Foy and Gargan said that, as they passed the girls, 'there was no smoke and no smell of burning', but that, only a second or two later, on hearing cries behind them, they turned to see Jacqueline wrapped in flames – 'like a stunt-man on TV', was Foy's dramatically vivid phrase.

The contradictions of the many witnesses, not helped by the coroner's fatuous interjections, and his even worse handling of those witnesses' contradictions, makes for astounding reading, even in the lunatic context of the older type of inquests involving SHC. And the strange ignorance of those questioned! Peter Hatton, Senior Administrator *in charge* [My italics!] *of health and safety at the college*, when asked about the special clothes provided for the cater-ing-classes, was unable to say whether or not the garments were inflammable!

The Home Office's chartered chemist, Philip Jones, gave what evidence he felt like giving – he rambled on about the 'spontaneous combustion' of haystacks, but that he had never known that type of combustion to happen 'in these circumstances'. This 'expert's' volunteered opinion that the poor girl's overall had been ignited by the cooker [after she had left the kitchen?] withered away under cross- examin-ation, and he willingly agreed that none of his evidence supported his theory:[51] 'Merely a *possible* explanation'; adding that 'my idea is by no means certain . . . no more than feasible, really . . .' An adjective very difficult to apply justly to the Alice-in-Wonderland fantasies of this witness.

Asked by a solicitor whether or not he was aware that the Chief Fire Prevention Officer of Cheshire had carried out independent tests, the Home Office 'expert' admitted that he did not know this. The solicitor did not press him to explain the ignorance . . .

At the request of the Fire Brigade, the Shirley Institute of Manchester had produced a thirty-page report of the tests that they had carried out in the investigation of Jacqueline's death. This authoritative document – authoritative, whether one accept its conclusions or not – was not exhibited in the inquest proceedings.

---

[51] At least, Mr Jones did not follow the example of the 18th Century philosopher, who, when told that his theory did not accord with the facts, replied, "So much the worse for the facts!"

The conduct and the findings of the inquest represent what is probably the last important inquest to be held on the old, traditional lines, where the jury's verdict is what the coroner thinks it ought to be – no matter what the evidence – and makes sure that the jury return the 'right' verdict.

Mr Glasgow, the coroner, welcomed his ideal witness in the person of P. C. Jenion, who agreed with the Home Office conclusion – a conclusion hard to recognize from Mr Jones's answers. Like the coroner, P. C. Jenion was a firm opponent of belief in SHC, and his comment, that Jacqueline's family had been 'upset' by newspaper speculation on a possibility that she had died of SHC, gave the coroner the lead that he required: he sternly bade the jury to 'ignore all the talk in the media about SHC'. The mindless jury obliged, and Mr Coroner, after taking six-and-a-half hours about it, came down hard on the 'fact' that poor Miss Fitzsimon had died as the result of her leaning up against the gas-cooker – no evidence having been offered that the gas-burner had *not* been turned off. The jury – why do juries seem to be so intimidated by bigoted coroners? – is it that juries, bored stiff after hours, even days, in court, will return any required verdict as the ungrudged payment for permission to get home? The verdict of this particular jury – ordered and obediently returned – was 'Death by Misadventure'; that is, Jacqueline *had* leaned up against a hot cooker . . .

The attitude of 'the media' is curious: after the verdict, the newspapers, lamblike, accepted the verdict, the *Daily Mail*, ignoring the various proffered theories, treated the girl's death as though it had been accounted for beyond all argument: 'Jackie, 17, had been leaning against a lighted cooker-burner before leaving the practical cookery exam.'

However obediently ('Don't rock the boat') the Press fell into line *after* the coroner-ordered verdict, it was the widespread mention of the possibility of an SHC death *before* the verdict which made this inquest so long and complicated. It isn't the first time that the Press has seemed to lose its nerve; but once having treated SHC as at least a mentionable possibility, allusion to the phenomenon, both in Britain and in the United States, is no longer journalistically forbidden. The Press, breaking an old taboo, is coming – has come, indeed – to the point at which, without exactly endorsing the acceptable and accepted reality of SHC, it is now free to mention it as a phenomenon to be reported. It is true that opposition to the acceptance of SHC as a proven fact is still apparent in many die-hard quarters of opinion, but, since the Fitzsimon inquest, with its blatant disregard of 'awkward' evidence, its almost bullying direction of the jury, and its obvious 'cover-up' generally, no such vigorous attempt to brush SHC under the carpet has been seen. So that the progress towards the Folkestone coroner's commonsense finding of SHC as a *possible* cause of death may now be seen as an inevitable development of that changed attitude, by Press and Public, to the still mysterious, still unexplained, and still immensely fascinating phenomenon of Death by the Fire from Heaven.

And one last indignant word from one of the closest eye-witnesses of Jacqueline Fitzsimon's combustion: Mr John Foy, the engineering student. He had left before the jury brought in their obedient verdict that Jacqueline had died – or caught fire, rather – by her leaning against a hot cooker, which set her overall smouldering.

'What a load of rubbish!' said Mr Foy. 'When we walked past [her] there was nothing. Seconds later, her back was a mass of flames!'

The local *Widnes Weekly World*, reporting the verdict of the Fitzsimon inquest, stated blandly, with an entire rejection of almost all the evidence, 'Rumours that cookery student Jacqueline Fitzsimon . . . died of spontaneous human combustion were not true, it emerged from an inquest last week.' No such craven desire to earn Mr Coroner Glasgow's – or any other coroner's – approval marked the sub-editor's handling of a strange death in Austria, reported, when I was on an American lecture-tour, in *Weekly World News*, of 18th November, 1986. Half the front page of this admittedly sensational newspaper announced this:

The most bizarre case of spontaneous combustion ever!
PREACHER EXPLODES
DURING SERMON
Horrified congregation sees evangelist
blow up in the pulpit.

And certainly the completely verifiable report on the inside pages justifies the 'scare' headlines on the front page:

> In the most bizarre case of spontaneous combustion ever witnessed, a fire-and-brimstone preacher exploded in flames – just as he warned his followers they were headed for the blazing inferno of Hell!

> According to news-reports published in Austria, evangelist Franz Lueger was incinerated into a pile of ashes before the horrified eyes of his congregation 'by flames that burst from within his own body'.

There were sixty people in the evangelist's church on the outskirts of Vienna, and as all, presumably, had their eyes fixed on their pastor, no incidence of SHC can ever have had so many – and so many fully attentive – witnesses. I have said elsewhere that the highly *selective* character of certain types of combustion is a sure indication of that spontaneity that we classify under the general heading of 'SHC' – and here, in the astonishing flare-up of Pastor

Lueger, we observe that characteristic of 'classic' SHC, where objects – furniture, bedding, clothes, etc. in the closest proximity to the victim's body (when Billy Peterson burned to death in his garage in Michigan, in 1959, not even his underpants were singed) are not burnt.

> Incredibly, though the evangelist was consumed by the intense firestorm, the Holy Bible he was holding was not harmed. In fact, not a single page was so much as singed . . .

It ought to be noted that no two SHC incidents are exactly alike; though certain characteristics, being generalized, indicate that we are dealing with an SHC death. A 'strange smell' is often noted – especially by the discoverer of the charred corpse; it occurred when a Pennsylvania gas-employee, Don Gosnell, called at the apartment of a retired doctor, to read the meter. He was greeted, the front-door being open, by finding the flat filled with 'a light blue smoke of an unusual odour' – and, in the bathroom, nothing of the doctor but the remains of a calcined leg. (The coroner, true to the then form, decided that Dr Irving Bentley had died of asphyxiation 'after catching fire while smoking his pipe!)

But to return to the pulpit-SHC of Pastor Lueger: again we have a witness's recollection of an unusual odour. Interviewed by the TV reporters, Frau Braun, a member of the congregation, told of a 'strange smell' in the church, shortly before the minister burst into flame.

'There was an electrical odour in the air', said Frau Braun, 'like a burning wire or a short in an appliance. There was a bright flash from [the pastor's] chest, and then he screamed and slumped forward. It was then he literally exploded into a ball of fire . . .'

Terrified, all the congregation rushed out of the church, thinking that the building, as well as the pastor, would be incinerated. 'But', said Frau Braun, 'it didn't; and when we went back, inside, nothing else had been touched by fire – just the Reverend'.

The 'classic' elements of a 'classic' SHC combustion are not, as my readers will have discovered much earlier in this book, only matters of unburnt clothing, strange smells, and so on: the responses of the authorities are generally sure indications that we are face-to-face with SHC.

Weekly World News, recording the fact that 'statements given to the police by each of the sixty church- members were identical', comments justly that this unanimity of evidence, seems to indicate only one possible cause for the incredible inferno – spontaneous combustion'.

That would be our conclusion, too, but 'authorities', whether British or Austrian, prefer to come to other con-clusions: the inquest on the fire-consumed pastor resulted in a verdict of 'death by a fire of unknown cause and origin'. An extract from the police-report makes interesting and (by now) not unfamiliar reading; as so often the case, the investigators are determined to discover some ordinary – plausible – normal cause of fire, even though, in most cases, no normal heat-source could effect the almost total incineration of most SHC victims.

> While it is true that there were no open flames or high voltage electrical wires in the immediate vicinity when Herr Lueger was incinerated, and while the inquest has uncovered no logical explanation for his horrifying death, the inquest hesitates to fix the blame on spontaneous human combustion . . .

Why . . . ? When it was plainly evident that SHC *had* killed the pastor.

> However [the report concluded] the inquest does recognize the possibility that some mysterious and unknown force may have played a rôle in Herr Lueger's death by fire.

The police are not the only ones to entertain individual opinions. Scoffing at the 'conclusions' of the police-report, Frau Braun said stoutly: 'Those of us who were there that terrible night know well what that 'mysterious force' is! It was the work of Satan. He got his revenge on Pastor Lueger for trying to save our souls . . .'

****

Now, in my searching for a cause – or, perhaps, several causes – of the Fire from Heaven (a quest not yet rewarded by a verifiable discovery) I did, as I have said, appear to have isolated two elements common to very many of the cases of SHC – and, in all probability, to *all* the cases, were we to be informed of *all* the facts of the victims' background. One of these elements involves both the location of the Fire's incidence and the *nature* of that location; the other involves the emotional state of the victim. The first element – discovered by me almost accidentally, in marking on a map the places where the Fire had struck – is that nearly every case was to be found in the close proximity of a large body of water: the sea, an extensive lake, a big river. The other element so strikingly common to most (if not all) of the deaths or gravest injuries attributable to an SHC strike, is the obvious emotional state of the victim at the time of the strike; as I have said (page 362): 'It is certain – to my way of thinking – that there is a constant *emotional* element predisposing to death or injury by SHC.' I have merely to remind the reader of such emotion-linked SHC deaths as those of Billy Peterson, of Detroit; of Glen B. Denney, of Gretna, Louisiana, and of Mrs Françoise Price, temporarily of the *sea-coast* town of Hove, East Sussex, England, to make my point. Both Peterson and Denny had already set about taking their lives; Mrs Price, a Frenchwoman who couldn't speak English, and hated her life in a strange land, went upstairs to her SHC death after what was described as a 'flaming row' with her husband. Now, why I recall here these three cases already discussed in detail is that, in the blazing pulpit-death of Pastor Lueger, I might hardly fail to see plainly the two 'predisposing' elements mentioned above: proximity to a large body of water – the mighty Danube – and the grossly emotional imbalance accurately, even if rather too journalistically, implied in the *Weekly World News*'s subtitle:

He's burned to a crisp during fire-and-brimstone sermon!

Unconsciously, the 'fire-and-brimstone' evangelist had whipped himself into such an emotional frenzy that (with the Blue Danube handy) he had made himself into a potential victim ripe for SHC's plucking – and if the violence of the conflagration ('Preacher explodes into flames in the pulpit!') is related to the intensity of the emotion which induced the fatal SHC, then the 'Preacher's' sermon must have been very 'fire-and-brimstone' indeed!

****

The phrase, 'fire and brimstone', has become familiar rather through Shakespeare than through the Bible, but the title of my book, *Fire from Heaven*, comes from the Bible; indeed, as I have recently realized, the Bible is full of references to – but more, full of a conscious awareness of – that 'Fire from Heaven'. In Chapter 6 of this book – 'From Sodom to Sydenham' – I make a brief allusion to the destruction of the Cities of the Plain:

Genesis 19:4

Then the LORD rained upon Sodom and Gomorrah brimstone and fire from the LORD out of Heaven.

And again I turned to the Bible in Chapter 10, to touch on the story of the three boys, (as told by the Prophet Daniel) who survived, unharmed, in 'the burning fiery furnace'.

Why, I believe, the frequent mention of the Fire from Heaven throughout the books of the Old Testament has not been examined, as it should have been, by (including me!) investigators into the phenomenon of SHC, is that there has been too common a tendency to consider the record as, at best, analogical; at worst, unhistorical.

What brought me back to the Bible record of this omni-prevalent Fire – dismissed by the majority of investigators because the authors of the Biblical books attributed it to a divine – a supernatural – origin, was the newspaper-recorded fact that, as late as 1986, a witness of the Fire herself believed in its supernatural origin: Frau Braun.

It was only after reading her 'explanation' of the Fire which had taken off her Pastor – 'It was the work of Satan' – that the dismissing of the Bible-recorded Fire because ancient historians attributed the Fire to 'the Lord' had blinded us investigators to the possibility that ancient speculation on the Fire's origin – speculation in keeping with the beliefs of the time – were irrelevant to our considering the *factuality* of the historical record. In AD 1986, a level-headed Austrian *Hausfrau* believed that the Fire which had consumed her Pastor had come from the Devil; in 500 BC, a Semitic people had believed that the Fire that *they* had seen had come from Heaven. The point to bear in mind, I sternly remind myself, was to view the historical record uninfluenced by the opinions of the time whether, in 500 BC, the Fire was believed to have come from God, or, in AD 1986, to have come from Satan, the fact remained that, in the Bible, no less than in the newspaper accounts of the 18th, 19th and 20th centuries, we had eye-witness accounts of what, to give but one example, the ancient historians reckoned to be God's fiery rebuke to the wicked:

> Ezekiel 28:18
> (God's judgement upon the Prince of Tyrus for his sacrilegious pride.)
>
> Thou hast defiled thy sanctuaries by the multitude of thine iniquities, by the iniquity of thy traffic; therefore will I bring forth a fire from the midst of thee; it shall devour thee, and I will bring thee to ashes upon the earth, in the sight of all them that behold thee.

Of course, even in the earlier books of the Bible, the concept of 'fire' is used metaphorically, but, as one looks up allusion to 'fire', one sees that that specific fire – the Fire from Heaven – is never so used: the terrifying incidence of that Fire, when used to punish, is always treated literally:

> Amos 5:6
> Seek ye the LORD, and ye shall live, lest ye break out like fire in the house of Joseph, and devour it, and there be none to quench it in Beth-el. [i.e. The House of God.]

The almost insuperable difficulty in extinguishing the fire of any typical SHC was early realized by those who hosed water on the flaming victim: the water seemed only to increase the fury of the combustion.

And the following short passage from the Prophet Jeremiah was certainly written in no metaphorical sense, but, in the Biblical idiom of recording past events in the future tense, it treats of what cannot be other than an actual happening:

Jeremiah: 49, 27
And I will kindle a fire in the wall of Damascus, and I shall consume the palaces of Ben-hadad.

Forgetting for a moment, the ancient Hebrews' referring *all* manifestations of the Fire to the Will of the Lord, and looking at their recorded experience of the Fire, rather than their religiously-influenced opinion of its origin, one gathers that they were not so much more familiar with the Fire than we are, as that they had no desire, common to British and American coroners, to pretend that the phenomenon did not exist. And – this is not so easy to explain – they seemed, not so much to be able to direct it, as to understand the predisposing conditions in which the Fire would be likely to appear. There is no real reason to doubt the description of the sacrifices, where the pieces of the animal offered as sacrifice were arranged in a certain manner, and the Fire from Heaven came down to consume (*totally*, the Bible takes care to emphasize) the sacrifice acceptable to the Lord. After all, there is another Fire from Heaven that, since the mid-18th-century, we have been able, if not to direct, at least in great measure to control. I refer to lightning which, since the invention, by Benjamin Franklin, of the lightning-conductor, has spared, and continues to spare, millions of Man's buildings from destruction.

****

The Bible-record clearly distinguishes two different types of Fire: a benign manifestation, as when the Lord sends down the Fire to shew His appreciation of the sacrifice offered, and that other not-at-all-benign type that the Bible sees as the Lord's rebuke for some moral obliquity offensive to His idea of justice. To the men who, over the centuries, gave us our Old Testament, the connection between the Fire in its harmful aspect and the Divine enforcement of morality – respect for the Divine Law – was, to these pious men, obvious. The Fire was God's enforcing weapon; His hammer to beat down unbelievers and those who had strayed or looked like straying.

> Jeremiah 21:12
> O house of David, thus saith the LORD: Execute judgement in the morning, and deliver him that is spoiled [i.e. despoiled] out of the hand of the oppressor, lest my fury go out like a fire, and burn that none can quench it, because of the evil of your days.

So the threat of the fury-generated Fire is plain enough, but, then, so, to the Prophet Jeremiah, is the perfectly acceptable justification for that threat: the possible 'evil of your days'.

The notion that a hit by the Fire is, in some ways, a 'punishment', survived well into recent times: in the 18th and – more particularly, the 19th – centuries, it was maintained, and widely believed, that the Fire was a punishment for excessive drunkenness. Indeed, this belief, which was against all evidence, since even small children and adult teetotallers were among the victims, may be with us still; at least, as the reader may see by turning back to Dr Gavin Thurston's opinion on page 24, the supposed connection between excessive alcohol consumption and the Fire had not been ruled out by the medical profession even as late as up to the beginning of the second World War.

The ancient Prophets had a much easier time with the Fire than we do, since they had no need to speculate on its origins and nature. They *knew* its origin; they knew its twin purposes – to accept acceptable sacrifices and to punish the wrongdoer – so that, in a way forgotten to us, they could live as it were comfortably with it – above all, for them it held no element of mystery, as it does for us. (That is, for all but persons of Frau Braun's conviction, who is as certain of the Fire's origin and purpose as was any Old Testament Prophet; the fact that Frau Braun gave – gives – the Fire a diabolical, where the Prophets gave it a divine, origin in no way lessens her likeness to – we may almost say, her identity with – those pre-Christian witnesses of the Fire, to whom, it being taken for granted, offered no cause or excuse for speculation.)

My acceptance that the Fire mentioned in the Bible, and mentioned in no allegorical fashion, was, if not precisely identical with, at least of the same nature as, the Fire which is the subject of this book: is a fact which takes the history of the Fire back into remote times indeed. I have used a cautionary phrase, 'if not precisely identical with', and this I explain by observing a most curious question – rhetorical, but using an image well-known to the Prophet's listeners:

Proverbs 6:27
Can a man take fire in his bosom, and his clothes not be burnt?

Now, one of the most important pieces of evidence that, in a fire involving a human victim – SHC – the proof that we are dealing with SHC is the fact that the victim's clothes, or the sheets in which the victim is lying, or the cloth of the chair in which he is sitting, are not burnt – sometimes, not even scorched. This book offers many examples of the

Fire which almost totally consumes the body, and leaves those surroundings in even the most intimate contact with that burnt body untouched. Billy Peterson died, a calcined corpse, within his unburnt, unscorched, underclothes; Mrs Thomas Cochrane, 'burned beyond recognition', was in an easy-chair 'stuffed' with pillows and cushions, none of which had been even scorched. Sometimes, as with Mrs Clark, an elderly pensioner who died a week after Mrs Cochrane (in 1904) at Hull, Yorkshire or with Jack Angel, a commercial traveller, the victim escaped immediate death, but the bedclothes escaped altogether. In Mrs Clark's case, she was found 'terribly burned, but still alive'. In that of Mr Angel, who had parked his motor-caravan at the Ramada Hotel, Savannah, Georgia, on 12th November, 1988, he also escaped immediate death, after he had awakened in bed, to find himself − four days later − with first-degree burns on his legs, groin, back and right hand. He survived, but the hand had to be amputated. Nothing in his 'motor-home' shewed any signs of fire; not even the sheets on which he had been lying.

Now, was this detail of the SHC phenomenon missing from the experience − and thus the careful record − of the ancient Biblical chroniclers, or did those chroniclers, like modern gossip-writers in the most 'popular' newspapers, mention only Names? Or was it really so in those days: that a man, Fire- stricken, lost his clothes, as well as his body, to the Fire? Unconnected with *our* particular Fire, but of interest, nevertheless, is the rhetorical question in the succeeding paragraph in Jeremiah: 'Can one go upon coals, and his feet not be burnt?' Throughout India and Arabia and the Far East, holy men can, and witnessed by hundred of the devout (or the merely curious) do just that. Sceptics from the West have witnessed this 'fire-walking', have photographed it, have examined the feet of the fire-walkers both before and after their fiery walk.

300

One may hardly believe that this fire-walking was not practised in Jeremiah's day, and that that being so, he would not have heard of it, as, in all still-primitive cultures, almost everything is known, for all that it would have taken longer to hear the news than it would to-day. But perhaps, in this respect, things were different, and that, not only did men who walked on coals suffer burnt feet, but also the Fire took the clothes as well.

This raises an important point: though, as the reader will have seen, victims of the Fire have been badly injured or have died in beds where the sheets have not been even scorched, there have been recorded cases of SHC – and not, from the record, a few – where the Fire has raged furiously in the surroundings, as well as in the victim. The case of 11-months-old Peter Seaton (of interest in that the London *Daily Telegraph* of 4th January, 1939, headed its report: *Spontaneous Combustion*) involved a Fire which took more than poor little Peter. When a visitor to the house, Harold Edwin Huxstep, heard screams of terror from the bedroom in which the baby had been put to sleep, and went upstairs to investigate, 'It seemed', said Mr Huxstep, 'as if I had opened the door of a furnace. There was a mass of flames, which shot out, burning my face and flinging me back across the hall. It was humanly impossible to get Peter out.'

And though, in the case of the distressed French lady, Mrs Françoise Price, the hotel-room in which she died of SHC, was untouched by the fire, the modern double bed size spring mattress that, somehow, she had pulled off the bed on top of her as she lay on the floor, had been consumed, so that nothing but the springs of the mattress remained. And in the case of Mrs Mary Reeser, of St Petersburg, Florida – still a 'classic' of SHC, and still the subject of 'scientific' examination – we have seen how the Fire not only devoured Mrs Reeser so thoroughly that

301

nothing but a foot in a black satin slipper remained, but also that the Fire left nothing of the easy-chair in which she was sitting and the standing-lamp-cum-table by which she was reading, save the springs of the chair and the metal core of the standing-lamp. More: the *twelve lbs* of human ash into which the full body of the *anxious* widow had been converted was, with her skull, 'shrunk to the size of a baseball', found in the pit that the Fire had eaten in the wooden floor – just as Mrs Rooney, of Seneca, Illinois; her 190 pounds reduced to no more than 'a calcined skull, part of a vertebra, a foot and a mound of ashes'; was found lying in the hole that the Fire, in taking Mrs Rooney, had burnt in the floor of the Rooney farmhouse kitchen.

When, as *should* happen, the full scientific apparatus is turned upon the solving the problem of SHC, the explanation of why, in some cases, the Fire attacks the immediate surroundings and in other cases not even scorches them, may well provide the clue to the nature of the Fire itself. (Though, whether the Fire includes the immediate surroundings in its combustion or whether it confines its disastrous esurience to the body of the victim, the Fire invariably satisfies two conditions: the [almost always] *totality* of combustion, effected as no ordinary heat- source could contrive; and – mostly by no more; though always by no less; than an unconsumed foot-within-a-shoe – an *identifying* relic of the victim.) A foot – and only (but always sufficiently!) a foot – was all which remained of Mrs Mary Reeser (July, 1951), of 'Mrs E. M., a widow', (January, 1958), of 'a slim lady, 85 years old' (November, 1963), or of Dr John Irving, of Pennsylvania (1966). Despite the (never unexpected) expressed 'doubts' of firemen, police, medical-examiners and – above all! – coroners, that death or severe injury by fire is the result of SHC, there is, to the objective viewer, no doubt whatever of the nature of the fire: SHC 'writes its own unmistakable signature', and though, in this addendum to the original book, I have welcomed the break-through by which a British coroner has come gently out with the opinion that the body of the person on which he was (to use the English legal phrase) 'sitting' *might* have been incinerated by 'Spontaneous Human Combustion', this writer wonders how on earth it took so long for a recognition of the truth to be admitted . . .

****

If one swallow does not make a Spring, one coroner's commonsense finding has by no means converted the whole obstructionist forensic array of Fire Brigade, Police, Medical Officers and Coroners to the acceptance of SHC's factuality. Though Pastor Lueger 'exploded' in the pulpit, in full view of his horrified congregation of sixty attentive worshippers, the Austrian police were not only reluctant to come out honestly with a verdict of 'Death by SHC' — they positively refused to do so. The appalling cover-up of the Jacqueline Fitzsimon inquest, I have already examined; but when one reviews that protracted inquest, with its *dramatis personae* of the witnesses who not only contradicted each other, but somehow managed to contradict themselves, one — even knowing that the whole intention of the inquest was to deny the reality of SHC — may only begin to doubt the reality of one's senses when the ear has to register this solemnly expressed opinion of an 'expert' at that same inquest: 'The human body', said this pundit, loth to admit, or advised to(?) deny the existence of SHC, 'is full of fats. And with clothing to act as a wick, certain circumstances could dictate that a person could incinerate in this way.'

(The Coroner, gravely and courteously thanked this 'expert witness' for his 'helpful evidence'!)

And yet, on second thoughts, isn't my sarcasm unjust-ified? For this 'expert witness' (as 'expert witnesses' invariably are) *was* what the coroner gratefully called him: 'helpful'. That he got up solemnly to give an 'opinion' which, in the chill clarity of the printed record, must be seen only as a mouthing of meaningless gobbledegook – having the *sound* of words – of carefully weighed, respon-sibly, even solemnly, delivered, but which sounds, on examination, are found to be just that . . . mere sounds, *was* 'helpful'. These 'expert witnesses' are masters of what Anthony Lejeune has happily called 'weasel' words; that type of word of which Humpty Dumpty was himself the prime master:

> ' . . .There's glory for you!'
> 'I don't know what you mean by "glory" ', Alice said.
> Humpty Dumpty smiled contemptuously.
> 'Of course you don't – till I tell you. I meant "there's a nice knockdown argument for you!" '
> 'But "glory" doesn't mean "a nice knock-down argument" ', Alice objected.
> 'When *I* use a word', Humpty Dumpty said in rather a scornful tone, 'it means just what I choose it to mean – neither more nor less.'

What a superb 'expert witness' Humpty Dumpty would have made! No . . . I was wrong to dismiss the 'expert witness' as having contributed nothing to the progress of the inquest on Miss Jacqueline Fitzsimon. Indeed, though the 'opinion' of the Expert Witness, using every non-commit-tal word in the language: 'could', 'might', 'should', 'pos-sibly', 'in certain circumstances', and all the bet-hedging rest of the non-committal vocabulary, may seem to us to be devoid of all meaning, the function of the Expert Witness in any 'official' enquiry is an important and indeed a necessary one. His use and uses are well understood, and always skilfully employed, by the official conducting the enquiry, and leading it, by tried and proven methods, to the conclusion that a coroner, say, has already decided shall be, the verdict of his own preference. We see, then, how an Expert Witness, with meaningless verbiage, puts up a wordy smoke-screen to confuse, say, a jury, and seems to be confirming the reasoning, not of the witnesses, not of the jury, but of the (sometimes very wild indeed) wilder guesses of the coroner.

When the truth of any happening – and here we are concerned with the face of SHC – is examined under these traditional circumstances, is it any wonder that that specific truth, suspected, challenged, misrepresented and finally (so far as officialdom be concerned) dismissed as a fiction, a mere myth, as it still is to the majority of people, should have to fight so hard for acceptance? The wonder is, not that a British coroner has had the commonsense to pronounce in that truth's favour, but that even *one* British coroner – following the admirable example of the Dublin City coroner of just on twenty years ago (though *he*, the pioneer, still remains unique) – should have been found to assert the undeniable factuality of SHC.

****

EPILOGUE

The inquest was hardly more than a formality, the verdict an
inevitability. The coroner had not got where he was by thinking,
and he shewed no inclination to start on this occasion.

Robert Barnard: *Posthumous Papers*

There are many Odysseys of the Odd, and this of mine
– On the Trail of Spontaneous Human Combustion – first
embarked upon over forty years ago, has, for the record,
clearly revealed, as the principal character, not any of the
broiled-to-charcoal Victims, but . . . the coroner.   It is,
though, in what, over the centuries, he has patiently
suppressed, or misrepresented, and not in what (with the
two honourable exceptions from Dublin and Folkestone
whom I have mentioned) he has declared to be the truth,
that the real importance of the coroner stands plainly
revealed.

For it is through him, and through him alone, that the
official opinion on any accidental death is released to the
public. And so (once again to quote the inimitably brilliant
Mr Robert Barnard): 'If the police said they were satisfied
that the death was accidental, that was good enough for
him, and should be good enough for the jury. It was.'

Of course, the 'explanation' for the coroners' general
suppression of SHC as the cause of death – the 'explanation' given to me in the Autumn of 1956 by the Coroner
of Burton-on-Trent, sounded plausible enough. Told to me
over drinks in the Midland Hotel, but 'quite unofficially, you
understand?', 'just between you and me?', 'off the record?',
the 'explanation' was credible enough – far more so than
some of the verdicts demanded of pliant juries by dominant
coroners. 'Naturally', all coroners knew of, and accepted

the proven reality of, SHC, but no coroner was willing to take hours to explain – or to try to explain – to an *unconvinceable* jury what they could never be brought to accept. So . . . out with the old familiar props, the rag-bag, of 'causes': the cigarette-end (still, in these late 'Eighties, like Johnny Walker, going strong), the lighted candle, the malfunctioning electric-light switch, the dead coals in the burnt-out grate – with all of which the reader should, by now, be familiar, too. But, somehow, over the years, the 'explanation' has come to seem a little *too* contrived, a little *too* facile – and thus a little less credible. For, according to my coroner friend, it is to save themselves unrewarding talk that the tribe of coroners avoid the inclusion of SHC among the 'probable' causes of death by the Fire. Yes, but here is the difficulty: as a class, even if (in Robert Barnard's view) they haven't got where they are by thinking, they certainly haven't got where they are by the closest-mouthed Trappistry: apart from disc-jockeys and drill-sergeants (who, after all, are paid to talk non-stop) there is no class more loquacious than coroners . . .' (Older readers may remember the case, in the early 'Thirties, of the London coroner who, 'sitting' on the body of the pitiful child-victim, talked so much – and against openly-expressed Police objections – that the obvious murderer could not be brought to trial.)

So that an 'explanation' of the non-mention of SHC as a desire to avoid a coroner's unnecessary talking, now fails, for me at least, to carry unqualified conviction. I feel that this conspiracy of silence has far more behind it than any desire to spare a coroner unnecessary talk. But what that 'far more' is – can be – I have no idea. I wish I knew . . .

Oh, sometimes a coroner will mention SHC – but only to warn the jury against their thinking that *that* might have caused the fiery death on which they were '*sitting*'. In the Jacqueline Fitzsimon inquest, 'The coroner had opened proceedings by advising [*read*: 'instructing', 'ordering'] the jury to ignore all the talk in the media about SHC' – and so, obediently, the jury concurred in the coroner's opinion and decision that the cookery-student's death (by SHC) was, in fact, caused by her leaning against the gas-cooker.

I am afraid that, for every courageously honest Dublin coroner, there will still still be a thousand and more coroners of the type who pronounced on Jacqueline Fitzsimon's death.

****

Over the more than four decades since I first began to study the phenomenon of Spontaneous Human Combustion, how far has my research into its causes gone? Not very far, I'm afraid: statistically, I seem to have determined that there is locational connection between a Fire-hit and the proximity of a large body of water, and recently, a closer examination of the post-mortem condition of the victims inclines me to see a *quantitative* relationship between the area of the water and the extent of the SHC injuries. And, too, though my demonstration (see the listing on page 129-30) of the persistence of a certain *sound* in a large group of SHC deaths occurring within a short space of time (1974-5), was 'laughed out of court' by the Editor of *Fortean Times*, I still feel that this 'coincidence' merits closer attention, just as, the following news-story, of date, 6th July, 1984, impels me to call attention to the large number of SHC cases in which the cab of a motor-vehicle features:

Driver
dies
in blaze

A lorry-driver was burned alive
when his cab burst into flames
in a Birmingham street.

Passers-by saw the man
making desperate efforts to get
out of his blazing cab, which
was locked from the inside.

Police were today trying to
identify the driver and establish
the cause.

. . . . . .

Motorist and a passer-by
rushed to free the man from
the cab, but were beaten back
by the heat.

The man, thought to be from
the West Midlands, was dead
when firemen got into the
cab . . .

'Death by accident', of course. What else . . . ?

****

Of all the many world-wide cases of death or grave injury
(the latter only a small proportion of SHC-hits), the majority
are concealed by the coroners' traditional findings, which
hardly ever – one might reasonably say, 'never' – are reported as such. Only in the pages of the 'Paranormal' press –
of which the magazine *Fortean Times*, is by far the best, is
SHC treated as a fact of life (or, rather, of death). As we
saw in the case of Jacqueline Fitzsimon's death by SHC, the
Press at first took up the *possibility* of SHC's factuality with

enthusiasm, but, after the coroner's stern, no-nonsense instruction to the jury to ignore 'all the talk in the media about SHC', the Press immediately and obediently backtracked, and they themselves, ignoring all that *they* had speculated about SHC, accepted Mr Coroner's verdict without argument.

****

I would suggest that the majority of investigations (one might justifiably put that last word between single quotes!) into deaths by SHC result in a finding that some cause – any cause, it would seem – other than SHC must be blamed for the death. But even were all the deaths by SHC to be reported from the coroners' courts as such, the possibly hundreds of cases reported would still be insufficient to maintain that SHC is a generally fatal visitation of pandemic proportions. Few people are scared of their dying by SHC, for the good reason that either the majority of people haven't even heard of SHC, or, if they have, share the opinion expressed by so many coroners: that there's no such thing.

Thus, there's no money forthcoming for any research into SHC; for even the most brilliant Marketing Men could not succeed in scaring people of SHC, as these mind-manipulators have scared people of cancer and AIDS – the latter to the vast enrichment of the prophylactic-appliance industry, for whose benefit the costly campaign was devised and successfully engineered – costly, because the placing of advertisements of the largest size was needed to ensure the support of the media; though, of course, the vast outlay of money has been recovered many times. I see, in a recent copy of *She* (the magazine, not Rider Haggard's novel) a double-page spread advertising what AIDS was – at least, in its scare-presentation – more or less invented to sell.

310

('AIDS deaths may total millions in Africa' was one head-line.) The theme of AIDS' fatality is hammered home by all the copywriters. Here is *She*'s advertiser's version:

> Not using a condom when you make love can be the kiss of death nowadays, whether you're straight or gay. And AIDS is to blame.
> In New York, it's already the biggest killer of women aged between 25 and 35.

. . . And very much more of the same thing. (I wonder to whom one should apply to check that AIDS is the biggest killer of women between the ages of 25 and 35? As an old Advertising Creative Director, and the author of what critics have been pleased to call '*the* all-time classic study of Advertising', I am always a little chary of accepting 'figures' presented without authentication or without quoting their source.)

So it's evident that no millions could be poured into the tracing of SHC's source or sources. Investigation will have to be carried out by some dedicated amateurs – dedicated to puzzle-solving, with no hope of any reward other than the satisfaction of having unveiled an ancient mystery.

My own contribution – apart from my establishing the link between SHC and proximity to water, and its obvious connection with a disturbed emotional condition, as well as having (in my opinion) widened the scope of SHC's history to include the Biblical record – has been, I feel, to 'air' the subject in this book, in its four editions. The more people who can be brought to a knowledge of SHC, as well as to the fact that so many reasonably intelligent people accept its reality, the more chance there will be that some gifted amateur will eventually solve the problem of SHC – perhaps even to the extent of providing some shield against its attacks.

311

That the writings of myself and others on the subject of SHC have got that subject discussed in often the most unexpected places: in the copy of *She* carrying the anti-AIDS advertisement, there is an article on SHC – specifically, on the Jacqueline Fitzsimon case. I was amused to see that 'Additional research by Blakemore Wright' produced two additional 'boxes' – one, a 3-inch single column, headed *Fire Drill*, the other an across-three-column 3-inch panel headed *Burning Issues*, quoting ten SHC cases, six of which were taken – quite without acknowledgement of the source, from my book. (But that is what is meant now, by 'research' – read and use what another has researched!)

However, all this dissemination of talk about SHC does get the knowledge more and more widespread, and far more people accept the factuality of SHC than they acknowledge. It was in the on-the-spot reports of the London Fire Brigade, with the frequent 'Spontaneous Combustion' given as 'Probable source of Fire', which first attracted me to the subject of the Fire from Heaven. Well, *She*'s 'Additional Researcher', Blakemore Wright, may not have acknowledged his indebtedness to *my* real research, but he does deserve credit for having written this:

> SHC believers are not cranks. Sufficient credence has now been allotted to the phenomenon to justify the establishment of formal research programmes to determine its validity and causes.

Ten – even five – years ago, SHC could not have been a subject considered interesting to a popular women's magazine; despite the 'conspiracy of silence'; despite the calculated obfuscation of coroners and other 'authorities', news of – and, more, acceptance of – SHC are gaining ground. Slowly, perhaps, but surely, for all that . . .

****

312

A news story from the (London) *Daily Express*, under date, 21st September, 1988, may well give students of SHC matter for deep reflection. I quote the story as the newspaper printed it (and significantly, printed it without Editorial comment):

Jockey's girl tells of car fireball

The heart-broken girl friend of top jockey Paul Croucher told an inquest yesterday how she found him burning to death in his car.

Jockey Tarnya [sic] Davis made a written statement because she was still too grief-stricken to give evidence in person about the death of 27-year-old Paul, one of the National Hunt's top 10 riders.

But in the statement, she told how they had met at a pub for a meal and a drink, after attending race meetings hundreds of miles apart.

Paul said he was very tired, and they got into their separate cars to drive to the home they shared in Lambourne, Berkshire.

'I didn't know how much he had to drink', said 24-year-old Tarnya.

She drove on ahead, but when Paul didn't arrive after five minutes, she realized something was wrong, and drove back.

'I saw an ambulance pass me, and then firemen spraying water on a car which was like a shell.

'I realized it was Paul's car, and I thought he had been taken away in an ambulance.

'But then the firemen told me the car had been completely burned-out, with one person in it.'

313

> The inquest at Newbury heard that Paul had more than double
> the legal limit [*of ingested alcohol*] before hitting a tree in a
> lane at Chaddleworth, near Newbury.

Well, perhaps . . . and perhaps not. The coroner
directed the jury to return a verdict of 'Accidental Death',
but, as a well-known lady observed at an enquiry in 1963:
'He would, wouldn't he . . . ?' And though that reference
to 'twice the legal limit of alcohol' *seems* relevant in this
case, I hear the echoes here of that (still with us) theory of
Catacausis Ebriosus – [i.e. spontaneous combustion through
addiction to alcohol]. The coroner has had his last word:
I leave it to my readers to have theirs . . .

****

In ending this revised and updated edition of the first full
study of Spontaneous – usually, but not always, *Human*
Combustion, I must point out, as I have done in the past,
that SHC is and remains always with us, though generally
newspaper accounts and coroners' instructions to juries
almost invariably, would have us think far otherwise. And,
if SHC be – and plentifully be – always with us, the traditional cover-up is also with us still. . .

I have pointed out, in an earlier part of this book, the
established connection between SHC and the proximity of
any large body of water – which is why anyone who reads
the newspapers in my Channel-coast part of England must
be struck by the number of 'lonely old folk' – 'OAPs', as the
newspapers like to call them, who are found to have
perished by fire in rooms untouched by that same fire.

These cases are so numerous, so similar one to the
others, and so similarly treated by Press and Coroners, that
one recent example may stand representative for all. Here

is how such a case was reported by the Brighton *Evening Argus* of 25th November, 1988:

OAP, 87
KILLED
IN BLAZE

> NIGHT nurses launched a
> desperate bid to save an
> 87-year-old woman from being
> burned to death

It came as no surprise to read, after the newspaper had told how the nurses had tried to reach the victim in the sitting-room of an old folk's home, 'but were driven back by choking smoke', that

> Police believe the woman may
> have dropped a cigarette or
> match which set light to her
> chair and nightdress.

The only comment that I have to make here is this: I wonder what 'the Authorities' will find to blame for SHC when the campaign against smoking shall have rendered the cigarette obsolete . . . ?

Drivers still in peril

Only the other day, hearing of a case in which a driver flamed to death in his closed car, despite the efforts of passers-by to rescue him, I looked through my file of SHC cuttings, and found this clipping from the London *Daily Express* of 6th July 1984:

315

Driver
dies
in blaze

- and here is the same story as that of the other day:

> A lorry driver was burned alive
> when his cab burst into flames
> in a Birmingham street.

The details, so often repeated, never seem to vary: 'Passers-by saw the man making desperate efforts to get out of his blazing cab, which was locked from the inside', and, as in all these flaming-driver cases, 'Motorists and a passer-by rushed to free the man from the cab, but were beaten back by the heat'. And, what is also a consistent detail in all such stories, the report ends with the news of the fiery death; *never* is the coroner's finding reported.

Excitement the trigger. . . ?

'Experts say it was a case of spontaneous combustion' is how the story of Anton Givers' unusual death was headed in *The Sun* newspaper (USA) of 1st November, 1988.

I have suggested, in considering several cases of SHC, that emotional tension seems often a major factor in initiating the fiery death, and certainly it appears that it was intense excitement which caused Givers to burst into flames as he sat watching a wrestling match on TV, leaving him 'only a pile of ashes'.

The curious aspect of this death by SHC is that, though Givers's wife, Maria, told how 'One minute I'm washing dishes in the kitchen, and the next minute I smell smoke coming from the living-room. Anton never cried out or anything. I never heard a sound, except for the brief crackling of flames', it would appear that the death was not as instantaneous as Mrs Givers's account suggests, and that Givers's death by SHC seems to belong to that type of SHC death which has a relatively slow beginning. For Givers, a garage-mechanic of Toronto, Canada, already had a high temperature. 'He told me,' said Mrs Givers, 'that he was feeling a little warm. He had a bad case of the 'flu, and his temperature was high, but I never thought anything like this would happen . . .'

What is distinctly unusual in this case is that 'medical experts' had no hesitation in diagnozing SHC; what is **not** unusual is that, as Mrs Givers said, 'The amazing thing is that Anton was burned to a cinder, but he barely singed the chair. It's still in front of the TV, just the way he liked it . . .' That's the certain proof that the burning was by SHC.

Water again . . .

Almost the earliest students of SHC noted that any attempt to quell its flames by hosing the victim with water seemed merely to intensify the blaze. But the death by SHC of pretty 22-year-old Marilee Mars, a senior at Le College de Ste Marie, outside Paris, seems to be unique in the history of SHC in that the water was actually pouring on her when she burst into flames − for she was standing under the *cold* shower as, according to the French researcher of the paranormal, Henri Clément, 'the young woman started to smoke, and then burst into flames under a heavy stream of water in the shower'. Professor Clément had no hesitation in assigning the correct cause of death to this tragedy, when he discussed it with reporters, and a comment of his makes it clear that, like me, he looks for emotional imbalance as a chief factor in initiating SHC. For, though Mademoiselle Catherine Laffont, a fellow-student and eye-witness, said that the victim appeared to be normal and happy until she began to burn, Monsieur Clément doubts the judgment of those who remember her as 'always laughing and joking around'. 'Mademoiselle Mars's friends say that she was a happy young woman. But I guarantee that she had deep-rooted problems that she couldn't face. They eventually manifested themselves in the flames which burnt her body' – a conclusion exactly in accordance with my own long-held views.

The Too-ardent Bridegroom

Many a fantasy, secret or publicized, has imagined one's dying – passing away, becoming painlessly extinguished, are better ways of putting it – at some ecstatic moment of supreme happiness. Certainly, welcomed or not, that is what happened to Madrid bridegroom, Paolo Rodriguez, as, toasting his newly-wed bride in a glass of champagne, the Fiery Death took him at this happiest of all moments, leaving his body, within the space of less than a minute, 'a handful of grey ashes'.

Young Paolo Rodriguez's brother-in-law, Roberto Diaz, one of the hundred horrified wedding-guests who watched Rodriguez explode into a fire-ball of intense heat, is quoted as saying:

'It was the most horrible thing that I have ever seen. I was standing only inches from him when, all at once, he became a human torch.

'I saw the pain come into his eyes as he was making a toast to Teresa, his beautiful bride. Then the flames burst out. The fire seemed to come from within – from inside his body.

'One minute he was alive and happy, and the next moment he was a pile of ashes. It was as if his body was being consumed

318

by the fires of hell. Teresa saw everything. She is almost crazy
with grief.'

Understandably. But, from the scientific point-of-view, this
well-attested case is of extraordinary interest, for rarely has
a death, with total consumption of the living body, been
witnessed by so many, so close at hand. And the force of
the totally unambiguous testimony to the facts of the death
have not permitted the investigating police to avoid a
verdict of Death by Spontaneous Combustion. But then,
what other verdict could the police have pronounced?
Especially as all the witnesses testified that the victim was
not near any kind of open flame. And if there had been
any doubt that the death was due to Spontaneous Combustion, one fact would have made the cause certain beyond all
conjecture. In the words of Madrid Police-Inspector Luis
Mendoza:

'. . . there is one very bizarre aspect of Paolo's death. His body
was consumed by a fire of the most incredible intensity – it
lasted less than a minute, yet all that was left was ashes.

'But' – and here is the certain proof that I mentioned above
– 'nothing else was burned; not even the rug where Paolo's
blazing body fell. It bears no sign of the fiery death – not even
the slightest singeing.'

Our second animal SHC

It is rare indeed to record an animal's becoming a victim of
SHC, and the only example that I have found when I was
writing this book was the *half*-SHC attack on the Dawsons'
pet cat, in the case of orphan Jennie Bramwell (look her up
in the Index), but though the cat burst into flames, as soon
as, in its terror, it had bolted through an open door and
reached the garden, the flames went out. Another animal,
reported in the London *Sunday Express* of 29th January,

319

1989, was not so fortunate. The half-humorous, half-sceptical headline in the newspaper runs thus:

Who
flamed
Roger
Rabbit?

- though the question should have been more accurately put as *What* – not *Who* – flamed Roger Rabbit?

At any rate, 'Roger' *was* flamed, and flaming in the middle of a West Country road, was spotted by Police Sergeant Colin Price, who was out on patrol in his car. According to the newspaper, Sergeant Price, seeing something burning in the middle of the road, 'thought it was a gas-leak fire'. It was not:

> 'He was astonished to find a dead rabbit blazing fiercely on the tarmac. As he tried to move the animal to the roadside with a shovel, a sheet of fire 3ft high burst from its carcase'. "It's the weirdest thing I've encountered in twenty years on the Force," said the Sergeant, and the newspaper adds: 'Now the rabbit's body is being tested at the Home Office forensic laboratory at Chepstow, Gwent'.

I wonder what 'the Home Office forensic scientists' will find – and if we shall ever be told *what* they find. . . ?

NOTES

Page 28

The classic *literary* allusions to Spontaneous Combustion, nine in number, are to be found in the works of Charles Brockden Brown (*Wieland*, 1798), Washington Irving (*Knickerbocker History of New York*, 1809), Frederick Marryat (*Jacob Faithful*, 1833), Honoré de Balzac (*Le Cousin Pons*, 1847), Herman Melville (*Redburn*, 1849), Charles Dickens (*Bleak House*, 1853), Thomas de Quincey (*Confessions of an English Opium-Eater* revised edition of the 1822 original: 1856), Mark Twain (*Life on the Mississippi*, 1883), and Emile Zola (*Le Docteur Pascal*, 1893).

The individual treatment of the subject in the above famous books varies, naturally, as the characters of their several authors. Washington Irving, Thomas de Quincey and Mark Twain merely mention that there is such a phenomenon as Spontaneous Combustion, without giving any details; the allusion of the last-named to the subject being:

> Jimmy Finn was not burned in the calaboose, but died a
> natural death in a tan vat, of a combination of delirium
> tremens and spontaneous combustion. When I say natural
> death, it was a natural death for Jimmy Finn to die.

Both Brockden Brown and Herman Melville describe the 'burning fiery death' in considerable detail, but neither states explicitly that this death is the well-known 'spontaneous combustion' – the reader is left free to think that the horror *may* be something different.

Charles Brockden Brown, an early master of the Gothic who had a profound influence on Edgar Allan Poe, probably encountered the subject of Spontaneous Combustion in *The Lily Magazine and British Review*, Vol 4 (May, 1790), pp 336-7, in which the phenomenon is reported and described.

As George Perkins[52] says, the *Review* 'does not hesitate to use the term "spontaneous combustion", and Charles Brockden Brown's reluctance to follow suit stems perhaps quite simply from a desire to clothe the incident in as much mystery as possible.'

This is an interesting comment by the American scholar, since it would imply that, by the end of the 18th century, Spontaneous Combustion had lost its 'mystery' for the general public, and that 'mystery' had to be revived by the Gothic writers' deliberate and skilful manipulation of the facts.

Like Poe, who in many ways may be regarded as Brockden Brown's literary disciple, Brown went out wholeheartedly to give his readers a full helping of Horror – and 'horrors'!

Wieland is a German pietist of the then stock model: a mysterious creature with a mysterious religion, to observe the mysterious rites of which he goes at midnight, alone, to a tumble-down wooden shack of his own making, that he calls his chapel.

His wife, who is used to his midnight devotions, is suddenly startled by a bright light which bursts out above the 'chapel', as well as by 'a loud report, like the explosion of a mine'. She hears shrieks of the most terrifying nature, but on running out to the chapel she finds herself in both darkness and silence; the light and the cries have both died away.

Somehow, Frau Wieland manages to carry the 'insensible' body of her husband into the house. Wieland's clothing has been burned to cinders, though the chapel is unharmed; and his body is not only frightfully burned but bruised as well. The wretched man endures two hours of the most terrible suffering before he dies: ' . . . the disease . . . betrayed more terrible symptoms, fever and delirium terminated in lethargic slumber . . . Yet not until insupportable exhalations and crawling putrefaction had driven from his chamber and the house every one whom their duty did not detain.'

There can be no doubt that the author of *The Facts in the Case of Mr Valdemar* had read his Brockden Brown – any more than there

---

[52] 'Death by Spontaneous Combustion in Marryat, Melville, Dickens, Zola and others', *The Dickensian*, 1964, pp. 57-63.

may be doubt that Brockden Brown had somewhere come across the details of the death of Father Bertholi.

That the descriptions of spontaneous combustion in Marryat's *Jacob Faithful* and Dickens's *Bleak House* are rightly considered the best in fictional literature is because each is based on a newspaper description of a real case; indeed, in respect of Marryat's description of Mrs Faithful's death, the author is no more than 'subbing' a *Times* report, Neither author hesitates to use the term 'spontaneous combustion' in talking of the death of Mrs Faithful or of Krook.

Le Cousin Pons appeared late in the year 1847, and its (not very descriptive) reference to spontaneous combustion *may* owe its inspiration to the strange death of the Countess von Görlitz at Darmstadt, which was widely reported in the contemporary French press.

But both Marryat and Balzac may have owed additional information to an article in *The Literary Gazette* (London)[53] of 28 June 1828, in which not only the phenomenon of spontaneous combustion, but also its symptoms' progress, were discussed.

Herman Melville, in *Redburn (1849)*, is another describer of spontaneous combustion who fights shy of giving it its proper name. Melville knew of spontaneous combustion, for the source of his description of the phenomenon in *Redburn is* undoubtedly John Mason Good's *The Book of Nature (New* York, 1831), a title that Melville included in 'A Man-of-War Library' in *White-jacket* (London and New York, 1860), p 169.

Melville was evidently a convert to the *Catacausis Ebriosus* theory of Trotter, Conolly, Carpenter, Stockwell, and so many others – that 'boozer's gloom' led inevitably to 'boozer's doom'. At any rate, when Miguel, the shanghaied sailor, is about to meet his end, Melville takes care to put him into an alcoholic stupor, and to provide him, for good measure, with 'a noxious odor'. As the rest of the crew look on the recumbent figure of Miguel, drunk and stinking on the deck, they are horrified to see that:

---

[53] The credit for the discovery of this forgotten but important item in the literature of spontaneous combustion must go to Mr E. F. D. Howarth, who called attention to its existence in an article that he wrote for *The Dickensian* Vol. 34 (1937-8) pp. 69-70.

> . . . two threads of greenish fire, like a forked tongue,
> darted out between the lips and in a moment, the
> cadaverous face was covered by a swarm of wormlike
> flames . . . the uncovered body burned before us,
> precisely like a phosphorescent shark in a midnight sea.
> This was Prometheus, blasted by fire on the rock . . .

These are unusual symptoms, even for spontaneous combustion, but that Melville has not forgotten the 'classic' description of the 'classic' phenomenon is shewn by his including one of the commonest characteristics of this type of death: he notes that there was 'no sound'.

Another unusual point in the Melville description is that the Fire from Heaven is not permitted to 'consume Miguel utterly'; the still flaming and stinking body is cast overboard.

As for Thomas de Quincey, the reference to spontaneous combustion appears only in the revised (1856) edition of *The Confessions of an English Opium-Eater*, in which (that is, the revision) he includes, as one of the 'Pains of Opium', the fear of the opium-eater that the drug, like alcohol, might lead to spontaneous combustion. This fear was not mentioned in the first edition of *The Confessions* (1822), and Gordon S. Haight (see *Bibliography*) makes the ingenious suggestion that the Dickens-Lewes controversy had caught de Quincey's attention, and that three years after the publication of *Bleak House,* de Quincey recalled this quite imaginary fear of spontaneous combustion in 'the pretended retrospect' of 1856. It is typical of de Quincey that he pretended to recall this 'fear', only to dismiss spontaneous combustion as a 'popular fantasy' – thereby ranging himself solidly on *Lewes's* side in the latter's controversy with Dickens.

Of the two descriptions of spontaneous combustion – Dickens's and Marryat's – Dickens's is the more widely known, but in the field of medicine it is Marryat's description of a death by spontaneous combustion which has been adopted as the standard *clinical* description by which other descriptions are always judged.

Jacob Faithful is the least successful of Marryat's novels. Published in 1834, when Marryat was forty-two, it describes the adventures of an orphan who begins his working life as a Thames waterman. Marryat's grandfather was an eccentric East Anglian physician, respected more for 'his genuine philanthropy than for his spurious therapeutics';[54] Marryat's mother was an American of German descent. Marryat got his interest in the macabre from both: medically from his grandfather, romantically from his mother's German folk-memories.

Both combined to give Frederick a more than normal interest in all that was strange; and in a period in which anything strange attracted attention, he noted more strangeness than most people. What makes his description of the death of his hero's mother so memorable is that Marryat copied all the details from a report in *The Times* of 1832.

> The lamp fixed against the after bulkhead, with a glass before it, was still alight, and I could see plainly to every corner of the cabin. Nothing was burning – not even the curtains to my mother's bed appeared to be singed . . . there appeared to be a black mass in the middle of the bed. I put my hand fearfully upon it – it was a sort of unctuous pitchy cinder. I screamed with horror . . . I staggered from the cabin, and fell down on the deck in a state amounting to almost insanity . . . As the reader may be in some doubt as to the occasion of my mother's death, I must inform him that she perished in that very peculiar and dreadful manner, which does sometimes, though rarely, occur to those who indulge in an immoderate use of spiritous liquors. Cases of this kind do indeed present themselves but once in a century,[55] but the occurrence of them is too well authenticated. She perished from what is called *spontaneous combustion,* and inflammation of the gases generated from the spirits absorbed into the system. It is to be presumed that the flames issuing from my mother's body completely frightened out of his senses my father, who had been

[54] *Vide* the article on Marryat in the *Dictionary of National Biography*.

[55] Here Marryat is innocently quoting *The Times's* report on which he based his fictional description.

drinking freely; and thus did I lose both my parents, one by fire and one by water, [as Jacob's father had flung himself overboard, and had been drowned] at one and the same time.

Marryat's description has been accepted by the medical profession as 'classic', because, as Dr Thurston pointed out in a letter to the *British Medical Journal* of 18 June 1938, 'Captain Marryat quoted five of the six points mentioned by Mr L. A. Parry, FRCS (*Journal*, June 4, p 1237)

1. The victim was a chronic alcoholic.
2. She was an elderly female.
3. In the cabin there was a lamp which might have occasioned the fire.
4. Little damage was caused to the combustible things in contact with the body.
5. There was a residue of greasy ashes.'

Marryat did not mention that the hands and feet escaped combustion. Evidently there were doubts as to the origin of the fire, for 'after much examination, much arguing, and much disagreement, the verdict was brought in that 'she died by the visitation of God'.

The *moral* implications of spontaneous combustion were to be stressed in a much more positive manner by Charles Dickens with the publication, in 1852, of *Bleak House*. In a quite extraordinary article, 'Bleak House: From Faraday to Judgment Day',[56] Ann Y. Wilkinson has permitted herself to be caught up, as Dickens himself permitted a similarly total catching up, by the analogous links between the death of Krook by spontaneous combustion and the inevitable cleaning-up by fire of the evil personified by Krook. As Miss Wilkinson says: 'The world of *Bleak House* is a physical one, which reflects its moral twin. It has physical laws which are almost exact analogues to moral laws – laws in the sense of descriptions of existing behavioral events, in either sphere – and the observer of the physical scene has some of the same

---

[56] See *Bibliography*.

Preconceptions, but more, the same Problems of interpretation, as the observer of the moral scene.'

I wish that there were space in this book to analyze Miss Wilkinson's profound and subtle analysis of the manner in which Dickens, strongly affected by his scientific reading, makes Krook's death an event both symbolic-supernatural and factually-purposive. What Miss Wilkinson has either forgotten or not known is that the emotion that comes through so powerfully in Dickens's almost rhapsodical description of the strange death of Krook is referable to an inquest that Dickens attended, twenty years before, as a reporter on the *Morning Chronicle.*

It would be absurd to claim that an obsession with spontaneous combustion, originating in an inquest of twenty years earlier, had generated the dark fantasy of *Bleak House;* for it would be hard to refute the protest that the death of Krook is but a trivial incident in a long book dealing with more important things than either Krook's death or Krook himself. But, as Miss Wilkinson points out, Dickens did not think it so.

She makes it clear that, in imagining the death of Krook by spontaneous combustion, Dickens is drawing on that obsession with fire, flame, combustion, combustibility, which so strongly influenced his choice of subjects as the editor of *Household Words.*

Two years earlier, Dickens had written to Michael Faraday, then 'popularizing' science in his Royal Institution lectures, and invited him to contribute to 'my new enterprise Household Words'. Dickens had already printed *The True Story of a Coal Fire,* and when Faraday responded readily to Dickens's invitation to contribute to the new journal and sent in some notes on the chemistry of a candle, Dickens handed them over to Charles Knight, to lick into readable shape.

The first article, based on Faraday's notes, 'The Chemistry of a Candle', appeared in *Household Words* in the issue of 3 August 1850 – two years before the Publication of *Bleak House,* but at a time when that novel was already due for serial publication. In other words, as editor, Dickens was printing articles on combustion even as he was writing the mysterious properties of fire into the text of *Bleak House.* If we bear the temporal coincidence in mind, we cannot fail to be impressed by Dickens's preoccupation with the mystery of combustion, whether he is reading Knight's article for press or actually giving us his

327

own views on the *mystical-moral* aspects of heat, and finding analogues between the coal fire and the human organism.

In the article prepared by Knight from Faraday's notes, young Master Wilkinson explains the chemical composition and the process of combustion of the candle, telling the reader how black soot 'is getting invisible and changing into air', and concluding with the observation that burning a candle is 'almost exactly like breathing', which prompts the highly significant question from Uncle Bagges: 'Man . . . is a candle, eh?'[57]

Faraday has said: 'Now, I must take you to a very interesting part of our subject – to the relation between the combustion of a candle and that living kind of combustion which goes on within us. In everyone of us there is a living process of combustion going on very similar to that of a candle . . . This is not merely true in a poetical sense – the relation of the life of a man to a taper . . .'

Household Words continued the articles, the next in the series being 'The Laboratory in the Chest', in the issue of 7 September 1850. This article, though written-up (rather than written) by Knight brings us nearer still to the 'facts' behind the romanticizing of Krook's death.

In the second article Uncle and Nephew are discussing bodily heat. Uncle wishes to know how it is that, if brandy-and-water cool down from boiling point – note the allusion to alcohol – why doesn't the heat of one's own body cool down?

'Why . . . for the same reason that the room keeps warm so long as there is a fire in the grate.'

'You don't mean to say that I have a fire in my body?'

'I do, though.'

And so the dialogue continues, Nephew answering every question of Uncle's, until at last Uncle remarks:

'It makes me rather nervous to think that one is burning all over – throughout one's very blood – in this kind of way.'

And then Uncle Bagges asks the question which links the series of 'instructive' articles directly with the terrible scene in *Bleak House:* '. . . shouldn't we be liable to inflame occasionally?'

---

[57] *Cf* Leonardo da Vinci's views, quoted on page 260.

Nephew Wilkinson gravely observes: 'It is said . . . that spontaneous combustion does happen sometimes, particularly in great spirit drinkers. I don't see why it should not, if the system were to become too inflammable. Drinking alcohol would be likely to load the constitution with carbon, which would be fuel for the fire, at any rate.'

We now observe that the 'rationalizing' of spontaneous combustion has taken on a new aspect. The poet, the romantic, the mystic, in Dickens still respond to this mysterious, and mysteriously frightful, phenomenon in a primitively human 'non-rational' way, but the necessity of his age to find a rationalizing explanation of this, as of all other phenomena, forces Dickens to use the handy tools of a novel (and so romantically interesting) scientific knowledge to supply the necessary rationalizing 'explanation'.

Dickens did not write the articles on the burning of a candle; but he was a stern editor, and nothing went into *Household Words* of which he did not thoroughly approve; nor was he above rewriting any passage to bring it nearer to his own journalistic and philosophical standards. This should be borne in mind when considering the 'loaded' nature of the passage quoted above: such phrases as, for instance, 'I don't see why it should not . . .', 'Drinking alcohol would be likely to . . .', ' . . . which would be . . .', and so on.

Yet in this 'scientific' type of argument Dickens once again demonstrated the reasons for the popularity that he has enjoyed to the present day: an intuitive understanding of what the people wanted even before they themselves were aware of their need; and, even more important, the ability to anticipate the demand for *authorized* opinion . . . and to supply it.

As Miss Wilkinson says:

> I have gone into this detail for two reasons: one, to show that Dickens was indeed thinking of, or at least aware of spontaneous combustion as an abnormal occurrence in the case of a 'system' becoming too 'inflammable' as early as May of 1850, and that the fanciful redactions of Faraday's lectures provided the first (specious) scientific authority for the possibility of spontaneous combustion, an 'authority' that Dickens later could hardly call attention to (one cannot believe he forgot about it: his memory

329

about articles in the Periodicals was always extremely accurate, especially since he read all of them, and reworked many of them, besides writing his own) because of the clearly unwarranted conjectures he had allowed Knight to draw out of the notes lent by Faraday.

And she continues:

In addition to this, we have now the material before us to consider as the gross matter to be refined – sublimated – by the chemical magic of Dickens's technique into symbolic art. What has happened in this process?

What indeed!

What has happened is that, in going from physical, natural, chemical fact, which, under a 'romantic' guise, is still importantly present in the novel, to 'analogy' or symbol, the idea of spontaneous combustion had spread out and become the final explosive vision of the whole system Bleak House treats of, a vision of the most astonishing power, portending the release of necessary and purgative, but dreadfully destructive energies. What I wish to show is that *this vision of destruction by fire* [my italics – MH] is absolutely worked out in the materials of the novel, and then translated into social and moral terms, and then, finally, raised to its historical and apocalyptic symbolism . . .

This imaginative and important study of Dickens's treatment of the phenomenon of spontaneous combustion – a phenomenon familiar to him from his days of newspaper-reporting – would well have strengthened its own arguments had its author gone a little more deeply into the *personal* circumstances, not only of Dickens, but also of Dickens's friends.

By 1850 Dickens had not been, nor was he ever to be, fully 'accepted socially'. He was a famous writer; he was admired by all; but society had not extended to him the cachet of membership.

Dickens – and this explains the curiously ambivalent nature of this novelist's view of life – was to be, until his relatively early death in 1870, a social outsider; admired 'this side idolatry' by the reading public of two continents, but feared and shunned by society as being 'not one of us'.

He knew famous people, including famous aristocrats, but he knew them 'in the wrong way' and in the wrong conditions. He knew Bulwer Lytton, Disraeli, d'Orsay, and the other lions of the day, but he knew them in the wrong houses – in Holland House, for example, the salon of the brilliant but *déclassée* Lady Holland – and he knew them all with their mistresses. As a mistress-keeper himself, Dickens was 'one of them'. He was never admitted to that society of which the Queen and Prince Albert were the impeccably behaved heads; had he but lived another ten years (which would have made him only sixty-eight), he would have been a welcomed member of the Prince of Wales's Marlborough House Set.

Dickens, then, was a outsider, and outsiders are given to developing, out of their resentment, opinions which are dear to them, not so much because they are personal, as because they appear to be antagonistic to the opinions of the Establishment. But Dickens's mysticism had not been properly evaluated, and it is impossible to consider Dickens's view of spontaneous combustion without considering the commonly held opinions of all those of his friends and acquaintances who had permitted themselves to become fascinated by Neo-Gnosticism and Neo-Alchemy – of whom Lytton was the best known and most powerful in influence. As gnostics and alchemists, they were obsessed by fire, in both its material and its mystical implications. Lytton – for we are talking now of a practical age, which bred practical men – converted his occult studies into the raw material of best-sellers, and one should note that among the more successful of his best-sellers was *The Last Days of Pompeii*, in which a city is blotted out by the lava and ash from a fiery volcano.[58] (Fire is 'taking its revenge' upon unheeding humanity.)

Though Miss Wilkinson does not mention this, Dickens's preoccupation with fire (to give it no stronger a description) may well have been a contributory cause of his early death. On a trip to Italy, Dickens climbed – by himself – the warm slopes of Vesuvius, and, once at the volcano's lip, advanced, despite the warnings of the Italian guides, until he was actually within the crater of the burning mountain. He was peering into the writhing magma, its coruscating glow half-hidden by the toxic smoke, when he collapsed, and, but for the prompt action of his guides, would have fallen into the crater – no less a victim to fire than his 'punished' villain, Krook, had been.

Bleak House had first appeared in serial form, and already a number of readers had written to the author, complaining of something apparently incredible in the matter of Krook's death. These letters were so numerous, their complaints differing so little in substance, that Dickens thought it prudent – indeed, necessary – to preface the bound edition of *Bleak House* with an explanatory-defensive rehearsal of the best-known facts of spontaneous combustion.

Leading the objectors had been the 'rationalist' Mr George Henry Lewes (1817-78), editor at different times of *The Leader* and of the *Fortnightly Review;* and for him Dickens in this Preface had a special word: ' . . . the possibility of what is called spontaneous combustion has been denied since the death of Mr Krook; and my good friend Mr Lewes (quite mistaken, as he soon found, in supposing the thing to have been abandoned by all authorities) published some ingenious letters to me at the time when the event was chronicled, arguing that Spontaneous Combustion could not possibly be. I have no need to

---

[58] Dickens's interest in the "Occult", and his friendship with Lytton and others of a similar interest, are described in detail in the author's *Charles Dickens; A Sentimental Journey in search of an Unvarnished Portrait*; London; Cassell & Co., 1953. The choice of material accepted for the two publications that Dickens edited – *All The Year Round* and *Household Words* – make Dickens's continued and deep interest in the Occult evident indeed, for Dickens was a most conscientious editor, reading every contribution submitted to him as editor, and being solely responsible for what was printed in either of the journals.

observe that I do not wilfully or negligently mislead my readers, and that before I wrote that description I took pains to investigate the subject . . .'

Dickens then cites some of the more famous cases, and ends his Preface with these defiant words: 'I do not think it necessary to add to these notable facts, and that general reference to the authorities which will be found at page 534, the recorded opinions of distinguished medical Professors, French, English and Scotch, in more modern days; contenting myself with observing that I shall not abandon the facts until there shall have been a considerable Spontaneous Combustion of the testimony on which human occurrences are usually received.'[59]

But, later in the century, another novelist – French, this time – was to shew that all the old superstitions concerning spontaneous combustion had by no means been swept away by the rationalizing of such romantics as Dickens or such materialists as Lewes. In *Le Docteur Pascal*, Zola causes a peasant-farmer to catch fire while he is sleeping in a chair; *the victim having been a heavy drinker*. It was to be many years before students of the phenomenon were to admit even the possibility that there might be no constant cause-and-effect connection between booze and a blaze-up.

Here is the tremendous scene of discovery from *Bleak House:*

'Yes, Tony?' says Mr Guppy, drawing nearer to the fire, and biting his unsteady thumbnail.'You were going to say, thirdly?'

'It's far from a pleasant thing to be plotting about a dead man in the room where he died, especially when you happen to live in it.'

'But we are plotting nothing against him, Tony.'

'Maybe not, still I don't like it. Live here by yourself, and see how you like it.'

---

[59] In *The Leader*, Lewes had stated that he 'objected to the episode of Krook's death by spontaneous combustion as overstepping the limits of fiction and giving currency to a vulgar error.' In a letter to Dickens, Lewes said: 'I believe you will find no one eminent organic chemist who credits Spontaneous Combustion.'

'As to dead men, Tony', proceeds Mr Guppy, evading the proposal, 'there have been dead men in most rooms.'

'I know there have; but in most rooms you let them alone, and – and they let you alone', Tony answers.

The two look at each other again . . .

Now, that this exchange is meant to warn us that something strange and terrifying is about to happen – is already happening – is clear. It is clear to Guppy and Weevle – 'The two look at each other again' – and it is clear to the reader. Mr Guppy goes to sit on the window-sill: . . .

Mr Guppy, sitting on the windowsill, nodding his head, balancing all these possibilities in his mind, continues thoughtfully to tap it, and clasp it, and measure it with his hand, until he hastily draws his hand away.

'What in the Devil's name, is this? Look at my fingers!'

A thick, yellow liquor defiles them, which is offensive to the touch and sight, and more offensive to the smell. A stagnant, sickening oil, with some natural repulsion in it that makes them both shudder.

'What have you been doing here? What have you been pouring out of window?'

'I pouring out of window? Nothing, I swear. Never, since I have been here!' cries the lodger.

And yet look here – and look here! When he brings the candle, here, from the corner of the windowsill, it slowly drips, and creeps away down the bricks; here, lies in a little thick nauseous pool.

'This is a horrible house', says Mr Guppy, shutting down the window. 'Give me some water, or I shall cut my hand off.'

He so washes, and rubs, and scrubs, and smells and washes, that he has not long restored himself with a glass of brandy, and stood silently before the fire, when Saint Paul's bell strikes twelve, and all those other bells strike twelve from their towers of various heights in the dark air, and in their many tones. When all is quiet again, the lodger says:

'It's the appointed time at last. Shall I go?'

Never has horror been handled in so masterly a fashion. The reader does not know that the thick yellow liquor which defiles Mr Guppy's idle hand is the body of Krook, liquefied by some dreadful alchemy. And, indeed, when the two men creep fearfully into Krook's room, and find him vanished in a cloud of evil-smelling smoke and the cat gone mad, we still do not know (or have not been told by Dickens) that the stagnant, sickening oil is . . . Krook.

The description of what the two friends find when they go in search of the 'burning smell' is not only classic as regards Dickens's creative skill; it is also classic in the sense that it is, for all its Gothic embellishments, an accurate description of a case of spontaneous combustion that Dickens 'sat in on' as a young reporter of the *Morning Chronicle*.

By an oversight, to which several readers have called my attention, I omitted, from my list of *classic* literary allusions to Spontaneous Combustion, Gogol's *Dead Souls*. It is true that the reference to SHC is casual and unimportant, so far as the plot is concerned; all the same, Gogol does mention the death of a character from this mysterious cause, and the famous Russian novel ought, of course, to have been included in my list.

Here is the passage, from the Constance Garnett translation, published in Penguin Classics:

'Last week my blacksmith was burnt . . . Such a clever black-smith! Could do a locksmith's work, too.'

'Did you have a fire, ma'am?'

'The good Lord preserve us from such a calamity, sir! A fire would have been worse. No, no, sir, he caught fire himself. Something inside him caught fire. Must have had too much to drink. Only a blue flame came out of him and he smouldered, smouldered, and turned as black as coal. And he was such a clever blacksmith, too . . .'

Note that, in the tradition of his time, Gogol does not hesitate to adopt the *catacausis ebriosus* theory: 'Must have had too much to drink.'

335

Pointing out that SHC victims are rare among young people, especially very young people, I mentioned in the second edition of this work that I knew of only one case of a pre-pubescent Fire-victim: that of the 11-month-old boy, Peter Seaton, of Peckham Rye, London. From information which has come to me since, it is clear that even the very young may no longer be regarded as fairly safe from the Fire.

The Birmingham (England) *Evening Mail* of 26 August, 1974, reported the death of Lisa Tipton, in a fire confined to one room of her parents' house in Highfields, Staffordshire. No real attempt was made to provide even a half-hearted 'reason' for the fire in which Lisa had died: it would have been difficult to pin the blame for the fire on her, since she was only six months old!

Only a month older was the boy, Parvinder Kaur, when both he and the baby carriage in which he was sitting blazed up. Rushed off to the modern Burns Unit at Birmingham's biggest hospital, the boy, obviously, could give no explanation of how he came to be alight; but, as his baby carriage had been in a corner of the Kaur's sitting-room, the official mind could suggest that 'kids could have been playing with matches' – an opinion for which no evidence was offered.

Part of a series of eight Birmingham/Birmingham-district SHC fires, extending over the period from 8 April, 1973 to 23 March, 1975, the death of little 7-month-old Parvinder Kaur involves a most curious coincidence: that, in the London *Evening Standard* of 6 January, 1978, the 'Stop Press' contains these three items of news – and *only* these items:

FOUR DIE IN
HOUSE BLAZE

A woman and three children died in house at Hull today. Striking firemen left picket line to attend blaze.

WOMAN FOUND DEAD

Mrs Inder Kaur, 50, was found dead on floor of her home in St. Leonard's Street, Bedford, today. She had burn marks on arms and legs, *although there had not been a fire in the house*. [My emphasis]

FISH SHOP BLAZE

Fire damaged Icelandic fish shop in Colin Parade, Edgware Road, Kingsbury, today.

There are, in fact, two coincidences here – one obvious, the other not so obvious. A baby, Parvinder *Kaur,* dies in a mysterious fire in Birmingham in 1973. Over four years later, in January, 1978, sixty miles distant Mrs Inder *Kaur* dies of burns in a fireless house: a death even more mysterious than that of the baby in the blazing carriage.

I have tried to establish a relationship between the 50-year-old woman and the 7-month-old child, both bearing the same East Indian name, but so far my efforts have been unsuccessful. Yet, even were there a relationship, the coincidence would not be less striking: that, four years after the baby dies in a strange fire, the middle-aged woman should follow in a 'fire' no more explicable.

The not-so-obvious other coincidence is that fire should strike a store full of such incombustible things as 'wet' fish and ice, and that the fire should strike it when a mother and her three children die in *Hull,* one of the centres of the Icelandic fish-industry.

I shall comment later on the fact of the eight Birmingham fires when I come to point out the now perceptible pattern of the Fire's striking, and how, when it strikes, it not only seems to concentrate upon districts, rather than scatter its flames impartially, but often engulfs whole families in its fiery embrace. I shall return to this multiple fire later, and in a different context, but I am indebted to my friend, the scientist and author Jacques Bergier, for details of one of the most remarkable of these multiple fires on record.

The story was the front-page lead in the *Nigerian Herald* of 27 December, 1976, and is interesting in that the 'smoke screen' usually available in such cases to obscure the truth and to prevent speculation as to the real nature of the Fire was supplied, in this instance, not by police, fireman or other 'experts', but by the one surviving victim of a family of seven. Apart from this not unimportant variation, the tragedy exhibits every indication of its belonging to a well-documented class within the overall pattern of SHC.

MYSTERY OVER
FIRE DEATHS
Poser for the police
by Kayode Awosanya

The death of six members of a family of seven by fire in Lagos . . .. has now become the greatest mystery.

An on-the-spot investigation yesterday revealed that everything in the small wooden room at Iponri on the Lagos Mainland remained intact.

Among the articles left untouched by fire were two cotton mattresses carefully placed on two iron beds . . .

Altogether, the room looked unaffected by the fire which killed the six persons . . . It was also expected that nothing, including the wooden walls and iron sheets on the roof, would have remained . . .

And although earlier reports claimed that the fire came from petrol which was sprinkled on the family through an opening in the wooden wall while they were asleep, *[this was claimed by the mother who survived]*, it became known yesterday that this might not be true at all . . .

The Third World has its SHC visitations, too.

338

Castor and Pollux, with Clytemnestra and Helen, were the offspring of Leda and Jupiter, in his guise of swan: the four were hatched, in pairs, from two eggs.

Grown-up, Castor and Pollux (who may well have been real persons, despite the myth of their generation and birth), joined Jason's expedition to find and bring home the Golden Fleece; and during the voyage to Colchis, in a violent storm, their heads were seen to be glowing with a lambent blue flame – on which the winds died down and the storm went away. On the return voyage, they cleared the Hellespont and the neighbouring waters from pirates; and from these two circumstances – the flaming 'halo' and the defeat of the pirates – they became, for Greeks and Romans, the 'patron saints' of sailors and their ships. A double 'St Elmo's fire' meant fair weather, and was named 'Castor and Pollux'; but a single flame denoted foul, and this was named after their sister, Helen, who had suffered ill-fortune at the hands of the Athenians.

It is evident that here we have a case of bio-luminescence shared by twins. (See Page 182.)

'St Elmo' may be a derivation of Roman 'Helen' (interpreted, under later Christian influence, as 'St Helen'), or it may be – and, more probably, is – from Late Latin *stemmula*, 'a little wreath' (or garland'), that is, *flammarium*, 'of flames'. Metathesis – that is, the inversion of letters or syllables within a word – was a common factor in the development of Spanish from Vulgar Latin: e.g. Spanish *milagro*, 'a wonder, a miracle', from the Latin *miraculum*. 'St Elmo' – 'Sant' Elmo' would regularly derive from a hypothetical *stemmula*, giving *stellamula* and, later, *stelluma*, which would develop to *stel'ma*, and so to 'S'nt'Elmo'.

The attack by 'the three fingers of fire' is notable as being one of the more impressive of the coincidences; but it is by no means the only one – or even the only impressive one.

On 8 April, 1938, the *Sheffield Independent* reported that Mr G. A. Shepherdson, a building contractor of Hull, was driving past a new housing project at Hessle, Yorkshire, when he turned his gaze from the road ahead for a moment to wave in a friendly manner to some workmen. He had hardly returned his gaze to the road ahead when the car was seen to slow down and come to a stop at the side of the road. Mr Shepherdson had burned to death 'with startling suddenness' – and nothing within the car, save the driver, was even singed.

And now for a truly startling coincidence, in which may lie *one* of the keys to a solution of the mystery of SHC.

A little more than ten years later, in January 1949, the *Sheffield Star* reported the strange death of a man in a car at – yes! Hessle. The car stopped and rescuers rushed to drag the flaming body of a man from the completely undamaged vehicle, the door of which opened 'without the faintest trouble'. The driver was dead; the body so badly burned that identification was impossible – nor has the man been identified to this day. As in the case of Mr Shepherdson, the car was untouched; the gas-tank intact. Save for the fact that Mr Shepherdson could be identified and the second driver not, the cases were precisely similar, even to the direction in which both cars were travelling.

Is there something 'weird' at Hessle, as there is undoubtedly something 'weird' in the 'Oregon Vortex'? Bear in mind that Hessle is only a few miles from 'England's Oregon Vortex', Lincolnshire (see Page 193), where – as in Oregon – gravitation behaves in a seemingly abnormal way. Is there something at Hessle which ignites the human flame inside a car, while the car remains resistant to the fire-raising force? If so, Hessle is not the only place where this may happen, as we have seen; but it is the only place that I know of where the grisly phenomenon has repeated itself to the very smallest detail.

Three *simultaneous* deaths have somewhat obscured the fact that *multiple* deaths are commonly found in even the most superficial survey of the phenomenon of SHC – that is, a number of deaths, perhaps spread over a fairly long period of time, but occurring within one well-defined and not very extensive geographical area. (I have referred elsewhere to this tendency of the Fire to 'concentrate'.)

Indeed, the Fire's tendency to concentrate upon a 'pin-pointed' area is very marked. In England, there are least *nine* such 'targets' – the area in which I live, the Eastbourne-Chichester coastal strip being, it would seem, the prime 'concentration-area'. The nine are as follows:

340

1 Blyth, Whitley Bay and Newcastle-on-Tyne	*North-east*
2 Hull and Scunthorpe	*N.E. more to South*
3 The Broads, Great Yarmouth and Ipswich	*East*
4 Binbrook and Louth	*East more to South*
5 Colchester and Chelmsford	*East: South of 4*
6 Brighton, Worthing, Bognor, Chichester	*S.E. to South*
7 Chester, Liverpool, Birkenhead	*West*
8 Birmingham	*Midlands*
9 Leeds and Sheffield	*North-central*

The concentration at No. 6 (Brighton, etc.) has been almost totally ignored by some researchers in favour of a concentration that they find more striking: that at Birmingham (inland, in the very center of England, but on the River Tame). One researcher noted eight cases of SHC between 8 April, 1973 (John McRory) and 23 March, 1975 (William Cashmore).

In fact, the 'concentration' reaches a higher total than eight, if we go back a little in time, and include such Birmingham deaths as that of Sarah Pegler at the end of 1938.

However, the evidence for concentration in Fire-attack is plain and inescapable, and this must be one of those established facts which will help us to explain the origin and behaviour of SHC. (My own future work in this field will include the preparation of comparable studies for non-British countries.)

Page 130

Indeed, if we add the following names, omitted from the list on pages 129-30, we may add five more examples of the sinister 'S' initial to the impressive total of nineteen:

G. A. Shepherdson, Hull, England (1938)	*death in car*
Mrs Sarah Butcher, London, England (1938)	*death in room*
Mrs Sarah Pegler, Birmingham, England (1938)	*death in room*
Mrs Selina Broadhurst, Wrexham, Wales (1939)	*death in room*
Mrs Dorothy Sample, Thanington, England (1976)	*death in room*

a total of five; but if we add the name of Mr Robert Sanders, principal witness at the inquest on Mrs Sample, then our total here increases to *six;* our grand total to no fewer than *twenty-five!*

And bear in mind that this sinister recurrence of the 'S-factor' is listed here for the British Isles only, by no means the only place where this so-far unexplained sound-fire link is to be observed – an excellent example from Hoquiam, Oregon, being the case of Mrs Sam Satlow. (See pages 199-200.)

Page 162

To be precise, Russell lists twenty cases, but one (that of Horace Trew Nicholas, of Hampton Hill, London, reported in the London *Daily Telegraph* of 28 December, 1938), *may* be explained otherwise than by invoking the force of SHC. Here, then, is Russell's list of nineteen cases covering, for Great Britain, the Period 1938-9. On the patterns revealed by the list, I shall comment later. Where given, the dates are those of the newspapers carrying the various stories.

1938

7 April	George Turner, Upton-by-Chester	Death while driving
8 April	G. Shepherdson, Hessle	Death while driving
12 June	Unnamed woman, Butterworth	Death from ignited clothing
30 July	Cruiser case, Norfolk Broads	SHC in cruiser
20 September	Phyllis Newcombe, Chelmsford	SHC while dancing
27 December	Mrs Florence Hill, Croydon	SHC at home
" " "	Mrs Agnes Flight, Brixton	SHC at home
" " "	Mrs Louisa Gorringe, Downham	SHC at home
" " "	James Duncan, Ballina, Ireland	SHC at home
28 December	Mrs Amelia Ridge, Sheffield	SHC at home
" " "	Sarah Pegler, Birmingham	SHC at home
" " "	Ellen Wright, Carlisle	SHC at home
" " "	Harriet Lawless, Warrington	SHC at home
" " "	Harriet Garner, Liverpool	SHC at home
31 October	Unnamed woman, Newcastle-on-Tyne	SHC at home
6 November	Mrs Butcher, son, Fred, London	SHC at home

1939

2 January	Mrs S. Broadhurst, Wrexham, Wales	SHC at home
4 January	Peter Seaton (baby), London	SHC at home
7 January	Mrs N. Edwards, Liverpool	SHC at home

Now let us examine some of the patterns emerging from this reasonably representative list; it will, I think, be more convenient to gather the cases together under headings.

SHC without witnesses

Mrs Florence Hill
Mrs Agnes Flight
Mrs Louisa Gorringe
Mrs Amelia Ridge
Sarah Pegler
Ellen Wright
Harriet Lawless
Unnamed, Newcastle-on-Tyne
Peter Seaton (baby)

SHC witnessed

Harriet Garner	Son, Joseph, deposed that he had found his mother lying amid flaming bedclothes; no fire or light in room; nothing to account for blaze.
Mrs Sarah Butcher and son, Fred	Would-be rescuers driven back by fury of the flames.
James Duncan	'A Pillar of flaming agony in his own bed-room. So fierce the fire, rescuers unable to approach.'
Mrs Selina Broadhurst	
Mrs N. Edwards	
Woman at Butterworth	
Cruiser case	
Phyllis Newcombe	
G A. Shepherdson	Death in car
George Turner	Death in car

343

Clothing inexplicably caught fire

Mrs Amelia Ridge	'Burned for no reason whatever; nothing could have caused it . . .'
Mrs Harriet Garner	Bedclothes: 'Nothing to account for blaze.'
Mrs S. Broadhurst	'Burnt to a crisp by her own clothes in circumstances where it was not possible . . .'
Mrs N. Edwards	'Burnt to death by her own clothes, which caught fire nobody knows how.'
Woman on cruiser	'Charred to ashes before her family . . .'
Phyllis Newcombe	Her dress flamed up as she was dancing.

Coincidence of name

Harriet Lawless and Harriet Garner
Dr John Irving and Dr Irving Bentley

Coincidence of Place

Harriet Garner and Mrs Edwards, both of Walton, Liverpool.
Dr John Irving and Dr Irving Bentley, both of Pennsylvania.

Witnesses/rescuers repelled by flames

George Turner	Blazing in cabin of truck
G. Shepherdson	Blazing in car
Mrs Butcher and son	'Would-be rescuers driven back by fury of flames.'
James Duncan	'So fierce the fire . . . the rescuers were unable to approach.'
Mrs Broadhurst	
Mrs Edwards	
Woman at Butterworth	'Her clothes inexplicably caught fire . . .'
Cruiser case	'Her family were totally helpless to save her . . .'
Phyllis Newcombe	'Her fiancé tried to beat out the flames, but the heat drove him back . . .'
Peter Seaton (baby)	' . . . as though I had opened the door of a furnace . . . a mass of flames which shot out, burning my face and flinging me back across the hall.'

The case of Horace Trew Nicholas, that Russell omitted from his list of nineteen, is certainly in a class by itself, though it has *some* resemblances to those cases in which Poltergeist activity is manifest.

As reported in the London *Daily Telegraph* of 28 December, 1938, Mr Nicholas, of Windmill Road, Hampton Hill, London, was walking along Windmill Road, when there was a bang, and Trew 'went up like a rocket'. He landed against the chimney of an adjacent roof, his clothes ablaze, his hair burned off (compare the case of Mrs Louise Matthews, of South Philadelphia, in 1960, when she lost all *her* hair) and his rubber boots melted on his feet. The 'experts' stated that a gas leak had caused the explosion. The Gas Light & Coke Company opened up its mains, but found no leak. Then the 'experts' suggested the malignant activity of 'sewer gas'. No such gas was detected, and the Coroner entered a verdict of Accidental Death, and closed the case. Was this SHC . . . or something different? At any rate, the case brings up another list of coincidences:

Coincidences of date

7 April, 1938	G. Turner dead in cabin of truck
8 April, 1938	G. Shepherdson dead in car . . . both from same cause
27 December, 1938	Mrs Florence Hill
	Mrs Agnes Flight
	Mrs Louisa Gorringe
	James Duncan
28 December, 1938	Mrs Amelia Ridge
	Sarah Pegler
	Ellen Wright
	Harriet Lawless
	Mrs Harriet Garner
	Horace Nicholas

I have quoted several theories on the origin of SHC: Russell's is unusual, to say the least. Having mentioned that ammonia and iodine form a highly explosive mixture, he goes on to say:

> The human system contains iodine and daily expels a certain amount of it. Urine is exceedingly rich in

ammonia. Couple these facts with carelessness in matters of hygiene, and you have a set-up which I do not for one moment offer as the true or likely cause of human burnings, but which serves to show what can happen.'

Well . . . what *can* happen? It is rarely that a theoretician advances a theory that he claims is unlikely. Rarely in the scientific investigation of phenomena – and Russell was a careful researcher – can so meaningless a sentence have been written.

Pages 167 and 202n
It is only fair to Dr Krogman that I should make his own position absolutely clear. In a private letter to me, he states unambiguously: 'I do not believe in Spontaneous Combustion.'

Page 193
Other foci of 'gravitational aberration' – with aberrations even more puzzling than those encountered in Lincolnshire – are to be found in North America, at three well-defined and now well-investigated places: two in Oregon (where, it will be remembered, the strange business of Mrs Satlow's partial combustion within a closed coffin occurred) and one in Colorado, roughly a thousand miles distant.

The three American foci are to be found at Sardine Creek, about thirty miles from Grant's Pass, Oregon; the second is – still in Oregon – some forty-five miles distant in the Siskiyou Mountains; the third is at Camp Burch, Colorado. Of the three, the first – the so-called 'Oregon Vortex' – is the best-known and by far the most puzzling (not to say alarming!). Here, as one observer remarked, 'Gravity seems to have taken leave of its senses' – a pithy summing-up of phenomena which seems, not merely to defy gravitation, but to mock it.

The 'Vortex' occupies an area of approximately 165 feet – the limits varying slightly through a 90-day period – and is centered upon an abandoned assay office, abandoned because of the erratic behavior of the scales used to weigh ore and dust from the mines. The human body is at once conscious, when entering the area of the 'Vortex', of a disturbing pull downwards, as though in response to a sudden and violent increase in gravitational attraction. A 28-pound steel ball, hung

346

by investigating scientists from the ceiling of the old wooden hut, hangs down, not vertically, but inclined towards the centre of the 'Vortex'; visitors to the hut find that they are leaning as much as 10 degrees out of true in the direction of that centre of attraction. Everything shows an inclination to move towards the center of the 'Vortex' – a glass will even run up a board in order to do so. Cigarette smoke blown into this gravitational oddity will eddy in a spiral, growing ever tighter until it disappears, indicating that there really must be a vortex, in fact as well as in name. Scraps of paper 'will spiral madly about, as though stirred in mid-air by some unseen hand': so the author, Frank Edwards, describes the phenomenon, in his *Stranger Than Science*.

Even the trees within the influence of the 'Vortex' lean towards its centre. But the phenomenon which is perhaps the most disturbing of all is the demonstration, by an ordinary photographer's light-meter, that light itself (in this case, its electrical equivalent) varies within the 'Vortex' appreciably from the light outside.

The effects are not so pronounced in the other two vortices – that at Camp Burch and that in the Siskiyou Mountains; but there are still striking aberrations.

The relatively milder gravitational aberrations of Lincolnshire *may* be explained by the fact that Lincolnshire is almost abnormally flat, while the three North American aberrations are to be found in some of the most mountainous parts of the West.

It is an odd coincidence that there should be a Salem not so far from the 'Oregon Vortex', and that equally odd things happened in Salem, Massachusetts, two hundred years before the white miners began to share the Indians' natural reluctance to frequent what the Indians held to be an accursed spot.

Page 205

Several readers of the first edition of this book have complained of what they designate as my 'credulity' in the matter of Palladino's and others' apparent ability to control their bodily weight. Dr Banesh Hoffmann, for all of whose opinions I can never have anything but respect, gently chides me in remarking that 'The phenomenon reported [by you] in the first paragraph of page 176 [in the first edition] can be found described in books on stage magic: it is done by means of electromagnets concealed under the stage. *This being the case* [my emphasis], I doubt that there is reason to conclude that the person in question could actually control her own weight.'

This objection to my accepting that a person *may* be able to control his or her own weight without the use of 'electromagnets concealed under the stage' carries with it, I am afraid, the disturbing implication, not only that *all* apparent weight control is 'done with magnets', but that all paranormal phenomena must, somehow, be explicable in our postulating the existence of a hidden mechanical contrivance. In all such objections to 'credulity', it will be observed that a different hypothesis is suggested – 'it is done by means of electromagnets concealed under the stage' – and then this hypothesis (no more proven than my own!) is henceforward treated as a proven fact. 'This being the case . . .'

But Dr Hoffmann's standing in the academic world is such, his opinion generally of so much weight, that I think that it should be examined here, since it does truly represent a widespread attitude to paranormal phenomena, *especially when exhibited on the stage or elsewhere in public.*

In October 1976, the British Broadcasting Corporation presented a television series on the 'Unknown', in the course of which the 'spoon-bending' Mr Uri Geller was attacked by a professional prestidigitator, 'magician' and 'illusionist', Mr Randi, whose deft performance illustrated all the wrong thinking behind the general objection to the mass of Paranormal Phenomena. Mr Randi's 'reasoning' went like this. 'If I can demonstrate that I may bend spoons and forks and keys, then the spoon-bending of Mr Geller *must* have been done as I say that I do it' – that is, by the methods of 'stage-magic' – 'and not by the way that Mr Geller says that he does it.' The proposition, as plausible as it is baseless, is that if a phenomenon may be reproduced by Mr Randi or any other professional conjurer, then that was how the phenomenon manifested itself in the first and in all other places. It would be hard to find a proposition less logical (or, since we are looking at a common point of view, more warmly defended).

Mr Randi, asked to explain the phenomenon of telekinesis (TK), by which, without apparent physical contact, a person may move objects – at present generally small, such as matchboxes – proposed that the

348

matchbox 'could have been' moved by means of an 'almost invisible' nylon thread, held between the Telekinetic's hands, and pushed against the matchbox. Now it is evident that, by means of an 'almost invisible' nylon thread, a matchbox may be made to *seem* movable telekinetically, but that does not – *cannot* – make it an 'explanation' applicable to all the recorded demonstrations of telekinetic force.

Does Mr Randi seriously suggest that when Mrs Nelya Mikhailova was put through a long and scientifically-controlled series of experiments designed to test her telekinetic powers, she bamboozled Dr Sergeyev and his colleagues of the A. A. Uktomskii Psychological Institute with such crude tricks as moving boxes with 'almost invisible' nylon thread; or, perhaps, that she sneaked in at night, after Dr Sergeyev and his team had locked up for the night, and then installed electromagnets beneath the table? Unfortunately for the plausible 'explainers' of the Mr Randi type, photographs of Mrs Mikhailova under the examination show that she is very far from being a free woman, since she is connected to recording instruments which register her rate of pulse, respiration, etc. She would need to be an exceptionally adroit trickster to deceive the Soviet scientists sitting all around her and watching her so closely!

At the end of the last century, Florence Cook, a professional medium, gained great notoriety, not so much in her producing 'spirit forms', as in her impressing some of the most distinguished of British scientists. She was 'exposed', to the satisfaction of all unbelievers, when the two most famous 'stage illusionists' of the day, Messrs. Maskelyne and Devant, announced – correctly, indeed – that they could 'reproduce' all Miss Cook's 'psychic' phenomena on the stage of their theatre at the Egyptian Hall, Piccadilly, London. There is no doubt that they could; but what no one asked the famous 'illusionists' then – and no one has asked since – is this: Could they have 'reproduced' Miss Cook's 'illusions' (as Maskelyene and Devant called them) *in the circumstances in which Miss Cook produced them?* It seems to me that the genuine possessors of paranormal abilities have shown a regrettable absence of enterprise and initiative in letting the Maskelynes, the Devants and the Randis of this world steal a march on them. What the Cooks, the Palladinos, the Cayces, the Mikhailovas, the Gellers and the Mannings should have done was boldly to say: Whatever the Maskelynes and the rest of the 'illusionists' have done, we can do, too

– *but without their special conditions:* their lenses and prisms and lighting; their mechanical contrivances and carpenter's effects – and their position at a distance of many feet from even the nearest of the audience. The genuine paranormals should have made the challenge – not left it to the professional stage 'illusionists'. But perhaps it is not too late for me to point out here that the challenge is decidedly one-sided – that what the Maskelynes have never done is to reproduce some paranormal phenomena in the same conditions in which they were originally produced.

Fresh thinking on this hotly debated subject is long overdue. In the mid-18th-century and early 19th century, three extraordinary mental calculators appeared: the English Jedediah Buxton (died, aged 70, in 1775), the English George Bidder and the American boy, Zerah Colburn, perhaps the most extraordinary of the three. These mental calculators could solve arithmetical problems – addition, subtraction, multiplication, division and the extraction of both square and cube roots – involving numbers containing as many as twenty-four digits; the problems presented verbally, and solved, within a few seconds, mentally.

Now, it would be quite possible for those who 'don't believe', in almost instantaneous mental calculation involving very high numbers to suggest a means by which the problems could be solved otherwise than mentally – that is, by a calculating device; the answers being supplied secretly to the 'mental calculator'. In the case of the farmer's boy, Zerah Colburn, who exhibited his talents in London and other places in Great Britain in the years immediately preceding the Anglo-American War of 1812-15, it would even be possible to suggest a system of communication between the 'real calculator' and the supposed mentally-calculating boy which involved electricity. (In 1812, the Russian general, Baron von Canstadt, defended Kronstadt and St Petersburg against an invading French fleet by means of underwater mines detonated *electrically.*)

In the case of, say, Zerah Colburn, we may imagine that, standing on a stage before a 'select' London audience, he is asked to give the square of, say, the number 623,351,089 – a number which, involving only nine digits, would have been 'child's play' for the boy mathematical wonder.

Let us imagine that young Colburn, in the accepted fashion of the day, stands with his fingers lightly resting upon a small round table, in which are some 'innocent' objects, such as a carafe, a waterglass, a book . . . perhaps a handbell or some other metal object . . .

Let us further imagine that, hidden behind a curtain off stage, is a normally competent cypherer, with an abacus, or merely a pencil and paper; one who is 'quick with figures'. With his abacus or pencil-and-paper, it is a matter of moments to add, subtract, extract square or cube roots.

The answer obtained by his rapid calculations, he then sends electrical impulses to the metal object through the table . . .

Three impulses . . . one, two, three . . . the digit 3.

Eight impulses . . . one, two . . . the digit 8.

And so on, until the number is 'impulsed' out through the electrically activated table or metal object on it.

Or, unseen by the audience, who are facing young Colburn, but clearly seen by him, is a dark-lantern with a rapidly adjustable shutter, on the principle of the modern Aldis lamp. The answers are flashed to young Colburn by means of this specially adapted dark-lantern.

Or . . .

But why continue? For, when young Colburn appeared before (and consistently astounded) representative committees of various bodies – including the Royal Society and the Senate of Cambridge University – he could not rely on his electrically-activated table, his informative dark-lantern in *their* committee rooms.

The truth which must be made clear is that, because a certain effect may be achieved in a certain way, that does not – cannot – mean that the effect may be achieved in no other way. Because the apparent increase of bodily weight may be achieved through the use of 'electro-magnets concealed under the stage', that does not mean that an increase of bodily weight cannot be achieved by any other means – including the use of paranormal powers. There are many ways in which any effect may be achieved – and this is a fact that the unbelievers would do well to accept.

It is a pleasure, then, in this atmosphere of incredulity in regard to the paranormal, to record the open-mindedness of one who, professionally, has mastered all the secrets of stage-illusionist deception, yet remains consciously accessible to the truth that strange

351

phenomena may remain inexplicable for all that the stage-magician may reproduce them.

Mr Bayard Grimshaw, of Rochdale, Lancashire, England, is a professional prestidigitator and illusionist, high in his craft. He is the author of *About Magicians,* and the editor of *The Budget,* the house-journal of the International Brotherhood of Magicians. Of Mr Grimshaw's claims to speak learnedly on stage-illusions there can be no doubt.

On my behalf, Mr Edward Campbell, literary editor of the London *Evening News,* wrote to him about that 'slow-vaulting' which, as I have remarked on Page 209, was certainly not the sole prerogative of Nijinsky.

There is a passage in Mr Grimshaw's answering letter to Mr Campbell which deserves, in my opinion, permanent record, not merely in relation to 'slow vaulting', but in relation to every phenomenon which cannot, in the light of our present knowledge, be explained. I quote Mr Grimshaw – asking the reader to bear in mind that he knows more about stage trickery than any of those who have adversely criticized the 'credulity' of those of us who accept the fact of – even if we cannot as yet provide the explanation for – paranormal phenomena.

It's odd that you should have remembered the 'slow vaulting' story from the time that I first told it in *About Magicians.* I agree completely with your theory. There are so many 'things in heaven and earth' that are anathema to the sceptic; but the intelligent, thinking, open-minded enquirer knows the difference between fiction and honest reporting, and remains open-minded. I have many brushes with the large body of magicians who seem to think that their knowledge of trickery qualifies them to 'expose' everything that doesn't seem to fit in with everyday humdrum affairs. And in, for example, the spheres of telepathy and 'ghosts,' I have so much personal proof that all the 'explanations' in the world leave one quietly convinced.

When such opinions of the paranormal can come from one who is acquainted with both stage trickery and the widespread belief that phenomena which may be imitated on the stage are thereby 'exposed' as fraudulent, we may confidently trust that the secrets of the paranormal will eventually yield to what Mr Grimshaw calls 'honest reporting'.

Pages 207-209

Through the kindness of Mr Bayard Grimshaw, illusionist, I am now able to give the details of that 'slow vaulting' that I saw before the first World War, and which had its 'first preview' at Nantes, in Brittany, in 1776, the year of the Declaration of Independence, but which, as an esoteric art, must have an unthinkably ancient history behind it.

'The most strange act I saw as a boy', a Staffordshire, England, reader wrote to *The Times and Recorder* (article of 20 January, 1939), was at a big fête at Trentham Park, when a Frenchman and his son did what was called 'slow vaulting'. They did all sorts of vaulting through the air with springboards, etc., but the strange thing was that the boy, who was in pantaloons like a clown, seemed to fly very slowly through the air. He made slow motions with his arms, and seemed to float slowly. If I remember rightly, his father was supposed to mesmerize him, and he finished his performance by jumping off a stage *as high as a house* [my emphasis], and slowly coming to earth, landing on his feet as light as a feather.'

That this 'slow vaulting' was a closely guarded secret of the French 'magicians' is stated in *The Romance of Magic* – a book now long out of print. There is no reason to doubt the validity of this claim, as it was a Frenchman, Monsieur Defontagne, who first gave a public demonstration of 'slow vaulting' – and invoked the authority of the Royal Governor to stage that demonstration under what is now called 'scientific control'.

Having perfected his technique, Monsieur Defontagne now sought someone to demonstrate it and, not incredibly, found no volunteers. The Frenchman then approached the Governor of Brittany, the Duc d'Aiguillon, to offer, 'in the interests of science', a pardon to any criminal who would submit himself to the experiments of Monsieur Defontagne. A condemned murderer of Port St Louis, Dominic Dufour,

353

aged about twenty-four, took up the offer. 'He underwent training with the inventor, and a number of experimental efforts were made. Then it was announced that the convict, under the inventor's guidance, had leapt off a 70-foot parapet.'

Obviously the time had now come for a public demonstration; and this was given, following the custom of those more spacious times, with a good deal of official ballyhoo, to emphasize the 'seriousness' of the occasion.

A contemporary account describes how, not only the paroled murderer, but the Duke and the King's Professor of Mathematics at the University of Rennes, ascended to the roof of the Arsenal, 145 feet above the Esplanade at Nantes. As a reasonable precaution against mishap to the criminal, a priest, the Abbé de Henry, came along.

There are some allusions in this account not easy to interpret: a reference to Dufour's wearing 'a suit of feathered tissue' – what could that have been? – and his being given a draught, just before being pushed off the parapet of the Arsenal, of 'a cephalic cordial', which seems an unnecessarily pompous way of describing brandy, if indeed it was brandy.

Now, 'as we all know', the gravitational constant of 32-feet-per-second-per-second – the rate at which a body (disregarding the resistance of the air for a moment) descends in free-fall – gives a time of no more than three *seconds* for an object to fall from the 145-foot-high roof of the Arsenal to the pavement below. But what happened?

'A strong cephalic cordial being given to [Dufour], he was pushed very gently off the parapet of the building in sight of more than ten thousand spectators; and after fluttering a little in a brisk wind, began to descend in a steady, uniform manner, amidst the acclamations of the people, whose joy for his success would have been immoderate, if not checked by some anxiety for the final outcome; which soon relieved them, for the convict landed upon his feet in perfect safety, being exactly two minutes and thirteen seconds in his descent'.

In other words, Dufour (under the instruction of Monsieur Defontagne) had so controlled the gravitational force of the earth that he had extended a 'normal' fall of only *three seconds* to no less than *one hundred and thirty-three seconds!*

Critics of 'wishy-washy liberal sentimentality' are often loud in their criticism of the soft way in which 'we' treat the modern criminal. It

354

seems to me, in reading old records, that the criminal of courage and enterprise didn't do so badly, either, in 'tyrannical' eighteenth-century France.

> '[Dufour] was immediately let blood and conducted through the principal streets, with drums and trumpets, to the Town Hall, where the magistrates gave a splendid entertainment to the many nobility and gentry who had come from all parts of the country to behold the extraordinary sight.
> 'A handsome collection was made by the company, and the prisoner relieved, with a certificate of his performance, to entitle him to the King's bounty and most gracious pardon, with which he set off the next day for Paris, to secure for it the Royal seal.'

Nantes to Paris is roughly two hundred miles – and, in those days, no easy journey. I like to think of the about-to-be-pardoned criminal, Dominic Dufour, paying his way by an occasional demonstration of the esoteric art which had saved him from the scaffold or – at least – the galleys.

The important point about such true stories is that the phenomena involved, however 'mysterious', were witnessed not merely by a small group of already half-convinced persons (one thinks here of Lord Adare and his friends testifying to the levitation of Daniel Dunglass Home), but by tens of thousands. The demonstration of 'slow-vaulting' at Trentham Park, a century and more after Dufour's descent at Nantes, was probably witnessed by even more people than had gaped at Dufour as he fell from the roof of the Arsenal at *one-forty-fourth* the 'normal' rate of descent.

That – apart from my own witness – 'slow-vaulting' (that is, the control of Earth's gravitational attraction) is a well-proven fact means at human skill has matched, in this matter at least, the 'gravitational aberration' apparent on the flat fields of Lincolnshire and in the mountainous regions of Oregon and Colorado. There is a growing body of opinion that *all* 'mysterious' – paranormal – phenomena are in some as-yet, unexplained fashion merely different aspects of the 'same thing' . . . whatever that may turn out to be. It is for this reason that, in investigating the phenomenon of Spontaneous Combustion, I have not neglected to look at 'slow-vaulting', levitation, telekinesis and

355

the rest. The Law of the Conservation of Energy makes no distinction among the various aspects of energy; to the Law, all energy is the same. Modern thinking is inclined to suspect the existence of a comparable Law of the Conservation of Energy in the Paranormal . . . I am sure that Russian official scientific thinking has already accepted the hypothesis that there is, that there must be, such a Law. But, assuming for the present that there is such a 'unification' of all paranormal phenomena as to suggest that they all spring from the same primal cause, then we must be prepared to accept that there may be as much conscious human will in all this paranormality as there is 'blind chance'.

Page 260

That variation in the classic SHC pattern in which the clothing, rather than its wearer, seems to be the victim of the Fire's attack, manifested itself recently in Brighton, England, a town at the very center of a Fire-frequented district. The account of Miss Sally Flack's alarming experience made an amusing story in the local newspaper, *Evening Argus*, and the young lady herself appears to have been more amused than frightened by her experience. With the presence of mind shown by the Nashville Professor, Mr Hamilton, Miss Flack managed to beat out the flames – but what if she had panicked . . .?

A GIRL CAUGHT
IN THE HOT SEAT

When Sally Flack jumped off a Brighton bus she was a real hot number. She was on fire.

Moments after she got on the bus at Saltdean her trousers caught fire. But she only noticed her hot pants when a fellow-passenger gave the alarm.

Sally, 18, managed to put herself out and was not hurt . . .

The cause of the blaze is a mystery. A Brighton Council official thinks a cigar-

356

ette-end may have got caught in Sally's
shoe . . .

On which one may only comment, 'He would!'

It is interesting to note the number of victims who do not 'notice' the Fire which has attacked them. The servant-girl at Binbrook Farm was unaware that flames were coming out of her back, and one of the eight Birmingham Fire-victims, Mark Bradbury, slept peacefully through most of the blaze which destroyed most of his legs and feet. (Note also the case − Page 111 − of the sleeping guest at the Air Terminal Hotel, London, on 12 September, 1974.)

And one wonders if those 'unaccountable' small burns − usually described as 'cigarette burns' − which seem to attack new (and mostly the more expensive) clothing and stockings and the upholstery of furniture are caused by cigarettes, any more than the fires which burn up mattresses and, too often, those who sleep on them. Though I do not smoke, I find that my clothing and furniture seems as vulnerable to tiny burns as the property of those who do smoke. Are these burns the 'micro-aspect' of that Fire which, in its more violent and voracious activity, will burn up humans, their houses and − as was noted at the time of the great Chicago Fire − even whole cites?

Page 265

' . . . and then we should have the problem of burning the body without touching the clothes.' In the investigation of any 'mysterious' − that is, not-yet-explained − phenomenon, no suggested explanation must be considered too fanciful; and a suggestion which was made to me some few weeks back has, as they say, 'caused me seriously to think'. It is this:

After having read my book, a friend of mine, Mr Richard Gluyas, a civil engineer by profession and a well-known London and Middle East businessman, asked me some further questions about those victims of SHC who had been burned inside their unburned clothing. When I assured him that there had been several such cases − all well-attested − he did not express the incredulity with which my account of such cases is too often met.

'Burned up, eh? Completely . . ..?'

'Some. Billy Peterson of Detroit was pretty well charred-up inside his completely unburned – not even singed – clothing; Mrs Satlow's corpse was half-consumed inside a closed coffin of which the satin lining was not even singed.'

'Contents burned, then, inside an unburned container?' Mr Gluyas did not hesitate to give me his, I think most eminently *practical*, solution: 'Why, my dear chap: simple! Ordinary microwave cooking . . .'

I recommend the suggestion to those scientists who are studying the problem of SHC. But perhaps the 'solution' has already been accepted; I understand that Mr Leslie Watkins of the London *Daily Mail* has already written a thriller in which the CIA causes the death of 'undesirables' by what appears to be, but of course isn't, spontaneous combustion . . .

Page 271

The Connection with Water – a breakthrough in research?

That the fire is closely linked with poltergeist activity is hardly to be denied; but statistical analysis of the cases after I had finished the revised version of *Fire from Heaven* has proved to me that there is a connection which is even more clearly demonstrated: the connection between the 'strikes' of the Fire and the proximity of water, whether of the sea, a river or a lake or inland waterway.

Like most other discoveries, there was a good deal which was accidental, even though I had been preparing to make a number of statistical analyses of the figures that I had already obtained. (For instance, I am working now on 'vulnerability' by age-groups.)

I was about to make a master-recording for the British Broadcasting Corporation, to be broadcast from their various stations in England; and I was asked to make a map showing the places where the Fire had struck. I made a rough sketch of the map of England, and began to mark out the Fire-strikes – and then I found that I was looking at something very interesting indeed.

I was struck by the large number of victims of the Fire who had lived by the sea or by important rivers – though by far the greater number of Fire-deaths occurred in seacoast towns or on the biggest of

English estuaries. Bearing in mind that only a small percentage of deaths or injuries by Spontaneous Combustion are ever reported in the Press, one must allow for analysis of comparatively small numbers of cases, though, fortunately enough for the purposes of serious research. In Britain alone, 53 per cent of the total number of cases recorded in my book occurred on the coast or on a large estuary, while a further 15 per cent occurred in towns distant no more than ten miles from the sea. A preliminary glance at the non-British, particularly American, Canadian and African cases, appear to reveal the same pattern, though a complete analysis will have to be undertaken as soon as possible.

The importance of this discovery – of the connection between the Fire and large bodies of water – cannot possibly be overestimated, since I consider it as giving us, for the first time, sound reasons for believing that at last we are on our way to a solution of this most mysterious of all mysteries. Ever since Science began to study the phenomenon of Spontaneous Combustion, theory after theory has been adopted and discarded in the effort to find a cause of the Fire: old age, adiposity, drunkenness, and so on. As I have said elsewhere, even Fort, though sensing the predisposing power of the emotions towards a Fire-vulnerability, overlooked the need to establish the optimum physical-environmental conditions – the ideal ambience, as one might say.

The count of (British) cases reveals the following:

			% of total of 66
A	On seacoast or estuary	35 cases	53%
B	Near seacoast or on river	10 cases	15%
C	On or near river, but distant from sea (ex-London)	14 cases	22%
D	London only (on River Thames)	7 cases	
			10% *
			100%

* Percentages ignore decimal points

Conclusion from the adduced facts

A connection between the incidence of the fire and the presence of water may be confidently accepted as an hypothesis not before considered or presented by any other researcher. Further – judging by the percentages given above – there appears to be a *quantitative* relationship. In other words, the greater the quantity of near-to-hand water (usually the sea), the more likelihood of the manifestation of the Fire – and the more vigorous its manifestation will be.

There is nothing in this new hypothesis which contradicts any of the assumptions already made in my book; to the contrary, it must have been my intuitive recognition of the Fire-Water relationship which caused me to discuss at some length (notably in Chapters 4 and 14) dowsing and related 'biophysical effects'. It might well be argued at any hypothesis may hardly be built upon an analysis of only sixty-six cases of Fire-strike – and those from Britain alone.

But even a hasty survey of the non-British scene, particularly the North American, seems to show the same sinister relationship between the fire and the presence of water. One may recall the appalling cases of Glen B. Denney of Gretna, Louisiana; of Billy Peterson of Detroit; of Mrs Mary Reeser of St Petersburg, Fla.; of the sixfold death in the Iponri family – this last, perhaps, the most frightful case of all.

Were these nine non-British victims of the Fire anywhere near water? Well, Glen B. Denney's factory and home were at Gretna, on the Mississippi, one of the world's greatest rivers; Billy Peterson's home town of Detroit is the largest exporting town on the Great Lakes; Mrs Reeser's St Petersburg is on that vast bay called the Gulf of Mexico, while the home of that luckless Nigerian family was at Lagos, on an even vaster body of water . . . the South Atlantic.

Page 281

Testimony of a similar type to that given by Miss Christine Harmer, who said of SHC victim, Mr William Seale, 65, that 'I think he got fed up not being able to go out . . . He was a lonely man', was given by the neighbour of yet another victim of that SHC which seems to come to the old and lonely.

Mr Herbert Mill, 88, had just been discharged from the hospital, and had returned to his home at Bognor Regis, in the 'strongly SHC' area which lies between Eastbourne on the east, and Chichester on the west, along England's Sussex coast. (Mr Seale lived in Brighton, about halfway between the two towns.) Said the local *Evening Argus*:

> An elderly man just out of hospital died in a fire in his Bognor Regis home early today. [Tuesday, 21st February, 1978]
>
> Two policeman made an unsuccessful bid to rescue [him] from the house in Burnham Avenue. They put wet towels over their faces but were driven from the semi-detached house by the choking smoke.
>
> PCs David Mills and Bob Smith smelled smoke as they passed in their patrol car at 2 A M. and discovered the fire. 'We knew an old man lived there', said PC Mills. 'The front door was ajar and we could hear glass exploding.
>
> 'There was nothing we could do. We closed the door and waited for the fire brigade . . .'
>
> The cause of the fire is not known, and Bognor Regis police said there were no suspicious circumstances.

In other words, the death of the lonely and unwanted through SHC is regarded, not, I think, unreasonably, as death from natural causes. A neighbour gave what must have been both an explanation and what may pass for Mr Mill's elegy:

> **ALONE**
> Mrs Arnold, who gave the policemen the towels, said Mr Mill went into hospital last Saturday and returned home last night.

> 'He lived alone', she said. 'We don't
> know anything about him. We hardly
> ever saw him.'

Elsewhere in these notes, I discuss my discovery of what appears to be an important factor common to most, if not all, the cases of SHC (but this cannot be the only common factor). It is certain – to my way of thinking – that there is a constant *emotional* element predisposing to injury or death by SHC.

Old, lonely, helpless people are often depressed – but then, so are younger people, younger people with friends and unimpaired physical powers. I doubt that the misery of any miserable old person may compare, in intensity of bitterness and suffering, with that misery which too often troubles the child and the adolescent.

'Obviously', one might say, what applied to 88-year-old Mr Herbert Mill would hardly have applied to 35-year-old Mrs Françoise Price, who died in an SHC fire of violent nature only six days before he did – both within the 'Fire Belt' of the Eastbourne-Chichester coastal strip, that fated strip within which Mr William Seale, that 'lonely man', perished eighteen months earlier, barely a mile from where Mrs Price died. But are the differences so 'obvious'?

I had the opportunity of discussing the death of Mrs Price with a chambermaid employed at the hotel in which the woman died; even for an SHC fire, the events were remarkable. The local newspaper carried this headline in its edition of Wednesday, 15 February, 1978:

WIFE DIES IN BLAZE AT HOTEL
Police this afternoon ruled out crime in the death of an attractive 35-year-old woman in a blazing Hove hotel room.

Her charred body, jammed against the door and partly covered by a mattress, was found by firemen at the Lawns Hotel, on the Kingsway.

Mrs Price had gone upstairs to her room, leaving her husband downstairs to follow. About an hour later, when he went to open the door of the bedroom, he could not get in; he smelled smoke, called the porter, who, in turn, called the fire brigade, which were unable to enter until after all hope of saving Mrs Price had long gone.

When found, Mrs Price's body was completely charred; and of the large mattress that she had somehow pulled off the bed, only the springs remained. (One recalls the statement of a member of the St Petersburg, Fla. mattress company who pointed out that that there is not enough material in any overstuffed chair – nor even in a big mattress – to cremate a human body. The basic stuffing of such articles of furniture, he said, consists in cotton, which is often combined with hair or felt or foam rubber; and that, though capable of being ignited, and of smouldering for a long time, they are, either alone or in combination, incapable of bursting into violent flame. See page 145.)

But in the case of Mrs Price, both she and the mattress were utterly consumed, as the horrified chambermaid told me. And one wonders *how* Mrs Price managed to pull a heavy mattress off the bed and cover herself with it?

Nor was this the only unusual aspect of the tragedy:

1. 'When police were called to the hotel just after midnight, Superintendent Bob Allen said: "We are treating this as a suspicious death."
2. 'But this afternoon, Detective-Superintendent Ian Eadie, head of Sussex Central Division Criminal Investigation Department, ruled out foul play after a preliminary report from Home Office pathologist, Dr Hugh Johnson.'

I pass this without comment.

Mrs Price was French, a foreigner in a strange land. 'She had a heavy French accent', said a neighbour. And perhaps another neighbour came as near as anyone to explaining how Mrs Price died when she remarked: 'Mrs Price was very attractive . . . but sometimes sad.'

Officialdom seems, in this case, to have learnt some of the lessons that forensic medicine has tried to ignore; but one sees the old obstinacy in this brief report – a mere six-line, single-column 'filler' – from the London *Daily Telegraph* of Tuesday, 17 January, 1978:

ARMCHAIR DEATH

Mrs Mary Watts, 82, a widow, was found
dead in a burning armchair at her home
in Stoke Albany, Northants, yesterday.
She is thought to have dropped a lighted
cigarette.

Is it not about time that some enterprising mattress-manufacturer
or maker of upholstered armchairs advertised his goods under the
slogan: 'Can't be ignited by a dropped cigarette'? But, then, what would
traditionally-minded officialdom do?

It really is extraordinary how Authority handles these constantly
recurring cases of SHC. A reader, Mr Terry Mazarella, of Canterbury,
Kent, sends me a cutting from *The Kentish Gazette*, 26 November,
1976, concerning the fiery death of an 82-year-old widow, Mrs Dorothy
Sample, whose end exhibits all those details which make it a classic
case of SHC: the charred and unrecognizable remains of an elderly
woman, the body identifiable only by the hallmark on the wedding
ring; the 'evidence' (mandatory at all coroners' inquests) that the
'deceased' smoked ('But not heavily', said the neighbour, Mr Robert
Sanders.); the *other* type of smoke noticed by the neighbour's wife,
who asked her husband 'where it was coming from'. The age of the
victim: eighty-two. The condition of the victim: elderly widow, who
relied on her neighbours 'quite a lot'.

The findings of the coroner's inquest follow the usual pattern:

'Two possible causes are that she was sitting in the
armchair smoking, fell asleep and set fire to the chair.
Depending on her clothes, they could have been ignited
by standing close to the fire.'

What highly inflammable clothes they must have been, to have had
the power, when well alight, to have consumed the body to a point
when it became 'a charred and unrecognizable' corpse.

One might have expected the verdict: 'Death by misadventure'.

The case interested me, not so much because it was so obviously
a classic case of SHC, as because once again that initial letter S *(see*

page 129) turns up, not only in Mrs Sample's name but also in that of the principal witnesses at her inquest: Mr and Mrs Sanders.

It is clear now that there are two *principal* predisposing factors in the making of that pattern in which SHC becomes inevitable: an 'emotional' factor (there is a more precise word; but 'emotional' will do for the present) and a factor constructed from and depending upon a certain well-defined physical environment. (Of course, the different-iation between emotional and physical is arbitrary and imprecise; but for ordinary argument, the differentation may justifiably be maintained – as when we say that people become victims of SHC when they *feel* in a certain way, and, at the same time, find themselves in a certain set of physical conditions.)

Charles Fort realized the predisposing vulnerability to SHC in that depression which comes from neglect, loneliness, fear, and so on. I am not so sure that he realized that there must be the predisposing power of environmental factors as well. I think that, in a statistical analysis of the *places* where SHC has struck, I may well have established the existence of at least one important environmental factor.

BIBLIOGRAPHY

Although mine is the first book to have Spontaneous Combustion as the main subject, the literature on this subject is plentiful.

The works – books and articles – cited below do not in any way exhaust the reserves of supporting literature: they are merely representative studies of, or observations on, a phenomenon which has had its own specialized research and medico-legal comment since the publication of Jonas Dupont's study of spontaneous combustion more than two centuries ago.

BOOKS

Adare, Lord, *Experiences with D. D. Home* (London 1924).

Bailey, Alice, A *Treatise on Cosmic Fire* (New York 1925, London 1925).

Beck, T. R. and Beck, J. B., *Elements of Medical Jurisprudence* (London 1838).

Bennett, Sir E., *Apparitions and Haunted Houses* (London *1939).*

Brewster, Sir David, *Letters on Natural Magic* (London 1832).

Brinton, Howard, *The Mystic Will* (London 1931).

Bucke, Richard, *Cosmic Consciousness (New* York 1905).

Burton, Jean, *Heyday of a Wizard (New* York 1944, London 1948).

Carpenter, W. B., *Principles of General and Comparative Physiology* (London 1839).

Carrington, Hereward, *Death: Its Causes and Phenomena* (New York 1921).

——————— and Fodor, N., *Haunted People (New* York 1951).

Casper, J. L., *Handbook of the Practice of Forensic Medicine* (London 1861-65).

Chalmers, N., Crawley, R., and Rose, S., *The Biological Basis of Behaviour* (London and New York 1971).

Constance, Arthur, *The Inexplicable Sky* (London 1956).

de Quincey, Thomas, *Confessions of an English Opium-Eater* (London 1822, revised edition 1856).

Dingwall, E., *Some Human Oddities* (London 1947).

Dupont, Jonas, *De Incendiis Corporis Humani Spontaneis* (Leyden 1763).

Edwards, F., *Strange World* (New York 1964).

Faraday, Michael, *The Chemical History of a Candle* (London 1861).

Fodor, Nandor, *The Haunted Mind* *(New* York 1959). ─────────

Between Two Worlds (New York 1964).

Forbes, J. and Tweedie, A., *Cyclopaedia of Practical Medicine,* 4 vols (Edinburgh 1833).

Fort, Charles, *The Book of the Damned* (New York 1920).

───────── *Lo!* (London 1931).

───────── *Wild Talents* (London 1931).

Gaddis, Vincent H., *Invisible Horizons* (Philadelphia and New York 1965).

───────── *Mysterious Fires and Lights* (New York 1967).

Gauquelin, Michel, *L'Astrologie devant la science* (Paris 1966) translated by James Hughes as *Astrology and Science* (London 1970).

───────── *The Cosmic Clocks* (London 1969).

Gideon, John, *Curiosities of Medical Experience* (London 1837).

Glaister, J., *Medical Jurisprudence and Toxicology* (llth edition, London 1964)

Good, John Mason, *The Book of Nature* *(New* York 1831).

Gould, G. M. and Pyle, W. L., *Anomalies and Curiosities of Medicine* (New York 1937).

Grey Walter, W., *The Living Brain* (Harmondsworth 1961).

Guy, W. A. and Ferrier, D., *Principles of Forensic Medicine* (London 1881).

Heywood, Rosalind, *The Sixth Sense* (London 1959).

House, Brant, *Strange Powers of Unusual People* (New York 1963).

Johnson, Walter R., *A Familiar Introduction to the Principles of Physical Science* (Philadelphia 1836).

Keel, John A., *Operation Trojan Horse* (paperback, London 1972).

Keele, K. D., *Leonardo da Vinci – Movement of the Heart and Blood* (London 1952).

Kilner, Walter, *The Human Aura* (London 1911).

Lair, Pierre, *Essai sur les combustions humaines, produites par l'abus des liqueurs spiritueuses* (Paris 1808).

Lambert, R. S., *Exploring the Supernatural* (Toronto 1955).

Von Liebig, J., *Letters on Chemistry* (London 1855).

Mackay, Charles, *Memoirs of Extraordinary Popular Delusions and the Madness of Crowds* (London 1852).

Mann, Dixon, *Forensic Medicine* (London 1922).

Michell, John, *City of Revelation* (London 1973).

Nichols, Beverley, *Powers that be; Authenticated Cases of Man and the Supernatural* (London 1963).

O'Malley, C., and Saunders, J. B. de C. M., *Leonardo da Vinci and the Human Body* (New York 1952).

Ostrander, Sheila and Schroeder, Lynn, *PSI – Psychic Discoveries Behind the Iron Curtain* (London 1970).

Paris, J. A. and Fonblanque, J. S. M., *Medical Jurisprudence* (London 1833).

Price, Harry, *Fifty Years of Psychical Research* (London 1939).

————— *Confessions of a Ghost-Hunter* (London 1936).

————— *Poltergeist over England* (London 1945).

Puharich, A., *Beyond Telepathy* (New York 1962).

Reichenbach, Baron Karl von, *Physico-Physiological Researches on the Dynamics of Magnetism, etc., in Relation to the Vital Force,* English translation, Dr John Ashburner (London 1851).

Rhine, J. B., *The Reach of the Mind* (London 1954).

Rhodes, Henry T. F., *Alphonse Bertillon; Father of Scientific Detection* (London 1956).

Russell, Eric Frank, *Great World Mysteries* (London 1957).

Sanderson, Ivan, *Investigating the Unexplained* (New York 1963).

Sandys, Sir John, *Companion to Latin Studies* (London 1910).

Sheahan, James and Upson, George, *The History of the Great Conflagration* (Chicago and Philadelphia 1872).

Stone, W. Clement and Browning, Norma, *The Other Side of the Mind* (New York 1967).

Taylor, A. S., *Principles and Practice of Medical Jurisprudence,* edited by Sir Sydney Smith and Keith Simpson (llth edition, London 1956).

Thouless, Robert, *Experimental Psychical Research* (London 1963).

Thulin, C.O., *Die etruskische Disciplin,* reprint (Darmstadt 1968).

Thurston, SJ, Herbert, *The Physical Phenomena of Mysticism* (Chicago 1952).

Trotter, Thomas, *Essay, Medical Philosophical and Chemical, on Drunkenness, and its Effects on the Human Body* (London 1804).

United States Army, *Index-Catalogue of the Library of the Surgeon-*

General's Office (Washington 1882). Lists fifteen books and over sixty articles of a scholarly nature, on the subject of spontaneous combustion, without mentioning articles in the popular press.

West, D. J., *Psychical Research Today* (London 1962).

Wilson, Charles, *Pathology of Drunkenness* (Edinburgh 1855).

Wilson, Colin, *The Occult.: A History (New* York 1971).

Wilson Knight, G., *Neglected Powers: essays on l9th and 20th century literature* (London 1971).

ARTICLES AND PAPERS

Apjohn, James, Spontaneous Combustion *(Cyclopaedia of Practical Medicine,* London 1833).

Batz, H. W., 'When Found' *(Dickensian,* XIII, No. 11, November 1917).

Bayless, Raymond, 'The Nature of Poltergeist Intelligence' *(Fate,* August *1965). Fate* magazine, published in the U.S., is a rich, responsible, and authoritative source of information on the paraphysical and the occult, as, indeed, are the magazines, *True Strange* and *True Detective.*

Becker, J., 'The Position of a Human Body, Burnt, but not Completely Destroyed by Fire' *(British Medical journal,* 1894, 1, p. 1297).

Blount, T., 'Dickens and Mr Krook's Spontaneous Combustion' *(Dickens Studies Annual,* 1, 1970, 183.211).

Boekhout, F. W. J., and Ott de Vries, J. J., 'Ueber die Selbsterhitzung des Heues' *(Centralbl. f. Bakteriol.* etc. 2. Abt. Jena, 1905, XV, pp. 568-73).

Brouardel, P., 'Etude médico-légale sur la combustion du corps humain' *(Bulletin de la société médico-légal de France,* Paris 1877-8, p. 336 et seq).

Budth, F., 'A Case of So-called Spontaneous Combustion' *(British Medical Journal, 1,* 1888, p. 841).

Devergie, A., 'Mémoire sur la combustion humaine spontanée' *(Annales d'hygiène et de médecine légale, XLVI,* 1951, 383,432).

Fortean Times, Issue No: 47, p.60: 'The Creation of a Myth? Postmortem on the Jacqueline Fitzsimon 'SHC' Inquest', by Peter Hough and Jenny Randles.

Gaskell, E., 'More about Spontaneous Combustion' *(Dickensian,* 1973, pp. 25-35).

Gee, D. J., 'A Case of Spontaneous Combustion' *(Medicine, Science and the Law,* vol. 5, 1965, pp. 37-8).

Grigor, John, 'Death of a Notorious Dram-drinker' *(Monthly Journal of Medicine,* Scotland, XV, 1852).

Haight, Gordon S., 'Dickens and Lewes on Spontaneous Combustion' *(Nineteenth-Century Fiction,* X, June 1955, pp. 53-63).

Hartwell, B. H., 'So-called Spontaneous Combustion' *(Boston Medical and Surgical journal,* 1892, CXXVI, pp. 12-21).

Hava, Adrian, 'An Account of a Case of Spontaneous Human Combustion' *(New Orleans Medical and Surgical journal,* April 1893-4, *ns,* XXI, pp. 721-31).

Josephson, C. D., 'La Combustion spontanée dans les oeuvres littéraires ou scientifiques' *(Acta Medica Scandinavica, LXV,* 1927, 430). Omits C. Brockden Brown, Herman Melville, Washington Irving, Thomas de Quincey and Mark Twain.

Knott, J., 'Spontaneous Combustion' *(American Medicine,* Philadelphia, 1905, IX, pp. 653-60).

Lendenem, F. C., 'A Case of Spontaneous Combustion in Man' *(Therapeutical Gazette,* Detroit, 1889, 3. v, p 387).

Middlekamp, A., 'A Case of Spontaneous(?) Combustion' *(St Louis Medical and Surgical journal, XLIX,* 1885, pp. 238-41).

Miehe, H., 'Ueber Selbsterhitzung' *(Med. Klin.,* Berlin, 1907, III, p. 520).

Oliver, J. B., 'Spontaneous Combustion – A Literary Curiosity' *(Bulletin of the Institute of the History of Medicine,* Johns Hopkins University, vol. 4, No. 6, June 1936, pp. 559-72).

Perkins George, 'Deaths by Spontaneous Combustion in Marryat, Melville, Dickens, Zola and Others' *(Dickensian,* January *1964,* pp. 57-63).

Reynolds, E. S., 'Spontaneous Combustion' *(British Medical journal,* 1891, I, p. 645).

Schauer, J., 'Ueber Combustion' *(Dermat. Centralbl.,* Berlin, *1914-15,* XVI, p.34).

She (monthly journal), issue of July, 1988, p.66: 'Deathly Hush-up' by Jenny Randles and Peter Hough.

Stein, C., 'Beitrag zur Frage der Selbstentzündung' *(Zeitschrift für Gewerbe-Hygiene* [etc.] Vienna and Leipzig, 1926, LXXI, p. 1860).

Stockwell, W., 'Catacausis ebriosus' [i.e. spontaneous combustion through addiction to alcohol] *(Therapeutical Gazette,* Detroit, 1889, 3. *s,* v. pp, 168-74).

Thurston, Gavin, 'Preternatural Combustibility of the Human Body' *(Medico-Legal journal,* London, 1961, 29, part 4, pp. 100-3).

Wiley, Elizabeth, 'Four Strange Cases' *(Dickensian,* May *1962,* pp. 120-25).

Wilkinson, Ann Y., 'Bleak House: from Faraday to Judgement Day' *(Journal of English Literary History,* Johns Hopkins University, vol. 34, 1967, pp. 225-47).

World Weekly News, issue of 18th November, 1986: 'Preacher Explodes During Sermon' (unsigned).

UNSIGNED

1. Article attacking Dr John Grigor's theory that spontaneous combustion was the cause of the death of a 'notorious dram-drinker' *(Edinburgh Medical and Surgical journal,* LXXVIII, 1852, 95.135).

2. 'Of the Death of the Countess Cornelia Bandi of Cesena' *(Philosophical Transactions* from the year 1743 to the year 1750, London, 1756, X, pp. 1068-77).

3. 'Of the Death of the Countess Cornelia Bandi of Cesena' *(Gentleman's Magazine,* VI, November 1736, pp. 647-48). (A more detailed version XVI, July 1746, pp. 368-9).

4. Article on Spontaneous Combustion *(Penny Encyclopedia,* supplementary vol. 1, 1845, p. 399).

5. Report on the trial at Darmstadt, of Stauff [in the matter of the Countess von Görlitz] *(The Times* of London, 18 April 1850).

6. News item: 'Girl Burned in Ball Dress' *(Daily Telegraph,* London, 20 September 1938).

7. 'Spontaneous Human Combustion' *(British Medical Journal,* 1938, 1, p. 1106).

CORRESPONDENCE

1. Dr G. Thurston to the *British Medical Journal,* 1938, 1, p. 1340: 'Spontaneous Human Combustion.'

2. Mr L. A. Parry, FRCS, to the *British Medical Journal,* 1938, 1, p. 1237: 'Spontaneous Combustion.'

INDEX

373

Saunders, J.B. de C.M., 259n
Schroeder, Lynn, 51n, 58n, 59n, 60n
Schurmacher, E., 105
Science,
    attitudes of (*to SHC*), 37-8, 283-4
    see also Medicine
    instruments, 47, 51-2
Seale, William, 111, 281-2
Seaton, Peter, 10-11, 39, 112, 282
Selectivity (*of SHC*), 11-12, 114-7, 141, 282-3
Semyonov, Dr N., 51
Seneca, Illinois, USA, 90
Sergeyev, Dr Genady, 9, 179n, 187, 349
Sex (*of SHC victims*), 38-9, 77, 98, 219, 226-7
Sheahan, James, 188
She magazine, 310-2
Shepherdson, G.A., 92, 341-2
Shirley Institute, Manchester, 287
Siberia, 268-270
Silk, Edward T. (*coroner*), 144
Simpson, Prof. Keith, 27-8, 103
'Slow-vaulting', 208-212, 352-3
Smell, absence of (*in SHC*), 82, 101, 144, 147, 167
Smoking, 38
Sochevanov, Dr N., 50-1
Sodom and Gomorrah, 69, 74-5
'Sodom to Sydenham', 69
'Sons of God', 134-5
Sound, 127-130
Spontaneous Human Combustion (SHC),
    attitudes to: *see* Medicine, Press, Science
    circumstances, 106-116
    definition, 6
    features, 39-44, 78-80, 86-91, 100-1, 104, 110-1, 112-4, 271-4, 281-3
    legal enquiry into, 158-9
    'near escapes', 176-7
    types, 122
    see also Car Deaths, Location,

Selectivity, Smell, Victims, Witnesses
Stauff (*suspect in Görlitz SHC case*), 157-161
Steers, Ellen, 110, 282
Stephens, Olga W., 174
Suicide, 82, 121, 262-3, 265-6
Sunday Express, 319
Sydenham, SE London, 69-70, 74
Symbolism, religious, 71-2, 88-9

Tardieu, A., 161
Taylor, Colonel, 194
Taylor, Dr J.E., 229
Telekinesis, 178-9, 191, 193, 249-252, 283, 355
Temperature,
    see Heat, *and under* Body
Thacker family, 215-6, 229
Theodoric the Great, 45, 187
Thomas, Dr F., 151n
Thompson, Edith, 109-110
Thompson-Bywaters murder case, 109
Thurston, Dr Gavin, 6, 26-8, 31-2, 40-1, 44, 150, 164, 164n, 213, 326
Thurston, Fr Herbert, 213, 260
Time (*dimension of*), 73, 267
Today magazine, article in, 169-172
Toronto, Canada, 317
Tucumcari, New Mexico, USA, 212
Tunguska, Siberia, 268-270
Turner, George, 12, 92, 96-7, 112, 124-8
'Twain, Mark' (Samuel Clemens, *US novelist*), 321
Tyrus, Price of (*Biblical*), 296

Ubbergen, Netherlands, 128
Ulrich, S.S., 91, 124-8, 176
Unidentified Flying Objects ('UFO's), 201
Upson, George, 188
Upton-by-Chester, England, 126, 127-8, 162

378

Uktomskii (Military) Physiological Institute, A.A., Leningrad, 179n, 187
Vesey, Peter, 92
Victims (*of SHC*),
    amnesia, 174-5
    characteristics, 9, 39-41, 91, 93-5, 101-2
    see also Age, Class, Health, Physique, Psychology, Sex
Vogt, Richard, 174-5

Wales, Principality of, Great Britain, 119-122
Watkins, Leslie, 358
Watt, Thomas, 227-8
Wattigney, Lieut., 82-3
'Weasel words', 304
Weekly World News (USA), 290-4
Wells, H.G. (*novelist and historian*), 276
Whiston Hospital, Cheshire, 285
White, Farmer, 195-6
White, Miss Lily, 9, 187, 260, 263-4
White, Mr and Mrs Nicholas, 226-7
Widnes, Cheshire, England, 285

Widnes Weekly World, 290
Wild Plum School, 237-240, 274
Wilkinson, Ann Y., 326-7, 332
Will, the human, 246-8, 251, 260-1, 264-5, 272, 281-3
    creative, 60
    to harm, 12-13
Williamson family, 189-190, 192-3, 215, 218
Wilson, Colin (*British novelist and occultist*), 105, 214, 237
Windrow, Dr J.E., 78n
Witnesses (*of SHC*), 174-5, 271-3, 343-4
Woolner, Thomas (*British sculptor*), 146
Worth, Mrs Olga, 174
Wouk, Herman (*US novelist*), 89
Wright, Blakemore, 312
Wu Ch'eng-en (*author of 'Monkey'*), 2

Yoga, 251, 254
Young, Thomas, 229-230

Zola, Emile (*French novelist*), 39
Zorab, George, 186
Zyl, Rev. J. van, 220-1

379

FORTHCOMING TITLES FROM SKOOB ESOTERICA

Michael Harrison: Fire From Heaven
A thorough exploration of the phenomenon of Spontaneous Human Combustion that is not without humour.

The Roots of Witchcraft
Reprint of classic in depth work on witchcraft.

Victor B Neuberg: The Triumph of Pan
Originally published by Aleister Crowley's Equinox Press in 1910. Out now

Three books by Vee Van Dam:

The Psychic Explorer
Concerned with astral projection and out of the body experience.   Out now

The Power of Mind and Consciousness
Creative visualization, meditation and subjective journeys through inner space.   Out now

Star Craft
Discovering auric energies and working with devas.

E Graham Howe: The Mind of the Druid
Meditations on the elemental origins of human psychology and faith. Out now.

Gerald Suster: The Truth About the Tarot
An illuminating, provocative, and instructive consideration of the tarot Concise, witty and wise.

Coming from Kenneth Grant

Remembering Aleister Crowley
What this memoir of the personal relationship between KG and Crowley in the latter's last years brings to light will change the perspective of occult history. A subtle wisdom and humour informs KG's commentary on their mutual correspondence.

Hecate's Fountain
Often Lovecraftian in ethos, the workings of Grant's Nuit-Isis Lodge have opened the gates to an influx of alien magickal intelligence, which lies behind Grant's revolutionary poetic and scholarly exegesis of Liber Al, and reveals the alchemic potential of our own bodies.

Subsequently the earlier volumes of the two trilogies will be reprinted.

Out now (with Steffi Grant)

Hidden Lore A4 Illus.   Limited to 1000
By their studies of Crowley, Fortune, Spare, Lovecraft and the Tantric tradition the authors have radically altered the direction of the 20th Century Occultism. A distillation in ten essays. With tipped-in colour plates of Steffi Grant's paintings, it constitutes a grimoire.

SKOOB OCCULT REVIEW
SUBSCRIPTIONS
'Food reading for the thinking occultist.' Pagan News
£8 per Year for 4 issues. Post free in UK.
If issue 1 required, add £2.